DO THE POOR COUNT?

Michelle M. Taylor-Robinson

DO THE POOR COUNT?

Democratic Institutions and Accountability
in a Context of Poverty

The Pennsylvania State University Press
University Park, Pennsylvania

Library of Congress Cataloging-in-Publication Data

Taylor-Robinson, Michelle M.
Do the poor count? : democratic institutions and
accountability in a context of poverty /
Michelle M. Taylor-Robinson.
p.   cm.
Includes bibliographical references and index.
Summary: "With specific focus on Brazil and Honduras,
examines electoral and nominating institutions and
clienetelism in Latin America, and the capacity of poor
people to monitor and sanction officials"
—Provided by publisher.
ISBN 978-0-271-03750-9 (cloth : alk. paper)
ISBN 978-0-271-03751-6 (pbk. : alk. paper)
1. Poor—Political activity—Brazil.
2. Poor—Political activity—Honduras.
I. Title.

JL2481.T39 2010
320.97283'086942—dc22
2010018457

It is the policy of The Pennsylvania State University Press
to use acid-free paper. Publications on uncoated stock
satisfy the minimum requirements of American National
Standard for Information Sciences—Permanence of Paper
for Printed Library Material, ANSI Z39.48–1992.

To FOREST

Contents

Tables

Abbreviations

CCT	conditional cash transfer program
DM	district magnitude
LB	Latinobarómetro survey
PR	proportional representation
SMD	single member district
SMD-P	single-member-district plurality
WVS	World Values Series survey

Brazil

CPMF	Contribuição Provisória sobre Movimentação Financeira
PFL	Partido da Frente Liberal
PMDB	Partido do Movimento Democrático Brasiliero
PP	Partido Progressista
PSDB	Partido da Social Democracia Brasileira
PT	Partido dos Trabalhadores
PTB	Partido Trabalhista Brasileiro

Honduras

COHEP	Consejo Hondureño de la Empresa Privada
CTH	Confederación de Trabajadores de Honduras
FHIS	Fondo Hondureño de Inversión Social
PARLACEN	Parlamento Centroamericano
PDCH	Partido Demócrata Cristiano de Honduras
PINU	Partido Innovación y Unidad Social Demócrata
PLH	Partido Liberal de Honduras
PNH	Partido Nacional de Honduras

PRAF   Programa de Asignación Familiar
PUD   Partido Unificación Democrática
TNE   Tribunal Nacional de Elecciones

Mexico

PAN   Partido Acción Nacional
PRD   Partido de la Revolución Democrática
PRI   Partido Revolucionario Institucional

Venezuela

AD   Acción Democrática
COPEI   Comité de Organización Política Electoral Independiente

Acknowledgments

Many people deserve my thanks and appreciation. It would not have been possible to carry out this study without the support and cooperation of many, many people in the Honduran Congress, ranging from the many deputies who graciously granted interviews to the staff who helped me navigate the informal rules of operation. While I cannot thank all the interviewees, there are a few people whose support and help must be acknowledged: Santiago David Amador and Johnny Handal Hawit, the leaders of the Liberal Party and the National Party in the Congress, both of whom gave invaluable assistance by urging their colleagues to grant me interviews and to fill out my survey. In addition, I thank Doña Ana and Doña Beatriz and their colleagues in the Secretaria Adjunta for their willingness to get me innumerable files and papers from the Congress Archive, and for granting me their friendship during the many weeks I worked in their office; they made working in the Congress fun. Doña Mercedes de Montes and her entire family, as well as Anna Acosta and her family, also gave me their friendship and support during all my various fieldwork trips to Honduras.

Many colleagues in political science also are due my thanks for their comments and constructive feedback during the long process that eventually led to this book. Kathleen Bawn, Ernesto Calvo, Damarys Canache, Scott Desposato, Kathryn Hochstetler, Wendy Hunter, Mark Jones, Marisa Kellam, Monika Nalepa, Nico Petrovsky, David Pion-Berlin, Randy Stevenson, Guy Whitten, Bruce Wilson, and Joan Wolf read chapters and offered very useful advice. Chris Diaz worked hard helping me with the initial coding for the deputy role analysis, as well as coding the target of hundreds of pieces of legislation. Maria Escobar-Lemmon deserves very special thanks for reading most of the book multiple times and for her unfailing support of this project, not just as a colleague but also as a friend.

Texas A&M University supported this project in various, essential ways, including sabbatical leave to write the initial draft of the manuscript, and several grants that funded fieldwork trips to Honduras. Funding from the

National Science Foundation (grant #Y460895) also made fieldwork in Honduras possible.

Sandy Thatcher at Penn State Press deserves my thanks for his support for this book over the long haul. I truly appreciate it, and I thank him for working with me.

Finally, I must thank my family for supporting me and this project. My mom has given never-failing emotional support from the very beginning of my studies of Latin America, and for this project in particular; I thank her too for taking me on my first trip to Honduras when I was a very impressionable child. My husband, Forest, deserves my immense thanks for his encouragement, for reading the entire manuscript multiple times, for helping to collect archival data, and for joining me on fieldwork trips to Honduras. Without him this project would not have been completed—I thank him so very much for all his help, both scholarly and emotional.

ONE

INSTITUTIONS, POVERTY,
AND DEMOCRATIC CONSOLIDATION

Do the poor count in Latin American politics? As voters, of course poor people count in democratic regimes. Winning poor people's votes can be essential to win elections. But do poor people count after the election—do the officials they helped to elect in fact represent them? This book explores whether, when, and how poor people count. It examines how the limited ability of poor people to monitor government officials, combined with how institutions can constrain the capacity of poor people to sanction, affect legislators' incentives to represent poor people.

Poor people make up a large percentage of the population in many Latin American countries (see table 1.1). There were eighty million "new poor" in the 1980s, and by the early 1990s 46 percent of Latin Americans lived in poverty (CEPAL 1992; Vilas 1997, 21). Following the economic crisis of the 1980s, many people formerly in the middle sectors became impoverished (Gold-frank and Schrank 2006, 13; Roberts and Portes 2006). Poverty rates vary across and within countries, but poor people constitute a large minority, if not a majority, particularly in rural areas. Understanding whether, when, and how poor people count in democratic politics will help explain challenges to consolidating democracy.

One of the problems is that poor Latin Americans typically lack resources that enable the middle class and elites to monitor officials, resources such as education and access to the information it provides (see table 1.2), as well as the means to form interest groups. In addition, institutions can make it difficult for poor people to credibly threaten to use democratic methods to punish elected officials who do not attend to their interests. Other methods to attempt to hold leaders accountable, such as mass protests, are still options for poor people, but they are often very costly to implement, particularly if the state responds to poor peoples' protests with violence. Will elected officials represent

Table 1.1 People living in poverty in Latin American democracies

	Human Poverty Index 2003[a]	2004 % of population[b]		2004 poverty rate[b]	
		Living in extreme poverty	Living in poverty	% of urban population	% of rural population
Nicaragua	24.3	42.3 ('01)	69.3 ('01)	63.8 ('01)	76.9 ('01)
Guatemala	22.9	30.9 ('02)	60.2 ('02)	45.3 ('02)	68.0 ('02)
Honduras	19.9	53.9 ('03)	74.8 ('03)	62.7 ('03)	84.8 ('03)
El Salvador	17.2	19.0	47.5	41.2	56.8
Bolivia	14.6	34.7 ('03)	63.9 ('03)	53.8 ('03)	80.6 ('03)
Dominican Republic	13.9	29.0	54.4	51.8	59.0
Ecuador	11.9	22.3	51.2	47.5	58.5
Brazil	11.4	12.1	37.7	34.3	54.1
Peru	11.4	18.6	51.1	43.1 ('03)	76.0 ('03)
Paraguay	10.3	36.9	65.9	59.1	74.6
Mexico	8.8	11.7	37.0	32.6	44.1
Venezuela	8.6	19.0	45.4	—	—
Colombia	8.2	24.2	51.1	49.8	54.8
Panama	7.8	14.8	31.8	22.4	47.9
Costa Rica	4.4	8.0	20.5	18.7	23.1
Chile	4.1	4.7 ('03)	18.7 ('03)	18.5 ('03)	20.0 ('03)
Uruguay	3.6	—	—	20.9	—
Argentina	—	—	—	29.4	—

SOURCE: column 1: UNDP 2003; columns 2–5: USAID and ECLAC, http://qesdb.usaid.gov/lac/index.html, accessed October 4, 2007.

[a] Human Poverty Index "measures poverty in developing countries. It focuses on deprivations in three dimensions: longevity, as measured by the probability at birth of not surviving to age 40; knowledge, as measured by the adult literacy rate; and overall economic provisioning, public and private, as measured by the percentage of people not using improved water sources and the percentage without sustainable access to an improved water source and the percentage of children underweight for age" (UNDP 2003, 61).
[b] Data for 2004 unless otherwise noted in parentheses.

poor people without the threat of being held accountable for their actions? When officials do work to provide representation to poor people, what form is that representation likely to take?

This is a study about representation, and in particular it asks if members of what is supposed to be the *representative branch* of government, the congress, have an incentive to represent poor people after Election Day. If the answer is "no," and poor people only matter while politicians and parties are giving them small "payments" (e.g., a bag of food, construction materials, a dental checkup at a campaign rally) to "buy" their vote, then poor people only receive attention from government for a short period, leading to a *representation gap* in democratic regimes. The extreme case of a representation gap

Table 1.2 Human development in Latin American democracies

	Human Development Index (HDI) 2007[a]	Adult literacy 2007 (% age 15 & over)	Gini index[b]	Internet users per 1,000 2005
Chile	0.878	96.5	52.0	172
Argentina	0.866	97.6	50.0	177
Uruguay	0.865	97.9	46.2	193
Costa Rica	0.854	95.9	47.2	254
Mexico	0.854	92.8	48.1	181
Venezuela	0.844	95.2	43.4	125
Panama	0.840	93.4	54.9	64
Brazil	0.813	90.0	55.0	195
Colombia	0.807	92.7	58.5	104
Ecuador	0.806	91.0	54.4	47
Peru	0.806	89.6	49.6	164
Dominican Republic	0.777	89.1	50.0	169
Paraguay	0.761	94.6	53.2	34
El Salvador	0.747	82.0	49.7	93
Honduras	0.732	83.6	55.3	36
Bolivia	0.729	90.7	58.2	52
Guatemala	0.704	73.2	53.7	79
Nicaragua	0.699	78.0	52.3	27

SOURCE: UNDP 2009, table H, 171–73; ibid., table M, 195–97; http://hdrstats.undp.org/en/indicators /147.html, accessed April 22, 2009.

[a] Human Development Index is a composite of three components of human development: health (measured as life expectancy at birth), knowledge (based on the adult literacy rate and combined primary, secondary, and tertiary enrollment ratio), and standard of living (GDP per capita) (UNDP 2007).

[b] Gini index "measures the extent to which the distribution of income (or consumption) among individuals or households within a country deviates from a perfectly equal distribution. . . . A value of 0 represents absolute equality, a value of 100 absolute inequality" (UNDP 2007, 366–67).

is where elites and the middle class are the only sectors of the population who can form interest groups to monitor government and sanction if policy moves too far from their preferences, thereby enabling them to be represented by the officials and parties they elect. In that extreme scenario, poor people are only represented when their votes are needed. At other times, their inability to monitor and sanction means that accountability—a hallmark of democratic government—does not work for poor people, and they do not receive representation because they cannot both observe and punish elected officials who ignore their needs. Poor people only receive representation after Election Day if an official or party coincidentally wants the same policies as poor people. Politicians can work on policies that represent small elite sectors of society because they are not concerned that poor people will hold them accountable.

The Main Argument

The main conclusion of this book is that the representation poor people are most likely to receive from their elected representatives is "clientelistic representation," but that even clientelistic representation may not be guaranteed. Clientelistic representation takes the form of both particularistic benefits for individuals and local infrastructure projects for a community of loyalists. This characterization of clientelistic representation is consistent with Kitschelt's (2000, 850) description of the difference between clientelist and programmatic types of citizen-elite linkage. Clientelistic politicians and parties "specialize in club goods and selective incentives," while programmatic parties "disperse rents as a matter of codified, universalistic public policy applying to all members of a constituency, regardless of whether a particular individual supported or opposed the party that pushed for the rent-serving policy" (ibid.; see also Kitschelt and Wilkinson 2007, 11–12; Magaloni, Diaz-Cayeros, and Estévez 2007; Hagopian 2009). A local infrastructure project may be designed to be excludable, as a club good, rather than a benefit for all members of a community. If demand to use the facility, for example a school or clinic, exceeds its capacity, politicians can use excess demand as an excuse to determine whose children get to attend the school or who receives an appointment with the clinic doctor, and only clients will benefit. Honduran deputies showed me letters they write to get a constituent/client an appointment with a social security doctor, and explained that while schools are free, poor families need scholarships to buy uniforms and school supplies. Desposato (2007, 110) describes the same behavior by state legislators in Piauí, Brazil's poorest state and one that has a strong clientelist tradition. A politician or party that utilizes clientelist linkages with citizens would ideally provide local public works projects to communities of loyalists where no excludability mechanism is needed, and such a project may be an efficient way to reward electoral support by overwhelmingly loyalist communities.[1] Still, politicians can be creative and

---

1. Cleary and Stokes (2006, 52) describe the PRI (Partido Revolucionario Institucional) using public works to intimidate voters in Mexico's Puebla state: "The PRI has not foresworn its traditional methods of clientelist mobilization and voter intimidation . . . it remains common practice for the PRI to threaten voters by claiming that if their neighborhood or town does not vote for the PRI, the government will withhold public services or halt public works projects." Cleary and Stokes (2006, 10) define clientelism more narrowly than I define "clientelistic representation." They view clientelism as "the trading of votes and political support in return for small, private payoffs to voters," but their case studies indicate that public works projects are used by parties to reward party loyalists, and that a community can also be intimidated by the threat of losing a service.

use some types of public works projects to reward supporters even in more diverse communities by designing the good to exclude nonsupporters, while the politician or party can still point to their local development accomplishments. As Roniger and Günes-Ayala (1994, vii) explain, "In societies laden with social inequalities, public policies—whether distributive, regulative, or extractive—are potentially discretionary and thus open to clientelistic use and abuse."

Clientelistic representation falls far short of the policy representation we commonly think that democratic accountability should prompt elected officials to provide. Poor people often lack the resources to monitor the policy activities of their elected representatives, and they are unlikely to value promises of policy benefits or claims that "I am working on policy X for you" because of their many past disappointments when politicians made policy promises and did not deliver. Unless they receive benefits from a policy before the next election, poor people are unlikely to reward representatives who say they are working on policy, even if the claim is true.[2]

There are two components to why poor people are unlikely to be able to hold officials accountable. First is the limited monitoring capability of poor people, particularly for monitoring what goes on inside the legislature (as well as the executive branch and government agencies). Second is that institutions in many Latin American countries (electoral rules, nomination procedures, and clientelism) make it personally very costly for a poor person to try to sanction policy work that does not represent their interests, and a sanction is unlikely to actually punish an official unless many frustrated people sanction at the same time. High sanctioning cost is another reason poor people may not bother to monitor. The result is that poor people are only likely to get policy representation from a legislator who happens to want the same policy as them; policy representation will not be forthcoming from the threat that officials not delivering policy for the poor will be held accountable. Yet even when a representative wants the same policy that poor people want, policy representation is not assured. The legislator must find a way to get the policy adopted and implemented before the next election so that poor people will want to reelect the official as a reward, and such policy work may encounter opposition from groups who have both a greater capacity than poor people

---

2. Poor people also often lack information to assess the likely benefit they would receive from a policy if it is enacted, or whether the bureaucracy will faithfully implement the policy. These problems give poor people more reasons to devalue policy promises.

to monitor what officials are doing and more ability to sanction policy work they oppose.

Clientelistic representation is simple for poor people to monitor. They can ask themselves if they received a personal benefit, or they can look at their community to determine if a public works project was built and they were able to use it. The first part of the accountability mechanism works for clientelistic representation. But if institutions make it personally costly for a poor person to sanction, a representative is unlikely to be punished for not delivering enough clientelistic representation. Thus poor people may not have a credible capacity to hold their elected officials accountable to deliver clientelistic representation. But there is a danger to legislators and parties that do not provide at least some clientelistic representation to poor people (i.e., the amount of clientelistic representation poor people have become accustomed to receiving from government). The danger is that poor people may become so frustrated with incumbents and their traditional parties that it becomes rational to sanction even if an individual's sanction will not punish the official or party. They are not going to lose nonexistent benefits of having a clientelistic connection to a politician or party, so why not take away their vote? If many poor people reach this conclusion, a traditional caudillo or party can lose an election. In sum, a legislator (or traditional party) runs a risk of being sanctioned by poor people who receive no representation and have no reason to think that they will receive benefits in the next term (if their party or representative was in the opposition during the current period). The sanction will only work if many frustrated people (not necessarily all poor) vote against the politician or party in the same election, so it is difficult for a strategic legislator to gauge how much clientelistic representation needs to be delivered to avoid a successful sanction, but the danger exists. Clientelistic representation, even though it does not fit conventional images of all that democracy should be, may keep a representation gap for poor people from eroding into a representation crisis, and thus may be a key to stability in a democracy where many people are poor (see Kitschelt 2000, 851–52, 873).

In Latin America, there is ample evidence of frustration with democratic institutions, established parties, and elected officials. It is not just poor people who are dissatisfied, as seen in the negative evaluations repeatedly reported by surveys (Lagos 2003, 144–45; Hagopian 2005; Seligson 2007, 89) (see table 1.3). In the 2005 Latinobarómetro survey conducted in eighteen Latin American countries, 86 percent of respondents said that political leaders are "not at all" or "only a little concerned" about the issues that interested them.

Table 1.3 Confidence in democracy and democratic institutions in Latin America (percentages from all Latinobarómetro surveys)

	1996	1997	1998	2000	2001	2002	2003	2004	2005	2006	2007
Satisfaction w/democracy (very or fairly satisfied)	27	41	37	37	25	33	29	29	31	38	46
Democracy is preferable to any other kind of government[a]	61	63	62	57	48	56	53	53	53	58	55
A lot or some confidence in:											
National congress	27	36	27	28	24	23	17	24	28	28	29
President	—	39	38	39	30	—	31	37	43	47	43
Judiciary	33	36	32	34	27	25	20	32	31	36	30
Political parties	20	28	21	20	19	14	11	18	19	22	20
Number of respondents	18,717	17,767	17,907	18,135	18,135	18,552	18,658	19,605	20,206	20,232	20,212

SOURCE: Lagos 2003, tables 7.2 (p. 145), 7.4 (p. 151), and 7.5 (p. 155); Latinobarómetro Report 2005, 56–60; Latinobarómetro 2006 and 2007 surveys.

[a] This question measures overt support for democracy, but it may include support for inconsistent or undemocratic values, such as the president controlling the media, governing without congress, or going beyond the law (Carlin 2006, 55–56).

Latinobarómetro in its 2005 report concludes that "the Achilles heel of representative democracy is precisely representation" (42). Electoral volatility is another indicator of voter frustration (Mainwaring, Bejarano, and Pizarro Leongómez 2006); in electoral districts where a majority of the potential electorate is poor, this can be interpreted as popular sector dissatisfaction.[3] Yet in some poor countries, traditional parties have maintained their dominance, and consequently seat volatility in the legislature is low. Seligson (2007, 95n14) notes that poor people's support for populism varies across countries. Development of theory to understand these cross-national differences is this book's objective. The theory posits that electoral institutions, nominations, and forms of clientelism interact to affect the cost to poor people of sanctioning, and thus when and how institutions give legislators incentives to represent poor people.

Institutions and Incentives for Representation

A key argument of this study is that it is not one but a *combination* of institutions that influences the sanctioning capability of poor and rich people and that constrains and influences the representation strategies that legislators can adopt. Multiple institutions create the political context of a polity, and institutions can "emerge at different times and out of different historical configurations" (Thelen 1999, 382). If we only considered one type of institution and the incentives it created (say electoral institutions), we would have an incomplete picture. Citizens must choose to expend effort on monitoring; but if they do choose to be so engaged, the institutions of their country will constrain their capacity to sanction. Legislators make choices about how they will do their jobs, and their choices are shaped by their institutional context. Experience with institutions creates expectations about the kind of job that legislators ought to do, such as whether they should check the president or be a local patron (Hall and Taylor 1996; Katznelson and Weingast 2005). For example, Desposato (2007, 118–19) shows how in Brazil, "even under virtually identical institutional environments, legislators can adapt fundamentally different political strategies in response to societal variables."

The institutions influencing sanctioning that I focus on are election rules, nomination procedures, and forms of clientelism. I introduce each briefly

---

3. Imputing the opinions of poor individuals from aggregate data risks ecological fallacy. But in districts where the vast majority of people are classified as poor by a country's census, it is less risky as the poor are almost all the people who could vote in those districts.

here. Election rules affect the sanctioning capacity of voters (poor and rich) because some types of ballots allow voters to select (reward or sanction) a specific candidate, while others require the voter to select only a party. Election rules influence a career-seeking legislator's strategy by creating incentives to seek a personal or a partisan vote (Mayhew 1974; Lancaster 1986; Cain, Ferejohn, and Fiorina 1987; Carey and Shugart 1995). While clientelism and personal vote seeking are not the same, electoral rules that create personalizing incentives are a common explanation for why and when politicians set up clientelist linkages with citizens (Kitschelt 2000, 852, 859). Other aspects of electoral rules, such as whether reelection is permitted, whether candidates can run as independents, and whether voters can split their ballot, also constrain legislators' strategies and influence citizens' capacity to hold their elected officials accountable.

Nomination procedures also affect the ability of poor and rich people to hold their elected officials accountable and influence the representation strategies legislators adopt. Candidates can be selected by voters in primaries, by local party organizations, at a party convention, or by national party leaders. If local primaries select nominees, a legislator has an incentive to represent the average primary voter to insure renomination (Fenno 1978). Where national party leaders select candidates, only people who have influence with those party elites can sanction or reward legislators at the nomination stage. Candidate recruitment and selection procedures influence the types of candidates who are likely to be selected by parties (Siavelis and Morgenstern 2008a). For example, if party leaders place local patrons in electable positions on the party list (expecting that the local patron will deliver their clients to vote for the party), nomination procedures can be an explanation for when politicians emphasize clientelist linkages with citizens.[4]

Informal institutions, such as clientelism, also influence the strategies of citizens and legislators (Kitschelt 2000; Desposato 2001; Taylor-Robinson 2006a; Kitschelt and Wilkinson 2007; Magaloni, Diaz-Cayeros, and Estévez 2007; Remmer 2007). Informal institutions are "socially shared rules, usually unwritten, that are created, communicated, and enforced outside of officially sanctioned channels," and they interact with formal institutions in various ways, such as modifying or filling in gaps in the incentives created by formal institutions

---

4. An "electable" position on a party list is one that the party is likely to win, particularly if the party does well in the election. Electable positions can be contrasted with "safe" positions—those that are sufficiently high up the list that the party can expect to win them even in an election where the party loses some of its typical support.

(Helmke and Levitsky 2004, 727). Voters can also be clients, and legislators can also be patrons. A local patron may be motivated to seek a seat in the legislature as a way to obtain resources for maintaining and attracting more clients. Poor people can easily monitor whether a patron/legislator delivered clientelistic benefits, but the nature of the clientelism institution affects the capacity of poor clients to sanction a patron who does not deliver. If clientelism works through party clientele networks, a poor person must sever a party network connection and set up a connection with a new network to obtain a new patron, so the number of available networks influences how costly it is for a poor person to sanction. If access to state resources for clientelism is likely to be limited to legislators belonging to the governing party, the viable patron alternatives for a client who is dissatisfied are limited, making it less feasible to sanction.

Incentives for legislators to act as patrons can come from multiple sources. As noted above, election rules or nomination procedures can prompt aspiring politicians to seek the backing of poor voters by offering selective material incentives to establish clientelist linkages (Kitschelt 2000; Desposato 2001).[5] Incentives to behave as a patron can also have a sociological, economic, or historical basis, where people have learned to connect themselves to a patron or broker to address their personal, business, or community needs, in particular to help themselves be recipients of state resources under conditions of resource scarcity (Valenzuela 1977). Where clientelism is part of the people's experience, politicians can be motivated to behave as patrons, even in the absence of personalizing electoral rules. Kitschelt (2000) reviewed various explanations put forth in the literature for why parties and politicians adopt clientelist or programmatic linkages: socioeconomic development, state formation and democratic suffrage, democratic institutions (electoral rules, executive-legislative relations, federalism), political-economic theories, and fundamental ideologies and ethno-cultural identities. He concludes that there are multiple causes for clientelist linkages, noting that "the choice of linkage mechanisms is not just predicated on formal democratic institutions but also on substantive economic and political power relations," and that "the institutional mechanisms that promote clientelist or programmatic linkage strategies

---

5. Patrons working in a democracy must find ways to monitor clients when ballots are secret. In chapter 2 I discuss ways patrons and patronage-based parties have developed to police the behavior of clients.

may be at least in part endogenous to such power relations" (ibid., 872; see also Boix 1999; Desposato 2007; Kitschelt and Wilkinson 2007, 42–43; Scheiner 2007).[6]

Institutions affect citizens' ability to punish politicians. Institutions also influence politicians' identities, self-images, and preferences for why they want to be in office, and place constraints on politicians' behavior. For example, in a society where people have more experience using clientelism as a means of addressing personal needs than they do using the ballot box, clientelism may prompt local patrons to seek a congressional seat—not to shape national policy, but to obtain access to state resources so that they can expand their local client base and their local status as a powerful patron. In a similar setting, politicians seeking congressional seats for the purpose of shaping policy may view clientelistic representation as the cheapest way to maintain the support of enough poor voters to obtain their party's nomination or to win election.

The institutions literature is underdeveloped with respect to the nature of the relationship between the elected official and the constituency. Whose interests should elected officials represent if citizens are heterogeneous in terms of their capacity to monitor and sanction? Who will legislators represent if the policy and service preferences of (some) constituents and party leaders conflict? Will a legislator represent all the people of the district, major campaign contributors, organized interest groups, party supporters, or clients? Where party leaders control nominations, whom do party leaders want backbenchers to represent and what form do they indicate representation should take? Do party leaders reinforce the "mobilization of bias" produced by formal institutions designed to favor the interests of traditional elites? Do they reward clientelistic representation over policy representation? Rational choice institutionalism tacitly assumes a more or less level playing field, one where all voters can hold legislators accountable. But to what interests will legislators respond in a society that is starkly unequal and where the playing field is anything but level?

---

6. These other explanations may motivate politicians to act as patrons and motivate parties to set up clientelist linkages in countries where electoral systems would not lead us to expect clientelist linkages (e.g., Austria, Belgium, Italy, Venezuela; for discussion of those cases, see Kitschelt 2000). They can also explain variance in support for clientelism in a country when electoral rules are the same across subnational units (Cleary and Stokes 2006, on Mexico and Argentina; Scheiner 2007, on Japan).

If party competition presents voters with genuine choices (i.e., parties offer different policy/service packages, covering the full range of citizen preferences), and diverse parties have a realistic chance of winning elections or becoming part of a coalition government, then over time all groups should have their interests represented.[7] If, however, the same party is in power for many years, or parties alternate but address the same limited subset of interests, then it is important to understand which groups officials from those parties have an incentive to represent.[8] If parties are only attentive to certain sectors of society, then legislators are only likely to represent those favored sectors if they want to build a career, thereby producing a representation deficit that impedes the deepening of democracy.

Certainly, institutions are not the only reason the poor often are not represented in Latin American democracies. A history of elite dominance of politics creates the expectation that politics does not work for the poor, and promotes a political apathy and fatalism that—particularly when paired with the lack of tools, such as education, that aid political participation—is hard to overcome. But institutions can create real obstacles to the representation of poor people by limiting their capacity to sanction. The literature about democratic accountability expects that elected officials will represent actors who can monitor their actions and who have the resources to sanction those who do not represent their interests (Fearon 1999; Ferejohn 1999; Rubenstein 2007). This book, therefore, examines the monitoring abilities of different socioeconomic groups and how institutions affect their sanctioning capacity, as well as how those groups and institutions influence legislators' identities and the strategies they adopt to achieve their political goals.

The remainder of this chapter lays out important themes of the book, and then provides an overview of the rest of the chapters. First, I explain my choice to focus on incentives that members of congress have to represent poor constituents. Then I consider how poverty affects democratic accountability, how the concept of representation can be applied to democratic politics in a context of poverty, and how poverty and consolidating democracy are related.

---

7. It is unclear in multiparty systems whether citizens can determine which party to hold responsible for policy decisions or outcomes they do not like (Powell 1989).

8. If voters do not have the choice to vote for candidates or parties with policy and service stances close to their preferences, then citizens cannot control government. All people can participate in elections, but due to limited electoral choices, an electoral mandate model of representation and accountability will not work (Powell 1989, 121). See Lukes (1974, 2005) and Bachrach and Baratz (1970) for discussion of how power is exercised in such systems.

Why Focus on the Legislature and Legislators?

This book studies incentives for legislators because the legislature is intended to be the representative branch of government, though in Latin America legislatures are often viewed with distrust. Latin American politics has little empirical knowledge about "the relationship between voters and parties or elected politicians" (Mainwaring, Bejarano, and Pizarro Leongómez 2006, 3). Many countries have made what should be important reforms to how legislators are elected, in order to try "to reshape the terms of the relationship between governments and citizens," but these measures have not generally been successful (Crisp 2006, 204). This study argues that part of the difficulty in strengthening the link between legislators and citizens may be that electoral rules are only part of how that link is created. Other institutions, such as clientelism and how candidates are nominated, may also play a role.

Descriptively, the legislature is relatively diverse compared to the executive and judicial branches. Its membership tends to have greater gender and ethnic variety. The legislature gives opposition parties at least some access to policy-making and overseeing the executive. So by studying the legislature we can observe how elected officials from different backgrounds and parties respond to poor people.

Other political actors of course play a role in representation and policy-making, though full-scale analysis of their role is beyond the scope of this book. Political parties that fit a responsible party model select a campaign platform; once elected, parties must decide what campaign planks to pursue first and with vigor, and which to postpone or let die a quiet death, and these decisions affect whether government addresses poor people's policy preferences. Mainwaring, Bejarano, and Pizarro Leongómez (2006, 2) explain that much research on representation, particularly in advanced industrial countries, focuses on parties with the expectation that party programs and "programmatic convergence between voters and legislators [are] at the core of democratic representation." But they argue that "such programmatic or ideological representation is very weak" in much of Latin America, especially with respect to programmatic representation of poor people (see also Mainwaring, Bejarano, and Pizarro Leongómez 2006, table 1.7, 26).

Presidents often set the policy agenda for government. The executive's job of implementing the law also gives the president control over state resources, which allows the president to distribute resources to target particular constituencies; therefore, presidents can influence whose interests receive policy or clientelistic attention. When legislatures and parties become discredited in the eyes of citizens, populist presidents may displace these institutions as representatives of the people, but such presidents have shown a tendency to overstep the democratic bounds of their office (O'Donnell 1994; Weyland 1999; Mainwaring, Bejarano, and Pizarro Leongómez 2006, 20). Government agencies make policy through regulation, and those decisions about how to implement laws affect whether the government represents poor people (see Weyland 2006). Incentives created by institutions, plus the career ambitions of bureaucrats, agency directors, and presidents, influence whether these actors work to address the policy and service preferences of poor people. Those strategy decisions and ambitions, however, must be left for future studies, although party leaders and presidents will be taken into consideration at many points in the analysis presented here.

This book starts from the premise that institutions constrain and create incentives for legislators, yet legislators still make choices (Scharpf 1989, 149–50). They do not all view their jobs in the same way, nor do they all have the same motivations for seeking a seat in the congress.[9] Institutions constrain legislators, allowing them to strategize how best to achieve their own goals based on what they expect others to do. The cultural approach in historical institutionalism explains that institutions also "affect the very identities, self-images and preferences of the actors," and that "behaviour is not fully strategic but bounded by an individual's worldview . . . it emphasizes the extent to which individuals turn to established routines or familiar patterns of behaviour to attain their purposes" (Hall and Taylor 1996, 939; see also Katznelson and Weingast 2005, 15).[10]

My analysis assumes that legislators, as well as poor and rich people, are rational actors who assess the costs, benefits, and potential for success of strategies for achieving their career or representation goals. In addition, my study assumes that institutions are products of a country's historical experience, and that experience shapes both politicians' views of how they can and should do their jobs and different types of citizens' views of what they can expect from government. Institutions are not just a set of rules that are plunked down in country X at time t, but rather are shaped by the past experience politicians and citizens have with those institutions. Following Hall and Taylor (1996),

---

9. Searing (1994) and Hagopian (2001) also analyze the different roles legislators adopt.

10. According to sociological institutionalism, "institutions influence behavior not simply by specifying what one should do but also by specifying what one can imagine oneself doing in a given context" (Hall and Taylor 1996, 948).

Thelen (1999), and Katznelson and Weingast (2005), I attempt to combine the insights and strengths of rational choice and historical institutionalism to understand how the institutional milieu in which legislators and poor and rich people operate affects whether, when, and how the poor will be represented in Latin American politics.

The Effect of Poverty on Accountability

How does poverty affect accountability in democracy? Scholars anticipate that integrating popular sectors into politics will both create support for democratic political institutions and economic institutions and deepen the quality of democracy (Hite 1997, vi; Wampler 2006).[11] Yet "the effect of poverty on support for democracy is under-theorized and is not generally distinguished from economic development" (Carlin 2006, 53).[12] O'Donnell (1992, 47) hoped that providing representation for poor people would make it possible to "challenge the predominance of patrimonialism and clientelism," but Latin American democracies have had little success integrating the poor into the regime.[13] For poor people, holding politicians and political parties accountable is often a luxury they cannot afford. With little or no education it is difficult for people to monitor politicians' work on policy. Poor people who are monolingual in an indigenous language face an additional impediment to monitoring. In the 2005 Latinobarómetro poll, 55 percent of respondents agreed that "politics is so complicated that people like us often do not know what is happening" (ranging from 40 percent in Venezuela to 69 percent in El Salvador and 68 percent in Paraguay) (40–41). Even when poor people organize groups to attend to their needs, their ability to monitor government policy may not increase, as many of the new popular associations that have proliferated

11. Morgan (2007) found that in Venezuela in 1998 lack of integration into established parties was a strong predictor of whether survey respondents supported new parties or were independents.

12. Carlin's (2006) analysis of Latin American countries in the World Values Survey found that an increase in poverty has a significant and negative effect on *overt* support for democracy, even with development and inequality controls. Overt support for democracy refers to a verbal statement of a preference for democracy (e.g., democracy is preferable to any other kind of government), while *intrinsic* support for democracy refers to the expression of democratic values (liberty, freedom of expression, interpersonal trust) (see Inglehart and Welzel 2003).

13. Even the innovation of participatory budgeting, which has been hailed as so successful in some cities, has not delivered on its promise of incorporating poor people in all cases (see Nylen 2003; Collier and Handlin 2005, 17; Goldfrank and Schneider 2006; Wampler 2006).

in Latin American cities are focused on local subsistence concerns (e.g., communal kitchens, organizations of street vendors, NGOs that provide social services to popular sector constituencies) (Collier and Handlin 2005). If poor people cannot monitor government, they are unlikely to attempt to hold politicians accountable. The chance of a sanction from poor people also is low when poor people lack effective low-cost tools for punishing officials (Rubenstein 2007).

There is no doubt that poverty and a representation deficit for poor people impede democratic consolidation. Yet how poverty affects whether people can hold their government accountable, and how legislators have incentives to represent poor people, has received little consideration.[14] Beginning to fill that gap is the focus of this book.

What Does Representation Mean in a Context of Poverty?

Representation is a broad concept, with meanings ranging from descriptive (a legislative body whose membership mimics the general population), to taking care of the interests of the represented group (the legislator acting as "delegate" rather than "trustee"), to policy congruence (legislators producing policy and services that follow from the preferences of their electorate) (Pitkin 1967).[15] Representation can mean that all actors get to take part in the deliberation of policy. They may not get exactly what they want, as making policy requires compromise, but at least their interests are represented in the deliberation that produces the compromise (Mansbridge 2003).[16]

14. The nature of the link between representation and accountability is a matter of debate. Stokes (1999) argues that in Latin America representation comes through accountability (retrospective representation), rather than in the form of mandate representation. Rubenstein (2007) discusses how "surrogate accountability" might help enable poor people to hold more powerful actors accountable.

15. Stokes (1998) cautions against viewing representation as policy responsiveness, because voters often lack the information they would need to evaluate *ex ante* the consequences of a policy.

16. Mansbridge (2003) offers a new typology of forms of representation. "Promissory representation" is where voters select a legislator based on campaign promises, and then at the next election sanction or reward the official based on whether the promises were fulfilled, which fits the criteria for democratic accountability. The three new forms of representation she describes—anticipatory, gyroscopic, and surrogate—break apart the direct relationship between the voter and the elected official. See Sapiro (1981) for discussion of whether representation needs to be descriptive. Schwindt-Bayer and Mishler (2005) argue that the correct interpretation of Pitkin's various concepts of representation is an integrated concept.

Where democracy operates in a context of poverty, do institutions give legislators an incentive to represent poor people in a way that comes close to any of these definitions? If elected officials want to use their office to represent poor people, is doing so a viable career-building strategy or a recipe for political suicide? Are efforts to make policy that enhances equity likely to be successful? Deliberative democracy assumes that all significant points of view can make themselves heard in the deliberation.[17] Yet according to Conaghan (1996), leaders operating in a context of poverty do not reach out to society or pay attention to citizen demands. She argues that democracy in Latin America lacks authenticity due to "imperial executives, foundering legislatures, corroded parties," and technocratic policymaking without consultation (34).

A different reason to question the validity of these concepts of representation is that poor people may care more about receiving particularistic services and local infrastructure than about national policy (Kitschelt and Wilkinson 2007, 25). Remmer (2007, 363) writes, "Research on the political economy of democracy takes programmatic linkages between citizens and politicians as its central point of theoretical departure. . . . For the majority of the world's voters, however, the electoral calculus is conditioned less by programmatic considerations than by patron-clientelism." Evidence supporting this point can be found in the demands popular associations often make for such things as food subsidies, land titles, work programs, or neighborhood infrastructure (Collier and Handlin 2005, 13). It can also be seen when governments design policies that provide targetable benefits, so that what appears to be a social welfare program is really something that can be used to benefit party supporters. This does not mean poor people do not have preferences about national policy, but that they may base their vote in the next election on concrete benefits they or their community received, rather than on policies whose impact is uncertain and will be difficult to monitor (Kitschelt 2000; Desposato 2001). Calvo and Murillo (2004) offer a complementary argument: parties with a support base that is composed of poor people will value patronage politics and campaign for votes by offering particularistic benefits, because poor people will value these cheap benefits. It is not efficient for middle-class parties to pursue such a strategy because their supporters will not view such benefits as valuable. Lyne (2007, 163) argues that voters (not just poor people) will only vote based on policy and collective goods when they "can ignore the effects

---

17. However, "influence can legitimately be highly unequal (at least under conditions in which the unequal exercise of influence does not undermine a rough equality of respect among participants, foreclose further opportunities to exercise equal power, or deny any of the participants the opportunity to grow through participation)" (Mansbridge 2003, 519).

of free-riding on their own welfare"—when they no longer find valuable what they will receive for their clientelistic vote. It is difficult to predict the results of a new policy—and even if a policy bill becomes law, implementation may be slow and enforcement lax. Thus, because the benefit is more certain and monitoring is cheap, poor voters may assess representation based on infrastructure projects for their community (e.g., a school or clinic) and personal benefits (e.g., a job, scholarship, building materials, or help for a sick family member).

A very loose concept of representation could be how citizens answer the question "What has government done for me lately?" A positive answer (e.g., I received assistance with a problem; my town got a paved road; or government agents are now enforcing the law that says women with small children should have child care at their workplace) could be representation. Representation as "acting in the interest of" (Pitkin 1967) could mean delivering a local service, a personal benefit, or a national policy (or enforcing an existing policy). According to Piattoni (2001, 3, 18), "politics is inherently particularistic" and "clientelism is just one of the historical forms in which interests are represented and promoted, a practical (although in many ways undesirable) solution to the problem of democratic representation."

Representation of poor people is not necessarily measurable as a policy impact that reduces poverty indices.[18] Poverty rates are determined by more than the policies a government adopts (e.g., trends in the world economy or natural disasters). A change in poverty indicators could result from resources invested in human infrastructure development a generation or more in the past, which are slow to produce results that show up in national statistics (Ross 2006; Dion 2007). Poor people can also have preferences about issues (e.g., access to drinking water, reduced street crime, respectful treatment from the judicial system) that do not show up in national poverty statistics.

Poverty and Consolidating Democracy

When democracy spread across Latin America in the 1980s, the initial concern was whether it would survive. Pacts and "perverse elements" (more on that

---

18. A number of scholars have explored whether democracy better serves poor people in Latin America than do authoritarian regimes, and the findings are mixed. Brown and Hunter (2004), Avelino, Brown, and Hunter (2005), and Huber, Murillo, and Stephens (2008) find that democracies spend more on social services than do non-democracies; Ross (2006) argues that these state funds may not benefit the poor, but rather may be welfare programs for the middle sectors (see also Kaufman and Segura-Ubiergo 2001). Iversen and Soskice (2006) find in industrialized democracies that different types of democratic institutions and party systems produce different class coalitions, thereby affecting whether democratic regimes will be redistributive.

below) lessened the fears of authoritarian incumbents and traditional elites so they would agree to a transition and insured that economic elites did not lose in policy debates (Karl 1986; Karl 1990, 11; Hagopian 1992; Valenzuela 1992; Casper and Taylor 1996; Hunter 1997). These deals may have been necessary to bring about a transition, but democratization is an ongoing process, and once installed a democratic regime enters the consolidation phase (Rustow 1970).[19] Survival may still be an important issue,[20] but "'who benefits' from democracy" has also become important (Karl 1990, 13).

Consolidating democracy requires, among other things, removing those perverse elements, which are undemocratic holdovers from the authoritarian past, and deepening democracy so that both the political elites and the masses decide they are better off with this form of government, even when they lose some elections and policy battles (Rustow 1970; Przeworski 1991; Valenzuela 1992). To consolidate, democracy needs "mass legitimation" (Linz and Stepan 1996) and participation (Burton, Gunther, and Higley 1992, 4), but what does this imply? Is it enough for all people to have the vote, or must they also receive representation in policy debates and be able to hold officials accountable?

If different sectors of society have unequal capacities to articulate their interests and to monitor and sanction elected officials, it will affect the chances of consolidating democracy. The existence of formal democracy (i.e., following the procedures of democratic institutions) does not mean political power is distributed equally to all people (Lukes 1974; Bollen 1990, 9; Vilas 1997, 11; Huber, Rueschemeyer, and Stephens 1999, 169). O'Donnell (1994) criticizes "delegative" democracy for violating the principle of checks and balances. Another criticism is that it insulates presidents from popular pressures so that they can implement painful economic policies, but elites still have a say if there is a mobilization of bias (Schattschneider 1960; Crisp 2000). According to Vilas

19. I apply a minimal procedural definition to categorize a country as having installed a democratic regime. The necessary attributes are "fully contested elections with full suffrage and the absence of massive fraud, combined with effective guarantees of civil liberties, including freedom of speech, assembly, and association" (Collier and Levitsky 1997, 322). Collier and Levitsky explain that some scholars add "that elected government must have effective power to govern" (433), because if the military enjoys reserved domains, elected leaders may not actually govern (Karl 1990; Valenzuela 1992; Mainwaring, Brinks, and Pérez-Liñán 2001; Bowman, Lehoucq, and Mahoney 2005). I view this attribute as part of *consolidating* democracy, which can occur after the democratic regime is installed.

20. Remmer (1995) questioned whether Latin America's democracies are really so fragile, given their ability to survive during the harsh economic times of the 1980s. Still, survival during hard economic times does not necessarily signal that democracy is deepening; it may simply mean that policy initiatives have not threatened the interests of traditional elites (Hagopian 2005).

(1997, 29), "Shrinking parliamentary and political party involvement in policy-making affects the average citizen much more than it does those who are high above the average. . . . Lobbying, 'media politics,' or bribery, strategies not available to every actor in the political system, substitute for open party competition." Associations formed to address immediate subsistence concerns certainly organize poor people and do appear to be a harbinger for popular democracy, but they generally do not enable poor people to insert their policy preferences into the debate on national politics (but see Hochstetler and Fried-man 2008). They have a large potential membership if they can form alliances across groups, but it is difficult to harness the potential political clout of their numbers. Decentralization *may* create institutional spaces at subnational levels of government (see O'Neill 2006), but people may still be dissatisfied with the representation they receive from the national government, which means democratic representation is still compromised (Mainwaring, Bejarano, and Pizarro Leongómez 2006, 31).

According to Karl (1990, 8), "The arrangements made by key political actors during a regime transition establish new rules, roles, and behavioral patterns which may or may not represent an important rupture with the past." These arrangements "become the institutions shaping the prospects for regime consolidation in the future" (8). Traditional political elites may be able to design institutions that enhance their political powers and restrain the power of groups whose interests conflict with their own. They may give other groups power only in issue areas where the elites and the masses have compatible policy preferences (e.g., building infrastructure in communities when wealthy contractors get to build the project) (Lukes 1974; Roett 1984; Moe 2005). Of course, elites can overplay their hand and poor people may not vote, thereby decreasing the legitimacy of elections with low turnout; they may turn away from established parties and vote for populist candidates; or they may parti-cipate by unconventional means that threaten the elites' control.

Deepening democracy takes time, as only through experience can people develop an effective attachment to the regime, not just to the current officeholders (Easton 1975).[21] The legitimacy of a democratic regime and its key institutions must be earned (Lievesley 1999, 18; Lagos 2003, 137–38). If poor people continually lose policy battles, they are unlikely to develop effective

---

21. Lodge and Taber (2000) use the image of a "running tally" of positive experiences with democracy, over time creating a deep-seated commitment to democracy and a reservoir of goodwill so that popular support will continue even when the regime goes through hard times and experiences policy failures.

support for democracy, because they will not conclude that they are better off with democracy than they would be with some other regime. Deepening democracy means extending citizenship and equal political rights to all of a country's people. In most Latin American countries, deepening democracy is made more challenging because it "must take place in a context of extreme inequality" (Karl 1990, 13; see also O'Donnell 1992, 19; Lagos 2003, 138; Hagopian 2005).

O'Donnell (1992, 46) asked, "Who will be represented, by whom, and how; and who will be (or continue to be) excluded?" In many countries or electoral districts, politicians and parties need the votes of poor people to win fair elections, and Latin American governments have largely adopted the norm of free and fair elections. But do the poor count beyond having their votes tallied in elections? Do officials remember their poor supporters when making policy and allocating state resources, or are poor people once again excluded? These questions are addressed in this book by examining poor people's ability to monitor, how institutions affect the capacity of poor people to sanction, and how institutions affect legislators' view of their job and whether their representation strategy should include poor people.

Overview of the Book

Chapter 2 uses a principal-agent framework to consider at a theoretical level whether it is rational for a legislator to represent poor people. First, I present a classical principal-agent model of democratic accountability to outline how accountability works, then how accountability can break down even when there is just one principal. Next, I look at the case of two principals with different preferences but equal capacity to monitor and sanction their agent. Then, I examine the case that is the motivation for this book: two principals, one that depicts elites and one that depicts poor people.[22] I then consider how electoral rules, nomination procedures, and clientelism influence whom it is rational for legislators to represent. The final section of the chapter presents a step return function (Croson and Marks 2000; Goeree and Holt 2005) for

---

22. The middle class could be a third principal; I distinguish the poor and rich principals based on their monitoring and sanctioning resources, however, and the middle class is more like the rich principal due to its capacity to monitor (if it chooses to become involved in politics). The middle class can also be viewed as a potential ally of the rich or poor principal, as in Iversen and Soskice's (2006) theory and empirical test of middle-class alliances under different institutional arrangements in advanced industrial democracies.

assessing when it becomes rational for poor people to rebel against a representation deficit, and when a poor person is likely to tolerate limited, clientelistic representation.

Chapter 3 examines macro-level observable implications of the theory using data from the World Values Survey and Latinobarómetro for nine Latin American countries. I categorize countries based on the sanctioning capacity of poor people created by electoral institutions, party nomination procedures, and the form of clientelism in their country, and evaluate whether differences in this sanctioning capacity help explain cross-national variation in how poor people evaluate their legislature. I hypothesize that public opinion polls will show that poor people have more confidence in their legislature in settings where institutions give them a greater capacity to sanction officials. The expectation is that, where poor people can easily sanction, legislators have an incentive to attend to poor people, which gives poor people a reason to have a more favorable view of their legislature relative to countries where institutions do not give legislators this incentive. The cross-national data largely support this hypothesis, and for countries where the sanctioning capacity of poor people changes over time, the intra-country data also support the hypothesis.

Chapters 4 through 7 present a multilayered, in-depth case study of Honduras. Honduras serves as a crucial test case (Lijphart 1971, 692; Gerring 2004, 347) for exploring whether, when, and how the poor count in democratic regimes because so many Hondurans are poor that there can be no question that the votes of the poor are needed to win elections. Poverty in Honduras resembles poverty in many Latin American countries, though its extent is generally greater (see tables 1.1 and 1.2). Poor people lack education, and many are illiterate or functionally illiterate in terms of the reading skills needed to assess political information. Many poor people have basic needs that are not addressed, including nutrition, clean water, electricity, and sewage service (see table 1.4).

Yet Honduras is a paradox because although it is very poor, the political system appears stable and poor Hondurans are actively involved in parties (Booth and Aubone 2007). Inequality has become more obvious in the last twenty-five years, as the rich have become more ostentatious in displaying their wealth, but inequality is not new. Two traditional parties were founded at the turn of the twentieth century, and they still receive most people's votes. Honduras has not experienced serious leftist guerrilla threats, or even violent protests by poor people against government policies. Hondurans protest, and strikes and demonstrations are frequent, but they are typically peaceful.

Table 1.4 Variation in poverty indicators across departments within Honduras

	HDI 2004	Average % illiterate	Years of education	% of households lacking Water	Sewer	Electricity	Homes with TV (%)
Atlántida	0.687	14.2	6.9	13.5	24.4	29.9	56.7
Bay Islands	0.726	4.3	7.6	10.5	14.4	10.5	64.6
Choluteca	0.627	25.7	5.4	23.1	42.6	64.0	26.9
Colón	0.636	22.3	5.6	16.5	36.0	47.7	32.9
Comayagua	0.629	20.9	5.8	19.6	40.7	48.8	40.6
Copán	0.578	34.2	4.3	22.9	43.0	59.8	25.8
Cortes	0.709	11.0	7.2	7.8	13.3	9.9	74.5
El Paraiso	0.619	27.2	4.9	34.4	35.6	62.7	27.3
Francisco Morazan	0.732	10.9	8.3	15.4	26.9	16.5	74.2
Gracias a Diós	0.635	22.0	5.4	45.9	72.9	86.9	5.5
Intibucá	0.582	28.5	4.9	32.1	43.0	81.6	13.2
La Paz	0.610	24.6	5.3	28.0	37.5	71.8	21.7
Lempira	0.554	36.5	3.9	27.5	51.5	86.7	6.9
Ocotepeque	0.600	28.8	4.7	17.6	42.2	59.5	27.6
Olancho	0.608	28.4	5.1	30.2	47.5	65.0	25.3
Santa Bárbara	0.597	32.4	4.6	18.0	38.5	57.6	25.3
Valle	0.649	25.3	5.8	23.0	52.7	52.3	36.7
Yoro	0.651	21.2	5.7	15.2	27.7	41.8	44.9
HONDURAS	0.664	20.0	6.2	18.3	31.7	40.0	48.0

SOURCE: Honduran National Census 2001; UNDP 2006, 30.
HDI = Human Development Index (UN)

This puzzle makes it interesting to explore whether elected officials in Honduras have an incentive to represent poor people and how, because one possible reason why poor Hondurans are willing to work within the system is that they do receive some clientelistic representation. The clientelistic benefits they receive could make them unwilling to risk losing those benefits to possibly obtain uncertain benefits from a major change in the party system.

Chapter 4 is an overview of Honduran history. The chapter highlights myths and misconceptions about Honduras commonly held because of its location in Central America. It explains the origin of the two traditional parties, their vertical organization and reliance on clientelism, and assesses the level of democracy in the present regime. It then analyzes the path-dependent development of electoral and nomination rules, showing how the vertical organization of the traditional parties and their continued need for access to the state's clientelism resources have sustained party leaders' control, even with regime changes, constitutional revisions, and election law changes.

Chapter 5 describes the institutions in Honduras's third-wave democratic regime, building on the path-dependent development of those institutions laid out in chapter 4. It applies the theoretical argument from chapter 2, examining macro-level observable implications of the theory to assess the capacity of rich and poor people to monitor. Further, the chapter explores how Honduras's combination of institutions affects the capacity of rich and poor people to sanction, the incentives that institutions give legislators to represent poor people, and the forms that representation is likely to take.

Chapter 6 presents a role analysis of Honduran deputies, examining micro-level observable implications of the theory to explore the ways legislators operating within institutional constraints choose to do their job. This chapter applies Searing's (1994) idea of legislators' informal preferences roles, which argues that even within institutional constraints, politicians still make choices (see also Scharpf 1989). The role analysis recognizes that, along with a "calculus approach" to human behavior, there is also a "cultural approach" that conceptualizes the relationship between institutions and behavior where "behavior is not fully strategic but bounded by an individual's worldview . . . which provide[s] the filters for interpretation, of both the situation and oneself" (Hall and Taylor 1996, 939). Honduran deputies have adopted three different roles or identities that fit the cognitive templates provided by institutions: *Congress Advocates* want to improve the quality of laws and strengthen the Congress; *Party Deputies* view their job as serving their party, particularly faction leaders; and *Constituency Servers* want to develop their communities and attend to constituents' needs. Chapters 4 and 5 explain the origins and the institutional setting of the current democratic regime and assess the constraints those institutions place on the representation strategies of legislators. Chapter 6 asks politicians operating within that setting how they view their job and the duties of a deputy, assessing which institutional incentives are of greatest importance to deputies who adopt different roles. I then make predictions about which types of deputies have an incentive to represent the policy, service, and particularistic interests of the poor.

Chapter 7 presents data about how deputies who adopt different roles view who their constituents are and their duties to those constituents. Analysis of the legislative records of deputies in the different role types shows that behavior differs across the roles. The chapter concludes with an examination of the implications of the different deputy roles for whether, when, and how the poor count in Honduran politics.

Chapter 8 begins with a consideration of the implications of the book's findings for policy outputs, in particular how an incentive for clientelistic representation affects policy, and includes brief case studies from Honduras's and

Brazil's conditional cash transfer programs. I then conclude, arguing that a representation deficit for the poor is likely in Latin American democracies because rich people and their interest groups will often punish those representing the policy interests of poor people. This occurs in part because rich people have more monitoring resources than the poor, and under many institutional settings have a greater capacity to sanction elected officials. Poor people may not support officials who try to represent their policy interests because their policy proposals are likely to be extensively revised and moderated just to be passed, and then are often not aggressively implemented. With their limited capacity to monitor the policy work of their elected officials, poor people are not likely to be aware of an official's efforts to produce programmatic policy on their behalf if the efforts do not deliver concrete benefits. But the representation deficit shrinks where institutions create incentives for clientelistic representation for (some) poor people, because people who receive clientelistic benefits have received a tangible indication that they matter to government. Thus clientelism may be a key to the stability of democracy in a context of poverty, albeit a democracy that may not fit our conventional images.

There is a representation deficit in Latin America because most combinations of electoral institutions, nominations, and forms of clientelism do not create incentives for elected officials to view their job as representing the interests of poor people in national policy. But it is not a *crisis* of popular representation, in the sense that institutions create *no* incentives to represent poor people. Multi-institution analysis indicates that some institutional settings create strong incentives for clientelistic representation. Other institutional settings may not *require* career-seeking legislators to engage in clientelistic representation but *permit* such activity by legislators whose role or cognitive template (which is prompted by the institutional setting) includes building a reputation as a patron. But even that source of representation may be dampened by other institutions that either create strong incentives for party loyalty or make it difficult for legislators to obtain access to state resources.

This study suggests that the role of clientelism and poverty in democratization in Latin America may be misperceived. Scholars often decry clientelism as the source of many of Latin America's problems, including the difficulty of consolidating democracy (see, e.g., O'Donnell 1992; Karl 1995; Stokes 1998, 2005; Huber, Rueschemeyer, and Stephens 1999, 181). Yet this study indicates that clientelistic benefits to the poor may be essential to democratic stability, and their removal can sow the seeds of popular discontent if they provide the only evidence of representation perceived by poor people (Scott 1969, 1155; Valenzuela 1977; Kitschelt 2000).

Do the poor count in Latin American democracies? The answer is a qualified "no," as institutions typically give elected officials little or no incentive to represent the poor beyond the delivery of clientelistic club goods and selective incentives. In contrast to the focus of some scholars on the extensive, growing poverty in Latin America as an indicator of unequal rights, however, this book concludes that poverty alone does not negate citizenship rights. Poverty interacts with institutions that affect the capacity of citizens to sanction their officials, constrain legislators' representation strategy options and roles, and often punish politicians for representing the poor in forms other than clientelistic representation.

TWO

THEORIZING REPRESENTATION AND
ACCOUNTABILITY IN A CONTEXT OF POVERTY

Principal-agent relationships are often used to study mechanisms of accountability in democratic systems, with citizens as the principal and the elected official as the agent.[1] Elegant in their simplicity, principal-agent models define boundaries and limiting conditions, such as the optimal payment to the agent (Barro 1973), and the level of monitoring that will motivate the agent to seek reelection and also produce the policy and services the principal desires (Ferejohn 1986). Scholars also ask whether elections are a selection game to choose a "good type" who will represent the voter's interests when making policy (Fearon 1999), or a moral hazard game to sanction incumbents who do not deliver the policies and services the voter desires (Ferejohn 1986, 1999).

Formal models of political accountability make simplifying assumptions that are suitable for economically advanced industrialized countries with a large middle class and high levels of education, but these are not necessarily appropriate in a context of poverty. In this chapter, I examine accountability in a democracy when extreme inequality differentially affects the ability of sectors of the population to monitor and sanction elected officials. First, I discuss assumptions in formal models of accountability that need to be relaxed in order to study accountability in this context. Next, I introduce the actors in a principal-agent accountability relationship set in a context of poverty. I then review the standard principal-agent model of accountability with one principal and one agent, and explore how two competing principals—each of whom has an equivalent capacity to monitor and sanction—affect the agent's strategy. I then examine how differences between capacities of poor and rich people to monitor—and how institutional constraints on the capacity of citizens,

---

1. The accountability of bureaucracies to elected officials is another principal-agent relationship, with the elected official as the principal and the bureaucracy as the agent.

particularly poor people, to reward or punish elected officials—affect the strategies of an elected official who wants to continue in politics. In sum, this chapter explores when legislators have incentives to represent poor people and when institutions produce a representation deficit for the poor. This chapter does not depict institutions from a particular country; rather, it considers the incentives that different electoral systems, party nomination procedures, and forms of clientelism create and how they influence politicians' decisions about whom it is rational to represent.

Studying Accountability in a Context of Poverty

To study democratic accountability in a context of poverty, two simplifying assumptions in principal-agent models of accountability need to be relaxed.[2] One assumption is that a single principal works with the agent. The second assumption is that all agents, or aspiring agents, are substitutable for the principal.

Formal models of democratic accountability generally adopt the simplifying assumption of a single principal, so the challenge for voters is coordinating the signal sent to their agent.[3] A lack of coordination allows elected officials to deviate from the preferences of citizens and obtain rents from government posts (Ferejohn 1999, 134). But what if people have different goals for government and therefore do not *want* to send the agent the same signal? This is not a coordination problem; it means the agent has more than one principal. Who will the agent represent? Moe (2005, 215) points to this question when he claims the key challenge of studying institutions is not just "whether rational individuals will cooperate in the face of collective action problems," which assumes individuals can reach a mutually beneficial agreement. If some people are losers from the arrangement, however, they do not cooperate with it voluntarily; their cooperation is due to coercion (Lukes 1974, 2005).

A single principal may be an appropriate simplifying assumption in democratic accountability models for developed countries where most people *can*

---

2. Rubenstein (2007) presents a model of *surrogate* accountability to address the problems that poor people or other weak groups have holding a stronger actor accountable. Her focus is not how institutions affect the sanctioning ability of an actor, though she acknowledges that institutions can exacerbate or mitigate the effects of poverty, but rather how another actor can help a weak actor to have the means to hold the powerful actor accountable.

3. An important exception is Bendor and Meirowitz (2004), who explicitly extend their model of delegation to include multiple principals.

monitor and sanction the agent if they choose.[4] If a politician knows that all types of voters and groups in society have the *capacity* to monitor and sanction, then the politician must find ways to make all principals perceive that government represents their interests (at least sometimes). If not, principal-agent theory predicts that the disaffected voters will sanction the politician, ending the politician's political career. But poor people have less capacity than do other citizens to monitor most types of actions by elected officials, and the sanctions they can impose are often blunt and costly to the poor people themselves.[5] When a large percentage of the population is both poor and has limited monitoring and sanctioning capability, it may be feasible for elected officials to not represent the interests of poor people.

The electorate in economically developed countries is heterogeneous (in terms of ethnicity, ideology, and religion, among other things), and groups have different policy and service preferences. In a context of relative economic equality, it may be a suitable simplifying assumption that groups have a similar capacity to make their preferences known and to monitor government (if they expend the effort). Politicians then have an incentive to represent (in the sense of working in the interests of; see Pitkin 1967) all the diverse people, because any group can reward performance that pleases them.

Modeling democratic accountability with a single principal assumes that all types of people have relatively equal capacity to monitor and sanction the agent. In one sense, this is true in a democracy. Anybody can ask, "What has government done for me lately," or "Am I better off now than I was at the time of the last election?"[6] All citizens must have the right to vote, and all votes must be counted equally, or else the country is not a democracy; therefore, in a democracy the vote is a sanction available to all people who meet the legal requirements.[7] But other monitoring and sanctioning resources may

4. Even where the population is educated and affluent, monitoring will not be perfect, as voters still cannot observe directly many of government's actions. In addition, many voters will accept slippage in the principal-agent relationship with government because they choose not to expend effort monitoring.

5. In Mexico under the PRI's rule, poor people who made demands and confronted government were less likely to be the ones who ultimately reaped the benefits of any policy concession (Fox 1994; Hellman 1994).

6. Ferejohn (1986) argues that suboptimal outcomes will result if voters use this individually rational decision rule when evaluating political incumbents. To achieve superior accountability, nonhomogeneous voters need to employ sociotropic or collective evaluative criteria.

7. The design of electoral institutions can determine whether the vote is a sharp sanction that can punish or reward specific officials, or a blunt sanction that can only be used on a party. This is discussed below. At this point, it is sufficient to note that ballot type should affect the sharpness or bluntness of the vote as a sanction available to both rich and poor people.

not be equally accessible. For example, campaign contributions provide rich people with sanctions unavailable to poor people. The poor might have their numbers as a sanctioning tool (they are a larger number of potential voters than the rich and middle class in many electoral districts in Latin America), but organizational fragmentation dilutes this potential (Gay 1990; Weyland 1996; Lievesley 1999).[8] Educated people can obtain and evaluate data to assess conditions. Uneducated people have less access to analytical information and may be limited to evaluating government performance by watching television or observing the condition and experiences of their family and community. Radio and television are becoming widespread, but media bias can limit the quality of this information for monitoring elected officials. The government may have power over the media (e.g., by controlling licenses or paying reporters), so investigative journalism is not necessarily available as a "cheap" monitoring resource.

Rubenstein (2007) discusses when surrogate sources of information can enable a weak actor to overcome the information deficit that short-circuits what she calls "standard accountability." She cautions that it is necessary to evaluate "how close did the surrogate come to gathering the *information* that accountability holders [in this case the weak actor] would have gathered?" (627–28). Surrogates can be quite effective at providing the weak actor with information about whether its agent has complied with rules (e.g., laws about fair treatment in the courts), but surrogates are less able to provide accurate information about whether the agent promoted the weak actor's preferences.

Another common assumption is that candidates or parties are substitutable, so a voter can always threaten to replace an incumbent. But this is a fragile assumption (Fearon 1999) that ignores voter allegiance to a party or the need for a patron. A strong party supporter would resist voting for an opposition candidate because of the psychic cost of voting against one's party. For a poor client, maintaining a relationship with a patron may be more important than sanctioning an elected official over policy.[9] How is voter control

---

8. A Global Barometer study of who votes in poor countries finds that the material status of voters does not predict propensity to vote. In Latin America, 78 percent of people who owned a full list of household goods (telephone, piped water system, etc.) said that they voted, while 74 percent of people who did not have all these goods also said that they voted (Bratton, Chu, and Lagos 2006, 9).

9. Patron-client relationships between voters and elected officials prompt the question of whether elections should be modeled as retrospective or prospective events. Principal-agent relationships typically assume that the principal responds to the agent's past behavior. For a principal who has a clientelistic relationship with the agent, the vote decision may be prospective, with the client voting for the agent expected to be the most helpful (Wilson 1990). Coppedge (1993) examined

over elected officials affected by the voter paying a high cost for switching agents, particularly if some types of voters incur a cost while others do not?

Principals and Agents in a Context of Poverty

The Agent

In formal models of democratic accountability, the agent is typically an incumbent representative.[10] Here, as well, legislators are the agent, because in democratic theory the legislature is intended to be the *representative branch* of government.[11] A growing body of literature shows that Latin American legislatures, which historically were viewed as marginal (Mezey 1979), are relevant players in the policymaking process. Cox and Morgenstern (2002) argue that presidents take into account the preferences of the legislature when proposing their own policy initiatives to insure they will pass. Presidents whose party lacks a majority must build coalitions by giving out cabinet posts and purchasing support from individual deputies and parties on individual bills (Amorim Neto 1998; Mejía Acosta 2003; Kellam 2007). Calvo (2007) shows that the Argentine congress can respond to the public mood and kill bills the executive initiates. Legislators themselves initiate bills with national and sectoral targets (not just local targets), and while some bills are trivial or symbolic (e.g., a bill to establish a national holiday), many address policy issues (e.g., changes to the penal or tax codes or electoral laws). Some deputies' bills win passage, and even if they do not become law they can attract attention, making the issue part of the national policy debate (see Taylor-Robinson and Diaz 1999; Escobar-Lemmon, Avellaneda, and Botero 2005; Micozzi 2009, for studies of legislating by deputies in Honduras, Colombia, and Argentina, respectively).

The legislature is an institution, but its members determine the larger body's actions (e.g., the median legislator or committee member, the governing party,

---

Mexico under the PRI and Venezuela when AD (Acción Democrática) and COPEI (Comité de Organización Política Electoral Independiente) dominated politics. He concluded that both major parties in Venezuela had to be attentive to poor people because the electorate could always just vote for the other party. In Mexico, the PRI was the only party whose patrons could deliver services and patronage, so a protest vote for another party was very costly to a poor person as it meant losing all possibility for particularistic benefits.

10. Models of democratic accountability are not explicitly based on the United States, yet assumptions typically fit the institutions of U.S. politics.

11. See chapter 1 for the rationale for this decision.

legislators acting as individuals). I assume that legislators respond to the incentives and constraints created by the institutions of their particular political arena, and that within those constraints they make choices about the job they will do (e.g., for whom they will legislate, or how they will allocate their time between institutional maintenance, constituency service, party work, etc.). Legislators should also consider whether they are likely to retain rich or poor voters' support for *attempting* to implement a policy (i.e., by proposing a bill or amendment, even if it is not passed), or if constituents will sanction if the bill fails.[12] An elected official's identity, self-image, and preferences are shaped by the institutional milieu, affecting whom the official represents and what form that representation takes. If citizens view legislators as unresponsive, they may develop a negative opinion of the legislature. They may begin to wonder why they are paying legislators' salaries, and the congress may lose legitimacy in the people's eyes. As table 1.3 shows, few Latin Americans hold their congress in high esteem.

Institutions also shape the identity and self-image of presidents and influence the initiatives that will become the hallmarks of a presidency—though a president who faces a term limit may be less constrained than a legislator who wants to continue a political career. Parties also work within the institutional milieu of their country, such as when deciding on an electoral strategy. Future research should explore how different institutional contexts affect executives and parties, as these actors must also confront monitoring and possible sanction by multiple principals.

The Principals

In a context of poverty, we can think of two stylized principals with different (though not necessarily conflicting) preferences and an unequal capacity to monitor and sanction.[13] The rich principal has abundant monitoring and sanctioning resources. The poor principal has few monitoring resources and sanctioning tools, which are often personally costly to use or require collective

12. Whether a constituent sanctions may depend on how badly the constituent needs the policy or service (e.g., I need an all-weather road to transport crops to market before they spoil vs. I would like to defend the Arctic National Wildlife Refuge). Constituents (rich or poor) who view a policy as a long-range goal requiring a public relations campaign to increase support for the issue should reward the legislator's efforts, provided they can observe those efforts occurring.

13. Actors with unequal monitoring and sanctioning resources may have compatible preferences. In that case, following Tsebelis's (1995) idea that two veto players with the same preferences can be viewed as a single veto player, the two principals become one, though they face a coordination challenge in policing their elected official.

action to affect the agent. Rubenstein (2007, 621–22) explains that there are three main elements of accountability: (1) setting the standards to which the agent will be held, (2) gathering information with which to evaluate whether the agent is fulfilling his or her duty, and (3) sanctioning so agents will have an incentive to meet standards. Though sanctioning is what gives the accountability relationship teeth, and thus limited capacity to sanction often appears to be the source of a principal's weakness, "all three elements of accountability—standards, information, and sanction—can be difficult to implement under conditions of inequality."

Each principal must choose the monitoring effort that achieves an acceptable balance between how far an agent's behavior differs from the principal's policy/service preference, and how much effort the principal invests in policing. Typically a principal will accept some shirking, since monitoring is costly and that cost subtracts from the benefit obtained from policy and services.

How much monitoring is optimal? The answer differs for rich and poor people because the relative cost of a unit of monitoring is greater for poor people. If a rich person has one hundred units of monitoring resources, the marginal cost of expending one unit is lower than it is for a poor person who has only ten units. Some monitoring is easy and cheap; for example, voters can ask themselves whether the streets feel safe, or if they received the promised job or assistance from the legislator. Monitoring whether a legislator who promised to promote rights for agricultural workers or to improve the quality of schools is following through with bills, amendments, and debate participation requires the principal to expend extensive monitoring resources. A rich person can afford to engage in resource-intensive monitoring, but a poor person likely cannot.[14]

Poor people, especially those with little or no education, may have little capacity to monitor elected officials. Limited reading skills make printed information inaccessible (e.g., newspapers, reports, congressional transcripts on the Internet). Monitoring policy negotiations and bill amendments requires access to information from inside policymaking circles that often operate behind closed doors. Poor people's monitoring may be limited to what they can observe about policy and services in their life, or information from NGOs whose policy goals overlap with the interests of the poor and who want to mobilize

14. A principal that has abundant monitoring resources may not use them, so rich people may be no more aware of officials' activities than poor people. For example, an educated person might utilize the Internet primarily for business or personal reasons, and never use it to track government policy development.

poor people for the group's cause (see Hochstetler 2000, 177–81).[15] By contrast, a rich person can join an interest group that employs staff to monitor government proposals and investigate their technical feasibility. Connections to government may allow rich persons or their interest groups to take part in policy negotiations.[16] In sum, poor people are likely to face a greater information asymmetry than are rich people. Simply based on the differences in their monitoring capability, we would expect agents to have less incentive to represent poor people than rich people.

Sanctioning tools also differ for the rich and poor. In a democracy, all citizens have their vote as a sanction, but votes are only one way to sanction or reward officials. As mentioned above, campaign contributions can be given as a reward or taken away as a sanction, and only rich people have the capacity to make contributions.[17] Influence on nominations can reward or sanction legislators, especially if the main hurdle for reelection is getting nominated in a safe district or securing a safe position on the party's list. A rich person may have business, family, or social connections with party leaders who control ballot access and list position. Poor people lack access to the inner circles of party power, and must vote for or against the candidate or list their party offers.[18]

As mentioned previously, sanctioning tools available to poor people are often blunt, costly to implement, or require participation by many people to be successful. Poor people can organize demonstrations to protest or support government policies or services—for example, women from a Lima barrio staging a sit-in at the Ministry of Health to protest the government not building

15. Evaluations of social fund programs provide evidence of how limited capacity makes it more difficult for poor people to obtain resources from government—even resources that are supposed to be targeted at poor people. According to Tendler (2000, 117–18), "Poor communities are handicapped in responding to [social fund]–like initiatives in that they require prior organizing, preparation of project proposals, and choosing and monitoring of outside contractors." This creates a "comparative advantage of communities that were better off—*within* the 'poor-designated' municipalities or subregions—in competing for funds."

16. "Business groups have increasingly organized intersectoral 'encompassing associations' to articulate and defend their class interests" (Durand and Silva 1998). "These associations play a significant role in the policy-making process, as they generally are granted direct access to governing officials" (Roberts 2002, 27).

17. Public financing for campaigns could help level the playing field in this regard.

18. Even with primaries, voters may still only have limited control over candidate selection. Extremists in the U.S. Democratic and Republican parties have acquired increased influence over the types of candidates offered to voters in the primary elections by directing campaign contributions to and grooming extreme candidates, while discouraging moderates (Fleisher and Bond 2004). Bachrach and Baratz (1970) and Lukes (1974, 2005) argue that elites band together to limit the choice set available to nonelites.

a promised health clinic in their neighborhood (Stokes 1995). Such unconventional forms of participation take time away from work, which means lost income, and organizers must invest their time to make the protest event happen. In addition, justice may not be applied equally to all people. Wealthy business leaders who request a meeting with a minister or congressional leader to discuss their opposition to a proposed policy are unlikely to be jailed for their efforts. If poor people take over a government building to show their displeasure with broken promises, they are just as likely to be arrested as to obtain a policy change or service. Collective action, such as a strike, is not only difficult to organize, but the repressive tactics often used against strikers or organizers raise the cost of this type of sanction. For example, when Ecuadorian banana plantation workers formed a union and went on strike in 2002, hooded, armed men dragged them from their homes, beat them, and shot several people (Otis 2003). If a poor person must pay a high personal cost to try to sanction elected officials, the poor person's sanctioning capacity is weaker than that of a rich person (more on this below).

This inquiry does not have to be limited to two competing principals. It could include various social classes and other societal groupings (e.g., ethnic or linguistic groups, industrial or union sectors). Since this book focuses on rich and poor people, however, it is useful to discuss how a middle class would fit into this analysis. The analysis assumes the competing principals have different policy and service preferences. When their interests differ from those of rich and poor people, the middle class is an additional principal competing for representation. Their success will be influenced by their monitoring and sanctioning ability relative to that of the other principals, as well as by politicians' policy and service preferences and career goals. If middle-class interests are compatible with the interests of rich or poor people, the monitoring and sanctioning capacity of the middle class can be added to the resources of this "partner," and the challenge then is to coordinate policy/service signals and sanctioning efforts. For simplicity, I examine a case of two principals—one rich and the other poor.

Accountability with One Principal

Accountability in a democracy can be thought of like a contract arrangement in business. A company hires an employee to do a task, and then evaluates

the employee's performance at a set time in the future.[19] In democratic accountability, the employer is the citizenry, and the employees are the elected officials.
In classical principal-agent theory, the principal is a unitary actor. This provides a useful starting point for considering how rational behavior by the agent
changes as we expand the principal-agent relationship to multiple principals
in a context of poverty.

   The citizen has a preference for a policy/service package, and the legislator
must decide what policy/service to provide. In formal models, each actor has
preferences over policy and a policy ideal point. In the discussion to come of
incentives to represent rich and poor people, it will be useful to consider
citizens' preferences for local services and particularistic benefits as well as
for policy, so I refer to a policy/service package. The legislator wants to benefit
from holding office, and we can assume legislators receive benefits from
various things, such as continuing their political career, receiving their level
of salary, maintaining the democratic regime, or enjoying an enhanced reputation as a local caudillo.[20] The citizen needs to decide how much to monitor
and, if dissatisfied, whether to try to sanction.

   If the citizen can elect a "good type," the legislator will produce the policy/
service package the voter wants without monitoring because they have the
same preferences (Fearon 1999).[21] If the citizen does not have enough information about candidates to select a good type, or if no candidate has the
same preferences, then the citizen must expend resources on monitoring.

   Unless the citizen can elect an agent who is a "good type," "constituents can
do no better than establish a threshold utility level and reelect the incumbent only if that level is attained. Obviously, the incumbent will follow her
constituents' wishes only if the cost of doing so is less than the (discounted)

   19. There are other aspects to accountability in a democracy, such as the judicial system's role
in ensuring the rule of law (Diamond 1997), or oversight committees and agencies monitoring
and sanctioning the bureaucracy (O'Donnell 2003). See Mainwaring and Welna (2003) for broad
coverage of the concept of democratic accountability.

   20. In transitional democracies, fears that people will not support democracy if their
policy/service interests are not represented, and that popular calls for a coup might bring down
the regime, could give officials an added reason to attend to peoples' demands. For similar
reasons, citizens may refrain from protesting government performance so as not to give the
military an excuse to move back into politics.

   21. Fearon (1999, 59) defines "a good type for a particular voter as a politician who (1) shares
the voter's issue preferences, (2) has integrity, in that he or she is hard to bribe or otherwise
induce to work against the voter's interests, and (3) is competent or skilled in discerning and
implementing optimal policies for the voter." An inducement to deviate from the policy
preference of the voter could take the form of a bribe, but it could also be a threat, such as a
guerrilla group threatening to kill an elected official, a strategy frequently employed by the FARC
(Fuerzas Armadas Revolucionarias de Colombia) in Colombia.

value of reelection, which depends both on the level of the utility threshold and the value of office" (Ferejohn 1999, 137). The legislator must want to continue in politics. The citizen must set the required minimum level of policy/ service provision so that the legislator places a positive value on a government career. The legislator must estimate the probability of reelection as positive and likely enough to be worth setting policy/service at a level that will please the citizen. If these conditions are not met, the legislator will not have a future time horizon, and the principal-agent relationship becomes a final-term game.[22] In a final term game, rational behavior for the legislator is to produce his or her personal preferred policy/service. Where legislators perceive no future political career, citizens will only receive representation if they can select a "good type" as their elected representative.

To make the principal-agent "contract" work—to hold legislators accountable—the citizen also needs the means to influence whether the legislator can continue a political career. The likelihood that the citizen can prevent a legislator from continuing in politics affects the legislator's probable benefit from holding office, which makes institutional design important to principal-agent accountability relationships.[23]

In sum, even a single principal often must accept representation that is not precisely the policy/service package he or she desires. Unless a legislator who is a "good type" is available, the principal has to expend resources on monitoring. Even abundant monitoring resources may not produce perfect representation; if the principal sets the acceptable level of performance too high, legislators will conclude that continuing a political career is not possible, and the principal loses the ability to sanction the agent.

Accountability with Two Principals
with Comparable Capacity to Monitor and Sanction

What happens to citizens' ability to hold legislators accountable when legislators represent people who want different policies/services, and both types

---

22. Term limits may not sever the accountability mechanism if legislators have progressive ambition (Schlesinger 1966) and performance in the current office affects chances of obtaining the next office. For example, Costa Rican deputies cannot be immediately reelected to the Legislative Assembly, but parties want to win the presidency, and they view constituency service as part of party strategy to win voter support. Parties give deputies an incentive to perform constituency service, since they can receive an appointed post if their party wins the presidency (Taylor 1992; Carey 1996).

23. Detailed discussion is given below regarding how the capacity of poor and rich people to sanction elected officials changes with different types of electoral, nomination, and clientelism institutions.

of citizens have equivalent capacity to monitor and to sanction? Because the people have different preferences, the challenge is not merely to coordinate. The legislator faces possible monitoring by both principals, and must decide what policy/service package to produce based on how the legislator prioritizes policy, continuing a political career (factoring in the likelihood of sanction for performance a voter or group evaluates as unfavorable), maintaining democracy, building a reputation as a patron, and so forth.

Competition among citizens or interest groups for attention can prompt a bidding war. Each principal can offer to accept a policy/service package that is further from what the principal really wants, while pledging to reelect the legislator so their needs are partially addressed (Ferejohn 1986, 10–11, 21).[24] The amount of resources a person or group invests in monitoring determines the slippage in policy/service provision they will notice. As the slippage they will tolerate increases, the legislator can provide less representation without fear of a sanction. If the policy/services different people or groups want are not very different, and at least one group will tolerate considerable slippage, a legislator may be able to adopt a policy/service package that satisfies everyone.

If such a solution is not possible, a legislator could ignore both groups at the cost of losing office.[25] But what if the legislator wants a political career? Each of the principals has an equivalent capacity to monitor and sanction, and if they invest equally in monitoring, the legislator cannot produce a policy/service that appeals to one without irritating the other. The reward the legislator will receive from representing one principal will be cancelled by the sanction from the other. Unless the principals begin a bidding war for attention, the legislator might as well adopt his or her personally preferred policy/service because the angry principal will surely sanction.

Politics, of course, covers many issues and service needs, so a legislator may be able to somewhat satisfy both principals before the next election. Both principals could conclude that overall the legislator did an acceptable job of representing them, so neither will sanction. This would be more likely if they did not always disagree; in fact, there are typically multiple opportunities for elected officials to represent people's interests as voters and interest groups hope to win some battles and expect to lose others.

24. Whether a voter can credibly commit to such a pledge is a valid question.

25. If a legislator plans a career outside of politics, a person who has the power to limit the legislator's job prospects could sanction the legislator. Similarly, in a violent society, the threat of violence could be used to punish an official. A legislator would have an incentive to represent the citizen who can get the legislator a desired private sector job or who could implement a violent sanction.

Representation and Accountability in a Context of Poverty

Who receives representation when constituents have different policy/service interests and *unequal* resources for monitoring and sanctioning? This describes the strategy choice of a legislator with poor and rich constituents. The institutional milieu shapes the legislator's reasons for holding office, and also constrains the legislator's strategy for building a political career.[26]

The differences between the policy/services that two different constituents want and between how vigilantly they monitor also influence the legislator's strategy. As discussed above, if voters' policy/service interests are not too far apart or if the voters have different but compatible preferences, a legislator may be able to represent both types of people and avoid sanction. Poor people's limited capacity to monitor national policies increases the likelihood of such a situation. If people want very different policies and services, however, and both monitor, then the legislator has to make a choice. It would appear that the legislator would always represent the rich person. After all, the rich person is more likely than the poor person to know whether a legislator is not fulfilling campaign promises. Monitoring asymmetry is particularly acute for national policies, while both poor and rich people can observe if the local public services and personal benefits they were promised have been delivered. Yet institutions affect the capacity of rich and poor people to sanction their elected representatives, which is the subject of the next part of the chapter. Even a tool as powerful as personal wealth is more potent in some institutional settings than in others, while some types of institutions can actually empower poor people, at least to some extent.

It is also necessary to consider the legislator's policy/service preferences and the value the legislator places on continuing a political career, gaining status as a local patron, and building prestige in the party. It is rational for a legislator to represent poor people if obtaining poor peoples' votes is a cheap way to win reelection (and reelection is important to the legislator). A distinct reason why providing clientelistic representation to poor people can be important to a politician is if the politician ran for congress to build a reputation as a local patron, which could happen even where electoral rules do not create personalizing incentives (see Kitschelt 2000; Kitschelt and Wilkinson 2007).

---

26. A legislator who wants to retire can represent whomever they want. If a legislator intends to work in the private sector, a principal with influence on the legislator's coming job prospects could influence the legislator's future.

How Institutions Affect the Capacity of Poor People to Hold Officials Accountable and Shape Legislators' Strategy

Here I consider how electoral rules, nomination procedures, and forms of clientelism shape legislators' incentives to represent poor people. Two points need to be underscored before examining each of these institutions. One, while it is easiest to think about individual institutions, it is multiple formal and informal institutions that comprise the real setting in which constituents and legislators must try to achieve their goals.[27] Two, institutions do not just constrain legislators; they shape how legislators define their roles in government and why they seek elected office in the first place (Hall and Taylor 1996, 939; Katznelson and Weingast 2005, 15).

Electoral Rules and Nomination Procedures

Formal rules, such as term limits and ballot type, shape legislators' expectations about reelection and affect the capacity of different types of constituents to hold representatives accountable. An incumbent facing a term limit may view the current post as a stepping-stone to another post, and if so, we can model the legislator's strategy as if he or she were running for reelection. In general, however, term limits sever the relationship that makes accountability possible in a democracy (Carey 1996). If reelection is legally possible but many incumbents lose, legislators will view reelection as unlikely, which weakens the incentive to please the voters.

Ballot type determines whether the legislator or party leaders control nomination and election chances, and therefore influences whether people can sanction a legislator directly. In single-member-district plurality (SMD-P) elections, the support of enough voters to come in first in the electoral contest is essential for reelection. Under open-list proportional representation (PR) elections, a legislator needs the support of enough voters to obtain one of the seats his or her party wins in the district. Under SMD-P electoral rules, if members of an ethnic group or union are numerically important in a district and they vote as a block, they can virtually ensure an incumbent's reelection, hence the power of union endorsements and the effort politicians exert to obtain them. Open-list PR electoral rules can make poor voters an important

---

27. Desposato (2006a) and Kitschelt and Wilkinson (2007) discuss how multiple institutions can interact and affect one another's endogenous development.

constituency because a candidate can buy their support cheaply by providing particularistic benefits or local infrastructure projects (possibly designed to work as excludable club goods), and poor people can vote for another candidate if their expectations are not fulfilled (Gay 1990; Hagopian 1990; Kitschelt 2000; Desposato 2001). With SMD-P and open-list electoral rules, people can use their vote to sanction a particular legislator, and voting is a low-cost activity, though it will only truly punish the incumbent if many constituents vote the same way. Where voters must vote for a party's slate of candidates and cannot disturb the list, as in closed-list PR elections, both rich and poor voters are stuck with the candidates the parties give them. An incumbent at the top of the list is likely to be reelected even if voters were not pleased with that legislator's performance. Only people who can influence the composition of the party's list can sanction legislators, so legislators have an incentive to represent those people who have influence with the party leaders controlling nominations.[28]

Even with SMD-P and open-list PR elections that give people the capacity to use their vote to sanction a legislator directly (not indirectly by sanctioning the legislator's party), voters are still limited to choosing a candidate running in the election. The choice of candidates determines the value of attempting to sanction, because it determines how much representation is likely to change. If all candidates advocate policies or promise services the voter does not want, a different representative will not enhance representation. Thus we need to consider nomination institutions.

If independent candidate registration is easy, a legislator can run for reelection without their party's renomination, which diminishes the sanctioning capacity of people with influence over the party's nominating committee.[29] Parties may choose candidates through primaries, which allow people (rich and poor) to use their vote to sanction a legislator. Voting in a primary is a low-cost activity for persons who feel that their interests have not been represented, but its success as a sanction depends on many people casting similar votes.[30]

28. Political insiders can limit the choice set available to political outsiders (Bachrach and Baratz 1970; Lukes 1974, 2005; Moe 2005). This can easily happen to poor people who lack influence with the party leaders who control nominations, while rich people have tools (e.g., connections or campaign donations) that influence those same party leaders.

29. Where party ID is strong, a legislator's chances of winning reelection may decrease without the party label to serve as a cheap signal to voters.

30. Nomination through primaries should advantage a principal with many potential like-minded voters, which could describe poor people in an electoral district with a mostly poor population. But Hagopian (1990) and Weyland (1996) argue that clientelism diminishes the ability of poor people to work collectively to signal their preferences to the state. How forms of clientelism affect the sanctioning ability of rich and poor people and legislators' strategy is discussed below.

If national party leaders control nominations and list position, a legislator should consider how a person with influence on party leaders will view their actions while in office.

Party system fragmentation, which is influenced by electoral institutions, also affects people's ability to sanction. In a highly fragmented party system, voters have many choices of parties and politicians with a reasonable chance of winning a seat in the legislature. This enhances opportunities to sanction an incumbent because there are many other parties for whom a voter can vote. It does not, however, guarantee that the voter (rich or poor) will receive greater representation from the new legislator or party. The new legislator may not be a "good type" whose policy/service interests resemble those of the voter, so once again the voter will need to monitor the legislator and have an effective means of sanctioning. Even if the new legislator has policy/service preferences that resemble the voter's preferences, the legislator will only be able to deliver on promises if the legislator is part of the president's coalition, which gives the legislator the opportunity to take part in policy decision making and access to resources from the executive branch for clientelistic representation. Where party fragmentation is high, it is unlikely that a politician or a party will be able to implement a policy pledge without building a coalition to support the bill, and coalitions typically require compromise that may mean the policy will be changed, watered down, or never actually delivered.

In sum, electoral rules and nomination procedures interact to influence the capacity of rich and poor people to sanction. If a legislator wants a political career and party leaders control ballot access and list position, then a person who has influence with party leaders can sanction the legislator. If people can vote directly for a specific candidate, both rich and poor people pay only a minimal cost (i.e., the act of voting) for attempting to sanction, but the sanction will only punish the legislator if many people vote the same way. These institutions also shape the legislator's preferences; for example, they may prompt a backbencher to want to become a party leader.

Forms of Clientelism

Clientelism affects the capacity of poor people to sanction and shapes politicians' career goals and strategies. Like Remmer (2007), I treat clientelism as a way that a politician can work to achieve professional aspirations, and not just as a function of the social composition of the electorate. Where clientelism is an important part of the institutional milieu of a country's politics—

particularly where it has a long history of influencing how people solve their problems—it may shape legislators' identities, prompting some to seek office to gain access to resources to expand their reputations as patrons.

Clientelism is an old institution in many Latin American countries, but it is neither static nor isolated from other institutions that became important in the recent democratic period (Kitschelt 2000). Clientelism is a system of exchange between unequal actors that has proven to be highly adaptive to urbanization, democratization, and economic change (see Valenzuela 1977; Kitschelt 2000; Roberts 2002; Calvo and Murillo 2004; Roniger 2004; Stokes 2005; Remmer 2007). Traditionally, clientelism flourished as a personal relationship common in rural areas, where the patron used his or her own resources to address client needs; yet clientelistic relationships have adapted to urban settings in democratic regimes. They still involve unequal actors, but the relationship may not be personal and often involves the exchange of votes and campaign work to boost the patron's prestige for immediate provision, or promise of future provision, of personal benefits or local infrastructure projects (Roniger 2004, 354; Kitschelt and Wilkinson 2007, 4; Remmer 2007). Clientelist politicians and parties provide selective incentives and club goods, the latter often taking the form of local infrastructure projects for a community of loyalist voters, or ones designed to exclude people who are not clients from getting to use the service (e.g., their children do not receive a scholarship to buy school supplies, or they cannot get an appointment with the clinic doctor) (Kitschelt 2000, 850).

In states that lack adequate resources for universal public services, clientelism is often used for connections that give people and communities access to public services (Valenzuela 1977, 154, 167; Roniger and Günes-Ayala 1994). Client-broker-patron relations are common, where the local broker is the connection between the client and the party. The broker obtains favors or services for the client and in return mobilizes party support (Lamarchand and Legg 1972; Kaufman 1974; Kettering 1988; Gay 1990; Hagopian 1990; Wilson 1990; Coppedge 1993; Brusco, Nazareno, and Stokes 2004, 77). Valenzuela (1977, 159–61) distinguishes brokerage politics from patron-client politics and interest group politics based on the nature of the transaction and its goals. Transactions that are individualistic in nature and have particularistic goals are classic patron-client relations, but brokers can also provide such services. Transactions that have categoric goals and are individualistic in nature (e.g., a public works project for a town) are examples of brokerage politics. Valenzuela expects brokerage politics to sometimes engage in transactions that are collective in nature but with particularistic goals, which can also characterize interest group politics (e.g., when a broker gets a legislator to file a private bill for a community). Both patron-client and brokerage politics can produce "clientelistic representation," and the recipient of benefits may be an individual, a local organization, or a community. A new incarnation of clientelism has come with neoliberal economic reforms as governments use social funds, often sponsored by the World Bank or the Inter-American Development Bank, to create jobs and reduce the harsh effects of economic restructuring on the poor. Social fund programs are intended to be demand-driven and formulaic in their allocation of funds to poor communities, but they can be a source of resources for clientelism. The banks accept this because it makes it more feasible for governments to adopt economic restructuring policies (see Gibson 1997; Schady 2000; Tendler 2000). I explain below that clientelism can take different forms that make it more or less costly for clients to sever connections to their patron or party.

Clientelism is often based on assumptions of loyalty and longer-term payoffs. Roniger (2004, 356) explains that "clientelist strategies not only are affected by immediate considerations of power and instrumentality, but often encompass longer evaluations of reciprocal benefits and commitment as the prerequisite to maintain ongoing relationships" (see also Magaloni, Diaz-Cayeros, and Estévez 2007). Auyero (2006, 180–81) characterized patron-client (or broker-client) relationships and networks in Buenos Aires shantytowns as long-term commitments, and he underscored the importance inner-circle members place on their friendship with their broker (see also Cleary and Stokes 2006). Stokes (2005, 318) notes that it may be appropriate to view clientelism as a repeated game where clientelist parties are old and well established in a community, though this assumption may not be appropriate where major parties are "young and hence less enmeshed in social networks." Roberts (2002, 9) explains that in party systems based on a segmented cleavage structure, parties mobilize supporters and "structure electoral competition by generating organizational identities . . . and/or constructing rival patronage networks." The rivalries across patronage networks are enduring, and "patronage networks and family or community socialization practices could lead individuals to develop stable party-mediated collective identities, particularly in nations were traditional oligarchic parties survived" (Roberts 2002, 13; see also Randall and Svåsand 2002, 22).

Clientelism can influence the career strategy of legislators where the state does not use universalistic or needs-based criteria to provide for basic services

(Scott 1969; Valenzuela 1977). "Legislators' strategy depends on voters' price and the amount of available resources. If a private-goods campaign is viable (legislators have sufficient private goods to attract votes), then such an approach will beat a public goods strategy" due to the ease of claiming credit for the services provided (Desposato 2001, 35).[31] Even politicians who support state reform and policy over patronage may revert to providing clientelistic benefits to win elections when they learn that their party can neither maintain voter support if it attempts to provide policy benefits, nor build a winning coalition to get the policies adopted and implemented (Geddes 1994; Hunter 2007). Context matters because electoral institutions can either reinforce or weaken clientelism (Kitschelt 2000; Roniger 2004; Kitschelt and Wilkinson 2007; Scheiner 2007). Yet electoral institutions are not the single determining factor of whether politicians pursue clientelist linkages with voters. Kitschelt and Wilkinson (2007, 43) write, "Given otherwise favorable conditions, it appears that politicians find a way to 'work around' electoral institutions, when other imperatives make it attractive for instrumentally rational politicians to build clientelistic principal-agent relations."

Clientelism as an institution can take different forms.[32] One way clientelism institutions can vary is by whether clients form a connection directly with a patron or are part of a party's clientele network. Where patrons have their own power base, clients can sell their electoral support to the patron who is the best provider, and if the patron fails to deliver, the client can vote for a new patron (Wilson 1990). The cost to a client of severing a relationship with an unsatisfactory patron is low because the client can search the "market" for another benefactor. Kitschelt and Wilkinson (2007, 13) refer to vote choice "elasticity" that is "a function of the probability that some competitor could offer the same or even more valuable targeted material goods to the constituency." The client does face uncertainty, however, about whether the new patron will provide more benefits. One dissatisfied client will not hurt the incumbent, but defection by many poor clients could end a legislator's career.

Where patrons are a link in a party's clientele network, the client must sever their relationship with their party and affiliate with another party to obtain a new patron. This is very costly for the client, for whom being part of a particular clientele network and party is part of their identity (Roberts

31. Yiannakis (1982) found that members of the U.S. House of Representatives from poor districts were more likely to present a particularized credit-claiming style than were members from more prosperous districts.

32. See Kitschelt and Wilkinson (2007) for an extended discussion.

2002, 9). The cost to the client of severing a relationship with the patron is higher under party-based clientelism than where many individual patrons or brokers are in competition for clients. Here again, party system fragmentation affects how institutions work. Clientelism in a highly fragmented party system can give clients options of alternative patrons if they are not satisfied with the services they have received from their current patron. High party system fragmentation may force patrons to compete for clients, while in a political system with low party system fragmentation, clients' options are limited.

If there are few parties that have a chance of winning the executive branch and its access to state resources, clientelism produces "political subordination in exchange for material rewards," and the poor are obliged "to sacrifice their political rights if they want access to distributive programs" (Fox 1994, 153, 152). The cost of switching patrons (really parties) will be particularly high where resources are scarce. A party may conclude that it must reward longtime supporters/clients first, so the new member of a party's clientele network may receive few, if any, benefits.[33] If the major reason a client has stayed with a party while it was out of power (i.e., while the client received no benefits from state coffers) is that the client expects to receive benefits when the party is back in power, then the party must deliver or risk losing active supporters. If government coffers are deep, it would be feasible to give rewards to new and longtime supporters, but if resources are limited they will be targeted to retain support of clients with a proven record of party activism. A client who is dissatisfied with the benefits provided by a party's clientele network can vote for another party, but severing a longtime relationship with a party will put the client at the end of the line for benefits from the new party's clientele network. The client will have to demonstrate affiliation to the new party by helping in campaigns, attending rallies, and becoming

33. This contradicts the argument made by Stokes (2005) that parties will target clientelism benefits at swing voters. But Stokes assumes that constituents have an ideological commitment to the party, which means voters would pay an emotional cost if they voted against their party. The voter's cost-benefit analysis will be different if party preference is not based on ideology, but rather on expectations of clientelistic benefits. It is also noteworthy that the one prediction of Stokes's formal model that is not clearly supported by her Argentine survey data concerns the party machine targeting benefits to swing voters and discriminating against supporters. Peronist sympathizers were likely to receive rewards, though the machine did discriminate against *ardent* supporters. According to Dixit and Londregan (1996), the choice of whether to distribute benefits to core supporters or swing voters is determined by whether incumbents can more effectively distribute benefits and collect taxes from supporters. They also expect that the less a group of voters is attached to a party by ideology, the more material rewards they should receive. Magaloni, Diaz-Cayeros, and Estévez (2007) also argue that parties invest clientelistic resources, especially particularistic benefits, in core supporters.

a local activist-organizer, and that takes time. In sum, party-based clientele networks weaken the sanctioning capacity of poor people who need a patron. The poor voter is not indifferent across parties, and the cost of sanctioning (the possible loss of patronage benefits) is high, so the patron can be less concerned that dissatisfied clients will quickly defect even if the clientelistic representation provided is not extensive.

This argument breaks down if the poor client receives *no* benefits from a patron/party. Then, even if the poor person is unlikely to immediately begin receiving benefits upon switching parties, the hope of eventually receiving some clientelistic benefit, combined with losing nothing, makes it feasible to switch parties—unless the former patron has the capacity to take vindictive action against the defector, in which case we would question the democratic nature of the political system.

A second important variable affecting the form of clientelism is whether patrons are dependent on membership in the governing party for access to state resources.[34] If governing party membership is required for access, then legislators seeking to build reputations as powerful local patrons will be particularly affected by their party winning the presidency, as it will affect the legislator's decision about seeking reelection. This variable also constrains the client's sanctioning options because alternative patrons are only valuable if their party will be in government. If the party system is fragmented and the executive must form a coalition to pass legislation, a patron can gain access to state resources by joining the president's legislative coalition in exchange for clientelistic resources. A legislator who can switch parties without personal political career costs can join a party with access to the state's clientelistic resources (Hagopian 1990; Desposato 2001, 2006b). These options increase the parties from which a client can choose when using the vote to sanction and decrease the risk to the poor client that a new patron will lack access to clientelistic resources.[35]

In sum, the cost to a poor person of sanctioning is affected by the form of the clientelism institution. If clientelism is based on direct relations between

34. See Calvo and Murillo (2004) for an analysis of how access to public funds affects the supply-side advantages of a patronage election strategy.

35. A similar perspective on how clientelism is affected by access to state resources refers to "externally" and "internally" mobilized political parties (Piattoni 2001; Roniger 2004). Externally mobilized parties do not occupy positions of power and therefore cannot use patronage to build support, so they try to appeal to voters with programmatic appeals. Internally mobilized parties have access to state resources, so they can choose whether to focus on patronage or policy (see also Hagopian 2009).

patrons and clients, dissatisfied clients can search for a new patron at low cost to themselves, provided there are alternative patrons.[36] If clientelism works through party-based networks, a client must establish a relationship with a new party to attempt to get improved clientelistic benefits—a more risky and costly prospect. If presidents must form coalitions to pass legislation, any legislator from any party could barter with the president to obtain access to clientelistic resources. If members of the president's party are the only ones who have access to state resources, this limits the market of patrons from whom the client can choose when attempting to sanction.

Clientelism may help legislators to represent both rich and poor constituents. The rich may want national policies that the poor cannot monitor, or that poor people view as unlikely to be implemented in a timely fashion or to directly affect them (e.g., increasing the safety of bank deposits or regulating private school tuition). In that case, a legislator can address the rich person's national policy preferences without the poor person wanting to sanction. Meanwhile, the legislator can deliver clientelistic benefits to poor people. Clientelistic benefits may be the policy/service package the poor person desires because they are cheap to monitor and their value is clear. The legislator's clientelistic work could also win favor with the rich person who receives the contract to build a local public works project. In this scenario, poor and rich people do not have incompatible policy preferences; they are interested in different things and representing both should be feasible, unless the government's budget is so limited that it cannot afford to fund both policies and services.

One final point about clientelism must be addressed: how is a clientelistic relationship enforced when clientelism operates in a democratic context? (Desposato 2001; Piattoni 2001; Roniger 2004; Stokes 2005). How can a patron, broker, or political machine insure clients are holding up their end of the deal when balloting is secret? Stokes (2005, 315) starkly states the importance of this issue: "If voters can renege, then machines should not waste scarce resources on them and clientelist politics breaks down." But as clientelism has proven itself to be robust and able to adapt to the new political reality of democracy, patrons must have ways to "police" their deals with clients, even if they are imperfect.

---

36. Ames (2001, 79) argues that this is why Brazilian deputies try to insulate themselves against incursions by competitors, "because the deputies know that barriers to entry, by eliminating competition, reduce campaign costs."

First, clients deliver not just votes, but also campaign activity for their patron. For example, clients are expected to turn out at campaign events organized by a broker. This participation can be observed as it is inherently public. How an individual client votes cannot be observed under democratic conditions of secret balloting,[37] but the patron (or the patron's agent, who may be the party's official observer at the polling place) can observe who actually turns out to vote (Nichter 2008), and this can put pressure on clients where precincts are small (Chandra 2004; Stokes 2005; Magaloni, Diaz-Cayeros, and Estévez 2007, 183–87; Scheiner 2007, 280–81). Stokes (2005, 317) explains that party poll watchers can be quite effective, especially in small towns and neighborhoods where people have known one another for a long time. It is "hard for voters to dissemble before people they've known all their lives: as one grassroots party organizer in Argentina explained, you know if a neighbor voted against your party if they can't look you in the eye on election day."[38] In a 2003 survey in Argentina, 37 percent of respondents said "party operatives can find out how a person in your neighborhood has voted" (Stokes 2005, 318).

Second, if a patron-client relationship is a repeated game, rewards can be conditioned on clients' inferred votes (see Schady 2000, 290).[39] Parties and patrons gather information about a client/voter's "predisposition for or against the machine" (Stokes 2005, 317). For a repeated game of clientelism to work, the party or patron does not have to have private resources to distribute goods to its clients even when it is out of power (Stokes 2005, 319), though it might be able to do so. The party can retain the loyalty of clients if clients think their party is likely to be in power in the next government and they will receive benefits then.

Third, parties or patrons can observe the final vote count at the precinct level. With this information, which is publicly available from the elections tribunal, they can determine whether a community they worked to organize voted as expected; and if it did not, the whole community can be punished (Chandra 2007).

Finally, patrons can use micromanaging methods to control how clients vote. Patrons can structure particularistic benefits so that part of the benefit

37. Some countries, such as Argentina, get around this problem by using party strip ballots provided by the patron (Stokes 2005).

38. Archer (1990) and Álvaro (2007) describe clientelism in Colombia where such intimidation practices are common and effective, particularly in rural areas.

39. Kitschelt and Wilkinson (2007, 8) explain that "clients and politicians gain confidence in the viability of their relationship by iteration, i.e., the repeated success of exchange relations that makes the behavior of the exchange partner appear predictable and low risk."

is not received until after the election, and then only if the patron is victorious (e.g., delivering only half of a pressure cooker before the election; see Ames 2001, 82).

Do Institutions Create Incentives to Represent Poor People?

The central question of this book concerns when legislators have an incentive to represent poor people. Poor people are typically at an informational disadvantage relative to rich people, except with respect to delivery of particularistic goods and local services. Again, poor peoples' sanctioning tools are often blunt and costly compared to tools rich people can use. Thus it appears more risky for a legislator to neglect a rich constituent than a poor one. Yet this conclusion needs to be more nuanced and take into account institutional context. A legislator who wants to continue a political career must consider the likelihood that *either* rich or poor people will notice shirking and be able to sanction. We must also consider how institutions shape legislators' identities and why they want seats in the congress.

If we think of a legislator's strategy decision as a game, first the legislator decides whether to represent rich or poor constituents, both, or neither. The legislator's payoff comes from how close the policy/service level is to the legislator's preference,[40] and how much the legislator values continuing a political career and the chance of getting to do so. Other components to the payoff could include the value of strengthening democracy or of rising within a party.

Next, poor and rich people decide whether to sanction. Their decision is based on awareness of the legislator's activities (monitoring) and how much they think a new representative would improve policy/service (V), the cost they incur for attempting to sanction (c), and how many people must sanction to end the legislator's career (n^*). This decision resembles a step-level public goods game "where N players decide whether or not to 'contribute' at cost c. If the total number of contributions meets or exceeds some threshold n^*, then the public good is provided and all players receive a fixed return, V, whether or not they contributed" (Goeree and Holt 2005, 208).

Particularly if we assume that a poor person incurs the cost of sanctioning regardless of whether sufficient people sanction for it to be successful (e.g., a

---

40. A legislator may first decide whether to invest resources in policy development (proposing bills, amendments, committee work), and then, if yes, select a policy.

client loses their relationship with their patron, a protestor risks arrest, a striker risks being fired), sanctioning is a costly activity for poor people, which makes them less likely to monitor elected officials, as they are unlikely to be able to do anything about performance they do not like. But poor peoples' cost for attempting to sanction can decrease under some conditions. If a legislator does not deliver on promises, losing the legislator as a patron does not hurt the poor person. The state may be able to arrest or attack protestors if their numbers are small, but if protests become large and frequent, attacking the protestors can be costly for the state. Still, uncertainty about how many sanctioners are needed makes it difficult for a poor person to decide whether it is worthwhile to sanction (Goeree and Holt 2005).

Croson and Marks (2000) propose a "step return," which is the ratio of social value to cost, or NV/n^*c. Based on this "step return function," the probability a poor person would sanction should increase with the number of people who are dissatisfied with the performance of elected officials (N) or the magnitude of the improvement in policy/service expected from replacing the official (V). The probability of a sanction attempt should also increase as the cost of sanctioning (c) or the number of sanctioners needed to make the sanctioning effort successful (n^*) decreases.

Rich people may have opportunities as individuals or by acting in very small numbers to end a legislator's political career (n^* is small). This, again, means that not only do rich people often have greater capacity to monitor, but it is easier for a rich person to assess the utility of sanctioning. For example, if party leaders control nominations, a rich person who has influence with party leaders can insure a legislator is not renominated, or is moved to an "unelectable" position on the party's list.

The largest benefit (V) for a poor or rich person would be a new representative who provides their ideal policy/service package. The cost of sanctioning (c) is determined by the sanctioning resources a rich or poor person can attempt to use and what benefits they would sacrifice by severing their relationship with the politician (which are determined by the country's institutions). Again, sanctioning costs are generally higher for poor than for rich people. Consequently a poor person is less likely than a rich person to view sanctioning as worthwhile, unless the poor person expects to get much greater benefits (representation) from a different representative, or the poor person in fact is receiving no benefits and does not expect to receive any, and many other poor people are similarly frustrated.

Some institutions limit a poor person's ability to monitor a legislator's actions and only allow poor people to sanction in ways that require collective action.

In this case, a poor person who thinks too few people will participate for sanctioning to succeed should not sanction because he or she would personally pay some cost (e.g., lost personalistic benefits or possibly lost infrastructure projects for their community) and would receive no benefit. Under such institutions, a legislator would seem to have little need to provide more than minimal representation to poor people to avoid a career-disrupting sanction. But some institutions do increase the value to a legislator of maintaining the support of many voters rather than the backing of a single party leader (e.g., nominations where party leaders consider a candidate's extent of local support when selecting nominees for the party's list).

These considerations predict that legislators will have little incentive to represent poor people in national policy. A representative elected under the banner of a party whose ideology defended the poor could work on reformist legislation without risking sanction by party leaders.[41] Still, if the legislator could not shepherd initiatives through the legislature and the policy implementation process, poor people would not benefit from the policy and would be unlikely to reward the legislator's efforts. Aside from the special case where a legislator is a "good type," the main way that (some) institutions give legislators an incentive to represent poor people is by providing particularistic benefits and local infrastructure projects for communities of loyalists. Such works are easy for poor people to monitor, and a legislator can claim credit for providing such services and make sure delivery occurs before the next election. Even clientelistic representation is not assured if poor people lack effective tools to sanction a legislator who does not deliver sufficient clientelistic benefits, or if the legislator does not have access to government resources to provide such representation because the legislator's party is in the opposition and party switching is costly.

In conclusion, poor and rich people have differing capacities to monitor the work of elected officials, and institutions affect the capacity of poor and rich people to sanction. Institutions also shape a legislator's career strategy, identity, and motivation for a congressional seat. How legislators define their jobs, combined with the constraints that are placed on poor and rich people and elected officials by institutions in a particular political system, determine whether poor people will be represented, and how.

---

41. Party rhetoric may include helping the poor, but as poor people often complain in Latin America, politicians and parties reach out to them at election time but forget their promises once in office (Posner 1999).

THREE

⟶⟶≫≫⟫≪≪⟪⟵

INSTITUTIONS AND POOR PEOPLE'S
CONFIDENCE IN THEIR LEGISLATURE

King, Keohane, and Verba (1994) urge researchers to find multiple observable implications of theory. For the role of institutions in a context of poverty, a variety of macro and micro observable implications exist. This chapter presents the first of several observable implications of when poor people count in Latin American countries by using cross-national data about poor people's confidence in their legislatures.

The theory presented in this book has two aims: One aim is to explore how combinations of institutions affect the ability of different segments of society to sanction elected officials. A second aim is to explore how combinations of institutions constrain the viable strategies of politicians and thus incentives to represent poor people. Because elected officials are expected to respond to the threat of monitoring and sanctions from citizens, one type of observable implication about how institutions affect representation of the poor is how poor people evaluate the institution in which those elected officials serve—the legislature. In this chapter I examine the hypothesis that more poor people will have confidence in their national legislature in countries where the institutional milieu makes it more feasible for them to sanction legislators than in countries where institutions make it costly for poor people to sanction.

The legislature is intended to be the representative branch of democratic government. While representative democracy is based on the principle of *one person, one vote*, in reality all types of people are not equal in ability to monitor and sanction representatives (Rubenstein 2007). Poor people have a

An earlier version of parts of this chapter was published in Spanish in *Perspectivas para la democracia en America Latina*, ed. Leticia Heras Gómez and John A. Booth, 353–83 (Toluca, Mexico: Universidad Autónoma del Estado de Mexico, 2009).

limited capacity to monitor what elected officials do in office, and by extension have limited ability to monitor the legislature, so they are less likely than
other people to sanction.

The theory of incentives to represent the poor predicts that the sanctioning
capacity of poor people will vary across institutional contexts. Some electoral
rules, nomination procedures, and forms of clientelism make it very costly for
a poor person to sanction, so such institutional settings create little incentive
for legislators to represent poor people. A legislator may still personally want
to help poor people, but in such an institutional setting the legislator is
unlikely to be rewarded for the effort, while rich people who have a greater
capacity to monitor may punish the legislator. Potential political aspirants
will observe what types of work in the congress are likely to promote a political career, and if their personal interest is to help poor people and communities, they will decide not to enter the political arena as a legislator (or will
exit after serving only one term).[1] In those types of institutional settings I
predict more poor people will have a negative evaluation of their congress
(relative to evaluations in institutional settings where it is more feasible for
poor people to sanction), because it is made up primarily of legislators who
have little incentive to represent them.

On the other hand, some electoral rules, nomination procedures, and forms
of clientelism empower poor people (again, relative to the sanctioning capacity
of poor people in other institutional settings) because a poor person does not
incur a high personal cost for sanctioning. A sanction by one disgruntled
poor constituent will not end a legislator's career, yet poor people's capacity
to sanction at low personal cost creates an incentive for members of congress
to attend to their poor constituents. In such an institutional setting, political
aspirants will observe that attending to poor constituents helps build a
political career, so politicians who want to represent poor people will enter
politics, and they will be able to build careers in government.[2] In these types
of institutional settings, I expect more poor people to have a favorable evaluation
of their congress, because it is made up of many legislators who respond to
incentives to represent them.

The analysis in this chapter will not detect if a poor person "loves their
congressperson but hates congress" (a well-known phenomenon in the United

1. In chapter 6, I show how this type of complaint prompted some Constituency Server deputies
in Honduras to opt to not seek reelection.
2. Strategic politicians may only provide clientelistic representation, however, because such
work is easy for poor people to monitor.

States), because the public opinion polls ask people how much confidence they have in their congress as a whole, not in their particular representative. In PR electoral systems, it is understandable why polls do not ask people to give an opinion about a local member of congress, because multiple members represent most districts, so it would be impossible to know which member a respondent was evaluating, though an opinion about a single member of congress may be driving a poll respondent's strong feelings. The theory developed in this book concerns how institutions affect the capacity of poor people to sanction, thus creating an incentive for legislators to represent poor people. If legislators do not face incentives to represent poor constituents because institutions make it very costly for poor people to sanction, fewer poor people presumably would love their congressperson and more would have a negative evaluation of their congress.

Public Opinion Data

To measure the opinion poor people have of their national legislature, I use data from the World Values Survey (WVS) and Latinobarómetro (LB). From the WVS I used the wave of surveys conducted in the mid-1990s, which included Argentina in 1995, Brazil 1997, Chile 1996, Colombia 1997/98, the Dominican Republic 1998, Mexico 1996, Peru 1996, Uruguay 1996, and Venezuela 1996.[3] From LB I use data from the same countries between 2001 and 2006.[4] I start using LB data in 2001 because many of the earlier surveys lacked national coverage. Popular evaluations of government institutions may fluctuate with current events or crises (e.g., a currency collapse or corruption scandal). To dampen the impact of such influences, I average the annual LB evaluations.[5] Table 3.1 provides the yearly data about percentage of poor respondents who gave a favorable evaluation of their congress. Although evaluations fluctuate somewhat across years even when institutions are constant, it is clear that more poor people have confidence in their congress in some countries than in others. For a few countries the sanctioning capacity for poor people created by some institutions changed between the time of the WVS and the LB data

3. The mid-1990s wave of the WVS also included El Salvador, but I do not include El Salvador in this analysis because the number of poor people in the Salvadoran survey is very small and does not appear to accurately describe the country's population.

4. The Dominican Republic only started to be included in the LB surveys in 2004.

5. I thank an anonymous reviewer for this suggestion.

Table 3.1 Poor people's confidence in their congress (yearly survey results by Latinobarómetro)

	% of respondents with no education or some primary school who have a lot or some confidence in their congress					
	2001	2002	2003	2004	2005	2006
Argentina	16.5	6.8	11.7	20.7	25.2	23.5
Brazil	27.8	27.7	30.2	38.6	28.2	35.1
Chile	33.9	27.5	21.1	25.4	29.2	30.3
Colombia	12.3	15.2	14.2	24.4	25.4	30.5
Dominican Republic	—	—	—	42.4	40.3	39.6
Mexico	26.3	25.1	21.5	21.9	35.2	29.9
Peru	23.3	25.0	8.8	14.6	13.7	17.7
Uruguay	47.4	39.3	25.3	37.9	54.1	40.5
Venezuela	41.7	35.2	19.7	35.8	51.1	57.1

NOTE: Latinobarómetro annual survey question: "Please tell me how much confidence you have in the Congress. Would you say you have a lot, some, a little, or no confidence?"

(e.g., the Dominican Republic, Venezuela, and to a lesser extent Mexico and Peru), so in effect they became new cases.

To study the opinions of poor people, I examine the subset of respondents who said that they had less than a complete primary education. This measure of poverty captures part of the difficulty poor people encounter in monitoring the activities of elected officials, compared to the monitoring capacity of better-off groups, if those who are more educated choose to engage in monitoring.[6] For example, lack of education, and particularly lack of strong reading skills, makes it difficult for poor people to obtain information about legislation that has been initiated, to evaluate the likely impact of a bill, or to track implementation of a law. According to Aoki et al. (2002, 233), "Inadequate education is [also] one of the most powerful determinants of poverty" (see also Psacharopoulos 1994; Brown, Brown, and Desposato 2002). No measure of poverty is perfect.[7] An alternative way to measure poverty is income,[8] but an income

6. See chapter 2 for an extended discussion of monitoring resources of poor versus rich people. See Rubenstein (2007) for the difficulties of using surrogates to monitor for those who lack monitoring capacity.

7. See the World Bank's *Sourcebook for Poverty Reduction Strategies* (Klugman 2002) for discussion of different indicators of poverty.

8. The WVS asked respondents to place themselves in one of ten income categories. I replicated the analysis for people who placed themselves in the three lowest income categories, and the percentages of people who said they have "a great deal" or "quite a lot" of confidence in their national legislature correlates at the 0.85 level with the findings of the analysis using education (illiterate or less than complete primary school) as the measure of poverty. The Latinobarómetro for 2004–6 asked respondents to "imagine a 10 step ladder, where in 1 stand the poorest people

measure is problematic for several reasons: cost of living varies around a country, income for rural people in particular is subject to seasonal variations, rural people often provide for some of their needs outside the monetary economy, and the income a family requires to provide for its needs depends on the number of dependents (IFPRI 2001, 17; IFPRI 1999, 4).[9]

Categorizing Countries on How Institutions Affect Sanctioning Capacity of Poor People

This analysis examines how electoral rules, nominations, and forms of clientelism empower poor people to be able to sanction elected officials or make it personally very costly to attempt to sanction. We can observe whether categorizing cases based on the capacity of poor people to sanction helps explain cross-case differences in how poor people evaluate their congress.[10] We can also take advantage of the institutional changes that occurred over time in some countries to explore if poor people's evaluations of their congress move in the direction that would be predicted given how the institutional changes affect poor people's sanctioning capacity: presidents in Mexico and Peru during the later period need a coalition, so more parties have potential access to executive resources for clientelism, which increases the options for poor people to find a patron and decreases the cost of sanctioning. In the Dominican Republic, changes in election rules increased people's ability to sanction. In Venezuela, President Hugo Chávez has not needed to build a coalition, but the type of candidates recruited by Chávez's movement is different from the type recruited by AD and COPEI, so most members of the congress need to serve poor constituents in order to be recruited by Chávez.

---

and in 10 stand the richest people. Where would you stand?" (No income category question was asked in the 2001–3 LB surveys.) For these three years of LB surveys, there is a 0.91 correlation between the confidence people on the three lowest steps and people with less than a complete primary education have in their congress.

9. Due to these challenges for determining which people are poor enough to merit inclusion, Honduras's conditional cash transfer program uses data about family consumption instead of income to determine who qualifies (IFPRI 1999, 4–5). In Brazil, researchers have developed an Index of Family Development (Indice de Desenvolvimento Familiar), which is a multidimensional index for measuring poverty, including "absence of vulnerability, access to knowledge, labor, availability of resources, child development, and household conditions" (Lindert et al. 2007, 45).

10. I thank Maria Escobar-Lemmon and Marisa Kellam for helpful comments as I developed this typology of institutions. Any errors are solely my own.

How Electoral Rules and Nominations Affect the
Sanctioning Capacity of Poor People

I categorize electoral rules and nominations as high, medium, or low to reflect an overall evaluation of the sanctioning capacity they create (see the chapter appendix, table 3.4, for case coding). Electoral rules give voters the ability to impose a sharp or blunt sanction, thereby creating incentives for legislators by allowing or disallowing voters to vote for individual candidates. Based on the theory presented in chapter 2, open-list elections with high district magnitude (DM) and personal lists empower voters, closed-list elections (especially with high party magnitude) weaken voters, and mixed systems are intermediate.[11]

I incorporate two components to whether nominations empower or weaken the capacity of poor people to sanction legislators: nomination procedures and the type of candidates that parties recruit. Nomination procedures are the formal rules and informal norms of how parties select candidates for the legislature. Based on the theory presented in chapter 2, when national party leaders control nominations, average voters' ability to sanction legislators is weak and people who have influence with party leaders are the ones who are able to sanction. When candidates can self-nominate or a primary is used, voters (including poor people) are comparatively empowered.

The type of candidates parties recruit can also affect representation of poor people. Siavelis and Morgenstern (2008b) created a typology of legislative candidate types based on to whom candidates (and then legislators) have an incentive to be loyal: party loyalists, group delegates, constituent servants, and entrepreneurs. I expect constituent servants and entrepreneurs to be more responsive to poor people than party loyalists or group delegates. Entrepreneurs need to find their own supporters, rather than relying on party ID to obtain votes. Constituent servants receive their party's nomination because of their reputation for working for their constituents. Whether entrepreneurs and constituent servants have an incentive to attend to the needs of poor people depends on their district. If a large percentage of people (or party supporters) in their district are poor, then these types of legislators have an incentive to represent poor people if they want to continue to be nominated by their party, thereby enhancing the sanctioning capacity of poor people. If other types of people make up a large percentage of their district, entrepreneurs and constituent servants may be recruited as a result of their

---

11. District magnitude is the number of representatives elected in a district. Party magnitude is the number of seats in a district that a party can typically expect to win.

connections to, say, middle-class voters who are co-partisans, instead of poor people. Party loyalists obtain their nomination by demonstrating their connection to their party (or faction) and its leaders; they do not need a personal reputation with voters, and so the capacity of poor people to sanction is decreased. Group delegates are tied to functional groups (e.g., a union or business association) and act as a liaison for that group to the party, which should make them less vulnerable if they lack support from poor people. (See Siavelis and Morgenstern 2008b for the detailed theory and descriptions of each candidate type.) Different parties in the same country may recruit different types of candidates. I code the country based on the type for the party (or parties) with the most seats (in other words, the recruitment type of the modal legislator). For example, in Brazil most major parties select entrepreneurs, but the PT (Partido dos Trabalhadores) selects group delegates or party loyalists (Samuels 2008). In Mexico, the PRI recruits party loyalists and group delegates, the PAN (Partido Acción Nacional) selects some party loyalists and some constituent servants, and the PRD (Partido de la Revolución Democrática) selects constituent servants (Langston 2008).

The following scenarios illustrate how nomination procedures and recruitment norms combine: if national party leaders control nominations, poor people have low sanctioning ability. But if party leaders recruit constituent servants, this reestablishes some connection to poor people in districts where poor people are a large percentage of the population, so the case is medium/low. Alternatively, if party leaders recruit party loyalists, the case is low/low.

If electoral rules have a different impact on the sanctioning capacity of poor than nominations, the country is placed in one cell with an arrow indicating that it verges toward another cell. For example, in 1993 Venezuela adopted mixed-member election rules for the Chamber of Deputies, creating an intermediate capability for poor people to sanction or reward legislators, but national party leaders continued to control nominations and they recruited party loyalists. In Mexico, mixed-member elections create an intermediate sanction capacity, but PRI national leaders retained control over nominations until the late 1990s and selected party insiders and group delegates with national party connections (Langston 2006), and at the time of the WVS the PRI still held a majority in the Congress. Mexico's prohibition of immediate reelection increases party leaders' leverage with politicians and further weakens any future local electoral connection as well as the sanctioning capacity of voters.[12]

12. Some electoral connection may still exist because most politicians do run for another office at some point in their career, and Mexicans think of politicians as being interested in reelection (Cleary and Stokes 2006, 91; Langston and Aparicio 2008).

How Forms of Clientelism Affect the Sanctioning Capacity of Poor People

As discussed in chapter 2, clientelism operates in various ways. I assess the competitiveness of the form clientelism takes in a country based on the cost to a poor person of trying to change patrons, and on the likelihood that patrons from multiple parties will have access to state resources, which increases the number of viable patrons. Categories of competitive, intermediate, or limited are a summary evaluation of how cheap or costly it is for a poor person to switch patrons (see the chapter appendix, table 3.4, for country coding).

One component to the competitiveness of the market of patrons is if a poor person must be part of a party clientele network to receive benefits. Party-based clientele networks raise the poor person's sanctioning cost, because sanctioning requires switching parties and building a reputation as a party supporter all over again; thus party clientele networks limit the competitiveness of clientelism, though the cost of such a switch depends on how many other party clientele options exist. The clientelism market is also limited if a poor person lives where a single patron exists as a monopolist (a politician's *reduto;* see Ames 1995). A voter with a strong ideological commitment to a party also faces a more limited clientelism market. The market of patrons is bigger if patrons are independent of parties, or poor people can select from various patrons within the party. This lowers the poor person's sanctioning cost because they are less likely to lose a clientelism connection by searching and voting for a new patron. To determine the form of patron-client linkages, I consulted country case studies.

A second component affecting the size of the patron market is the breadth of legislators with access to state resources. If only legislators from the president's party are likely to have such access, a poor person has few viable choices of patrons, thereby raising the cost of sanctioning and limiting competition. If legislators from many parties can expect to cut deals with the executive, poor people have more viable choices of patrons, making clientelism more competitive. To determine if clientelism resources are likely to be available to legislators from multiple parties, I examined whether the president's party typically had a majority in the legislature and whether it was a disciplined party, contrasted with presidents normally needing to form a coalition to pass legislation.

Competitiveness of clientelism is a combination of how a case fits both components. For example, if clientelism benefits go only to members of party networks, the case is limited; but if the president needs a coalition, allowing more than one party to gain access to state resources, the case moves toward intermediate, as in Mexico after 1997 when the PRI lost its majority in the Chamber of Deputies, and in Peru after the end of Alberto Fujimori's presidency. Country placement represents the institutions faced by the average poor person in that country around the time the survey was taken. For example, if it is common to have a market of patrons from which to choose, but in some places a single caudillo controls access to government resources, the country is coded as competitive even though some poor people do not have a choice of patrons. Similarly, if the norm is one-party government but for one term the president lacks a majority and must seek coalition support, the case is coded as limited because voters could not anticipate that multiple parties would have access to resources.

One additional point needs to be addressed directly: does the form of clientelism have an independent impact on the sanctioning capacity of poor people, or is it a product of electoral rules, so that the clientelism dimension of the analysis is endogenous to the electoral rules/nominations dimension? In some respects, how the form of clientelism affects the sanctioning capacity of poor people is related to electoral rules. In systems with closed-list PR elections, poor people typically have to become affiliated with a party-based clientele network, while where open-list or preference votes are used a client can often form a relationship directly with a patron. Electoral rules also influence whether a president is likely to enjoy the backing of loyal party backbenchers (Shugart 1998). Yet the number of party clientele networks or of individual patrons available to a poor person is not just a function of electoral rules, any more than the effective number of parties in a political system is completely determined by electoral rules (Cox 1997; Morgenstern and Vazquez D'Elia 2007). Cleavages in society influence the number of parties that win seats in the legislature, and parties can have factions competing for voter support. Informal barriers to candidates entering an electoral district can influence the number of individual patron options available in a district. In addition, not all parties that seek election under the same electoral rules set up the same type of linkage with voters or recruit the same types of candidates. Some parties operating in a country can set up clientelist linkages, while others have programmatic linkages (Kitschelt and Wilkinson 2007; Hagopian 2009). A party whose traditional constituency is the urban or rural poor may instruct its elected officials to provide clientelistic representation to maintain the party's base, even where electoral rules do not prompt legislators to seek a personal vote. Roberts (2002, 19) has argued that clientelistic representation may be promoted by economic liberalism (see also Calvo and Murillo 2004). Similarly, Hagopian (2009, 8) explains that where neoliberal economic reforms expanded the marginal sector of society (the informal sector and the rural poor), these marginalized people can be constituencies for clientelistic representation and prompt parties to pursue clientelistic linkages with voters.

The number of parties and the types of linkages to voters that parties use affect the choice of patrons available to poor people. The number of competing networks or individual patrons may range from zero to several. In sum, electoral rules could give poor people the capacity to sanction, but poor clients may still face a limited market of patrons, thereby decreasing their sanctioning ability. Alternatively, electoral rules might make it virtually impossible for a poor person to sanction a legislator who does not attend to his or her personal needs; further, the electoral rules may also create strong incentives for deputies to be loyal to their party, but a party may insist that its backbenchers perform constituency service and distribute patronage to clients (Hagopian 2009, 4). A country's electoral rules create incentives for all parties in the country, but parties and their individual legislators still make their own decisions about whether to specialize in programmatic or clientelistic representation, and not all parties or deputies in a congress have to make the same choices.

Findings

The theory predicts that because institutions affect the capacity of poor people to sanction, institutions influence legislators' incentive to represent poor people. Where institutions enhance poor people's sanctioning capacity, legislators have an incentive to attend to the needs of poor people and will observe that doing so is rewarded. I hypothesize that where such institutions exist, more poor people will have confidence in their congress. Where institutions make it costly for poor people to sanction, legislators have reduced incentives to attend to the needs of poor people. I hypothesize that where such institutions exist, fewer poor people will give a favorable evaluation to their congress.

Tables 3.2 and 3.3 show the percentage of respondents in the WVS and LB, respectively, with little or no education who said that they have a great deal or quite a lot of confidence in their congress. Evaluations vary across countries. In the WVS from the mid-1990s, 53 percent of poor respondents in Uruguay and 10 percent in Peru gave a positive evaluation of their legislature. In the averaged evaluations for 2001–6 LB surveys, positive evaluations

Table 3.2 How institutions empower poor people and their evaluation of their congress (World Values Survey, 1995–98 wave)

Sanctioning capacity from election rules and nominations	Competitiveness of clientelism			
	Competitive	Intermediate	Limited	Row avg.
High	Brazil (44.7)			44.7
Medium		Colombia (22.1) ↑		22.1
	Uruguay (53.3)	Chile (39.1)		46.2
	↓ Venezuela (36.9)		↓ Mexico (32.4) ↓ Peru (9.9)*	26.4
Low			Argentina (12.8)* Dominican Republic (12.9)	12.9
Column avg.	49.0	32.7	17.0	

NOTE: (1) Numbers in parentheses indicate the percentage of respondents with no formal education or incomplete primary school education who said that they have "a great deal" or "quite a lot" of confidence in their congress. (2) If institutions have different impacts on the sanctioning capacity of poor people, the case is placed in a cell that is subdivided, with an arrow indicating that the case verges toward another cell.
*Case also includes respondents with complete primary education because so few respondents had less than a primary education.

range from 41 percent in the Dominican Republic and Uruguay to 16 percent in Peru.

The figures array countries based on poor people's sanctioning capacity. Rows offer a gross measure of how election rules and nominations give poor people an ability to sanction. Columns indicate the competitiveness of the form of clientelism, which affects the cost a poor person will incur for attempting to sanction (the chapter appendix, table 3.4, provides country coding information). If institutions have different impacts on the sanctioning capacity of poor people, the case is placed in one cell with an arrow indicating that it

Table 3.3 How institutions empower poor people and their evaluation of their congress (Latinobarómetro 2001–6 surveys)

Sanctioning capacity from election rules and nominations	Competitiveness of clientelism			
	Competitive	Intermediate	Limited	Row avg.
High	Brazil (31.3)		Dominican ← Republic (40.8)	36.1
Medium		↑Colombia (23.2)		↑Venezuela (40.1)	31.7
Medium	Uruguay (40.8)	Chile (27.9)	← Mexico (26.7) ← Peru (16.0)		27.9
Low				Argentina (17.4)	17.4
Column avg.	36.1	25.6	27.8	28.8	

NOTE: (1) Numbers in parentheses are average values for 2001–6 LB surveys indicating the percentage of respondents who are illiterate or had incomplete primary school education who said that they have "a lot" or "some" confidence in their congress. (2) If institutions have different impacts on the sanctioning capacity of poor people, the case is placed in a cell that is subdivided, with an arrow indicating that the case verges toward another cell. Some cases are in different cells from those in table 3.2 because of major institutional changes that occurred after the WVS.

verges toward another cell. For example, in 1993 Venezuela adopted mixed-member election rules for the Chamber of Deputies, creating a medium capacity for poor people to sanction or reward legislators. National party leaders continued to control nominations, however, and they recruited only party loyalists, thereby decreasing poor people's ability to sanction (see table 3.2). After Hugo Chávez came to power, legislators for his movement were recruited to be constituent servants, thereby increasing their connection to poor people in districts with large poor populations (see table 3.3). Some country placements change from table 3.2 to 3.3 due to changes in election rules (the Dominican Republic), nominations (Venezuela), or competitiveness of clientelism

(Mexico, Peru, Venezuela). Countries whose institutions place them toward the upper-left portion of a table would be expected to have more poor people who state that they have confidence in their legislature than countries in the lower-right portion.

In Brazil, 45 percent of people with little or no education in the WVS, and on average 31 percent in the 2001–6 LB surveys, said they have confidence in their congress. Election rules, nominations, and the form of clientelism enhance the sanctioning capacity of poor people, and thus should create incentives for legislators to be at least somewhat responsive to poor voters. Brazil's institutional setting likely would not create incentives for legislators to work on the *policy* concerns of poor people, but it gives many legislators incentives to deliver clientelistic benefits to poor voters, as that is a logical way to obtain their votes and build a career. This combination of institutions should also attract people to the Congress (particularly as candidates of traditional parties) who want to build their reputation as a strong local patron.[13]

In Uruguay, 53 percent of respondents with little education in the WVS, and on average 41 percent of like respondents in the LB surveys, give a positive evaluation to their congress; several aspects of the institutional setting enhance the sanctioning capacity of poor people, which should create incentives for legislators to be responsive to poor voters in order to enhance the weight of their faction within their party. Presidents' regular need to build a coalition to pass legislation gives many legislators access to state resources. Combined with many competing factions within parties, this produces a competitive form of clientelism that increases options for poor people.

By contrast, in Argentina and the Dominican Republic, 13 percent of respondents in the WVS with little education indicated that they have confidence in their congress.[14] Multiple institutions in both countries made it very difficult for poor people to sanction legislators who did not attend to their needs, and the institutional setting should attract politicians who want to build a party career more than people who want to work for poor constituents (Jones

---

13. Many scholars who study Brazilian politics make similar arguments about the incentives for clientelism but the lack of incentives for legislators to work on policy (e.g., Geddes 1994; Weyland 1996; Ames 2001; Desposato 2001, 2006b).

14. For Argentina, the WVS analysis also includes respondents with complete primary education because only two survey respondents out of 1,280 had less than a complete primary school education (neither indicated a positive evaluation). If I included respondents with a complete primary education in the WVS analysis for the other countries, the percentage of positive evaluations is virtually identical in most cases, though in Brazil positive evaluations decrease to 36.9 percent, in Uruguay they decrease to 46.7 percent, and in Mexico they increase to 41.4 percent.

et al. 2002; Carey and Reynolds 2007). Poor people's evaluation of their congress remained negative in Argentina, with an average favorable evaluation for the 2001–6 LB surveys of 17 percent.

The Dominican Republic shows a large increase, with an average of 41 percent in the 2004–6 LB surveys (LB did not conduct surveys in the Dominican Republic before 2004). The direction of the change is consistent with the theory of incentives to represent the poor, since in 2002 the Dominican Republic began using rules for electing its congress that increased the sharpness of the sanction available to most voters. In the eight largest-magnitude provinces (containing 58 percent of seats in the lower chamber), candidates in 2002 ran in electoral districts instead of running as a group for the entire province.[15] Voters got the option of casting a preference vote for a single candidate, while previously they had to vote for the party's entire list. In addition, the capital became a separate electoral unit, creating a middle- and upper-class district (the capital) and a lower-class district (the surrounding province) (Sagás 2003). These changes increased the need for candidates to obtain personal votes, and candidates appeared to recognize this since they got the elections tribunal to include their nicknames on the ballot so that it would be easier for constituents to recognize them (Sagás 2003, 794). The changes make districts more homogeneous, and make it more feasible for poor voters to sanction or reward individual legislators. In addition, they should enable intra-party competition for clients, creating a more competitive form of clientelism. Changes in electoral rules may take a while to affect legislator behavior, particularly those legislators who began their careers under the old election rules, but reelection rates were low in the Dominican Republic (Hartlyn 1998, 153–54). Changes in responses to the Proyecto de Élites Latinos Americanos (PELA) surveys done by the University of Salamanca indicate that deputies responded to the new incentives. Before the changes in election rules, Dominican deputies gave more "national" responses to questions about whom they represent (average score of 3.77 on a six-point scale, where 6.00 is the most "national" response), while deputies elected under the new rules offered more

---

15. DM in the twenty-three *circumscripciones* that were created ranged from 2 to 8 (average 3.8) and party magnitude was 1.3 for PLD (Partido de la Liberación Dominicana), 1.7 for PRD (Partido Revolucionario Dominicana), and 0.9 for PRSC (Partido Reformista Social Cristiano). In the twenty-four small provinces that did not have electoral districts, DM ranged from 2 to 4 (average 2.5), and party magnitude for the PLD was 0.5, 1.4 for the PRD, and 0.7 for the PRSC. With the electoral rule changes that made party magnitude close to 1 in almost all districts, it is possible for partisans to identify "their" representative.

local-oriented responses (average score of 2.94) (Marenghi and García Montero 2006, 41–42; Valverde 2009).[16]

In Peru during the Fujimori period, a low percentage of people with little or no education (10 percent) indicate confidence in their congress, which comports with Peru's institutional context.[17] The only institution that should enhance the sanctioning ability of poor Peruvians is open-list elections with high DM, but nominations and the form of clientelism in mid-1990s Peru gave poor people little real capacity to sanction legislators. After 2001, clientelism has become somewhat more competitive because the president no longer can enforce legislators' loyalty (Conaghan 2001), and presidents' parties have won far less than a majority in the congress, creating more viable patron options for poor voters who want to sanction. Low voter party ID also may give legislators an incentive to behave like entrepreneurs (Schmidt 2003, 2007), which should increase the influence of poor people, at least when they reside in districts with large poor populations.[18] These changes could explain the increase to an average of 16 percent of Peruvians with little education saying they have confidence in their congress.[19]

Chile, Colombia,[20] and Venezuela (the latter only in the 1990s) are intermediate cases on both the electoral/nomination and the clientelism dimensions. Relative to the spread of country evaluations in table 3.2, an intermediate percentage of people with little education in these countries indicate that they have confidence in their congress—though for the WVS data from the 1990s, notably fewer Colombians than Chileans or Venezuelans indicated that

16. The PELA surveys ask deputies various questions about whom they pay attention to when doing their job, and the authors developed an index of "representation focus" ranging from 0.00 (most local) to 6.00 (most national) focus. The average for all countries is 3.37 in the earlier study, and the Dominican Republic had one of the highest scores (though Mexico, with a score of 3.97, was higher). In the later study the regional average is 2.47, and now the Dominican Republic's score is in the middle. Only Uruguay had greater movement in average scores (from 2.92 in the 2000–2005 congress term to 1.35 for the term beginning in 2006).

17. For Peru, the WVS analysis also includes respondents with a complete primary education because only seventeen respondents out of 1,501 had less than that (none gave a positive evaluation of the congress).

18. Peru also broke up congressional elections into twenty-five districts, instead of one national district, though open lists are still used. DM for Lima is 35.0, and for the other districts the average DM is 3.5 (Schmidt 2003, 2007).

19. The Peru average presented in table 3.3 uses 2002–6 data because in 2001 the LB survey only covered 52 percent of the population. When 2001 is included, the Peru average is 17.2 percent.

20. The Colombia average presented in table 3.3 uses 2001 and 2004–6 data because in 2002 and 2003 the survey only covered 50.5 percent and 50.7 percent of the population (conflict territories were not included in the survey). When those years are included, the LB average for Colombia is 20.3 percent.

they have confidence in their congress. One possible explanation for the higher percentage of positive evaluations in Chile could be the capacity of the state and a relatively strong economy to deliver social welfare programs and services to people in need, as Concertación governments implemented many programs to alleviate poverty (Angell and Graham 1995; Weyland 1997). Poor people seeing legislators as possible assistants for obtaining welfare benefits would contribute to a more favorable evaluation of the legislature (Durston et al. 2005, 170–73; Moraes 2008).[21] Historically, Chileans expected members of Congress to provide clientelistic benefits to their constituents and their district, though the 1980 Constitution (and also a 1970 amendment to the 1925 Constitution) greatly reduced their capacity to do so (Valenzuela 1977, 153–55; Faundez 1997, 315; Siavelis 1997, 360; 2000, 153–55). Despite the legal changes in the power of deputies (such as their capacity to influence the budget), Chileans still expect personal service from deputies, so much so that Siavelis (2000, 154–55) expressed concern that deputies' lack of legal power to perform constituency service is harming popular opinion of the Congress. In Venezuela in the 1990s, AD and COPEI were still attempting to use their political machines to get out the vote (Saez strikes a deal 1998), even though the diminished state resources during the oil crisis made efforts at clientelistic representation much less success-ful. In part because they knew that voters could switch their support to another party, both parties had built extensive clientelistic networks when oil provided ample resources (Coppedge 1994; Molina and Perez 1998, 10; Roberts 2003, 46; Canache 2004, 36), and the 1996 poll may still reflect those past efforts.

In table 3.2, relative to the other cases, more Mexicans with little or no education than would be expected gave a favorable evaluation to their congress (32 percent). Election rules, nomination norms, and the form of clientelism present in Mexico in the mid-1990s each gave poor people quite limited sanctioning capacity, and the ban on immediate reelection also limits the sanctioning capacity of voters. An explanation may be that the Mexican survey was taken in 1996—a year before the PRI lost its majority in the Chamber of Deputies. Thus poor people were still operating in a political system dominated

21. In 1998, Hagopian (2001) surveyed Chilean legislators about their view of their role as elected representatives, asking them to rank six role options. "Resolving pragmatically people's problems" was the most commonly selected role, indicating that Chilean legislators see their job as helping constituents. The PELA surveys consistently find that Chilean deputies have a local focus to their job. Deputies in the 1997–2001 term had an average representation focus score of 2.40, which was the most local in the study, and in the 2006–8 PELA study the average representation focus score for Chilean deputies was 1.99, which was lower than the regional average of 2.47 (Marenghi and García Montero 2006; Valverde 2009).

at the national level by the PRI, which was known for buying poor people's support, and it continued to utilize such voter mobilization methods in the 1990s (Coppedge 1993; Fox 1994; Magaloni, Diaz-Cayeros, and Estévez 2007). By the next decade, poor people's evaluations of the Mexican congress, relative to the other cases, are more in line with expectations of the theory, with an average positive evaluation of 27 percent for the 2001–6 LB surveys. By this time, presidents had to build coalitions to pass bills, thereby expanding patron options for poor people. Also, more deputies were being elected from PAN and PRD, both of which recruit constituent servants (Langston 2008), which should create greater links between poor voters and officials in districts with large poor populations.

Venezuela appears at first as an outlier in table 3.3, since on average 40 percent of people for 2001–6 with little or no education express confidence in their congress. Poor people's ability to sanction was further constrained since President Chávez's movement controlled the congress and he did not need a coalition to pass legislation, which shrinks the market for patrons. But Chávez's movement recruited constituent servants into congress and sent clear signals that he wanted them to help the poor.[22] Thus poor people may have many "good types" in the congress, working on their behalf.

Conclusion

Various factors may affect how people evaluate their congress, ranging from the health of the economy to a recent major corruption scandal. But this macro-level analysis indicates that institutions can also help explain variation in poor people's evaluations of legislatures. A single institution does not produce the whole picture because multiple institutions affect the capacity of poor people to sanction. But when viewed in concert—as the institutional milieu in which poor people attempt to fulfill their personal and community needs, and as that which shapes political aspirants' reasons for wanting a seat in the legislature and their strategy for building a political career—institutions can help us to understand when more poor people are likely to evaluate their legislature favorably.

22. Elites now had little capacity to sanction, they did not like the programs Chávez and his movement were developing, and they were not the type of people to whom constituent servant legislators were supposed to give attention.

If we only examined electoral institutions, we would expect that open-list (or personal-list) systems with high district magnitude would give voters a sharp sanction because a relatively small number of voters can determine who receives a seat in the legislature, and those voters can use their vote to reward a specific legislator. Closed-list systems with high magnitude would provide the weakest sanctioning capacity. Mixed-member systems would be intermediate because legislators elected in single-member districts could be rewarded or punished by voters, but those elected on party lists would be insulated (Lancaster 1986; Carey and Shugart 1995; Carey and Reynolds 2007). Based only on their electoral institutions in the mid-1990s, the cases would be arrayed in the following order from strongest to weakest capacity for poor people to sanction:

High: Peru ⟶ Brazil ⟶ Colombia ⟶ Chile
Intermediate: Venezuela ⟶ Mexico[23]
Low: Dominican Republic ⟶ Argentina ⟶ Uruguay

Categorizing cases just on the basis of electoral institutions places Peru and Uruguay at the incorrect ends of the spectrum, indicating that other institutions may affect poor people's evaluation of their legislature. As stated earlier, according to Kitschelt and Wilkinson (2007, 43), "Given otherwise favorable conditions, it appears that politicians find a way to 'work around' electoral institutions, when other imperatives make it attractive for instrumentally rational politicians to build clientelistic principal-agent relations." Those other imperatives may come from party recruitment norms and the forms of clientelism that sharpen or weaken the sanctioning capacity of poor people. For example, in Uruguay, *sublemas* within parties increase the patron options available to poor voters. Presidents' need to form coalitions to pass legislation also expands patron options for clients, making that form of clientelism more competitive. In Peru during the Fujimori period, lack of political competition limited the clientelism market, and Fujimori's ability to control legislators from his movement made those lawmakers more loyal to him than to their constituents, thereby weakening poor people's sanctioning capacity. In Peru, *un*favorable institutions reduced the sanctioning ability created by open-list elections with high DM.

Average confidence ratings from the cases in each row in tables 3.2 and 3.3 show that the percentage of poor people who say they have confidence in their national congress decreases as election rules and nominations give poor people a weaker capacity to sanction, though the decrease is not monotonic in table 3.2. (Since some countries are placed in a row with an arrow indicating that it verges toward another row, table 3.2 shows averages for three sub-rows in the middle row, and table 3.3 indicates averages for two sub-rows in the middle row.) Averages for the cases in each column also show that the percentage of poor people who say they have confidence in their congress decreases as the form of clientelism makes it more costly for a poor person to sanction, though in table 3.3 the decrease is not monotonic. (Table 3.3 has averages for sub-columns to differentiate the cases coded with arrows, indicating that they verge toward the next column.)

Multiple institutions can affect the capacity of poor people to hold their legislators accountable. This chapter tested the hypothesis that when the electoral rules, nominations, and form of clientelism present in a country enhance the capacity of poor people to sanction legislators, more poor people will have a favorable evaluation of the congress compared to cases where institutions make it more costly for a poor person to sanction. While this macro-level study does not explore what type of representation poor people receive, the analysis on the whole finds that more poor people say they have confidence in their congress when more institutions give them a sharper and more easily used sanction.

23. Both Mexico and Venezuela had mixed-member electoral rules for the lower house of congress by the mid-1990s, but in Mexico the PRI was able to steal elections, dampening the ability of voters to use their vote to punish elected officials and parties. In addition, the ban on immediate reelection in Mexico means voters can only sanction legislators who run for another office.

Table 3-4 Appendix: Explanation of case coding

Case survey years	Electoral rules[a]	Nomination procedures	Type of candidates parties recruit	Party clientele or market	Access to state resources[d]	Coding sources
Argentina 1995 WVS 2001–6 LB	closed-list avg. DM = 10.7 *low*	party leaders or primaries *low*	party loyalist *low*	party network *limited*	small coalition needed *limited*	Gibson 1997; DeLuca et al. 2002; Stokes 2005; Jones 2008
Brazil 1997 WVS 2001–6 LB	open-list avg. DM = 21.2 *high*	state party leaders until '02 renomination was automatic *medium*	PP, PTB, PMDB, PFL, PSDB entrepreneur, PT group delegate, or party loyalist *mode—high*	market *competitive*	coalition needed *competitive*	Ames 1995; Desposato 2006b; Hunter and Power 2005; Hunter 2007; Samuels 2008
Chile 1996 WVS 2001–6 LB	open-list DM = 2 *medium*	national party leaders *low*	party loyalist/ constituent servant *medium*	party network and community organizations *intermediate*	president's coalition *intermediate*	Siavelis 2000; Durston et al. 2005; Navia 2008
Colombia 1997–98 WVS 2001–6 LB	before '06 personal-list in '06: open-list avg. DM = 4.9 *medium*	self-nomination *medium*	entrepreneur *high*	party broker network *intermediate*	unruly parties *intermediate*	Archer 1990; Shugart and Mainwaring 1997; Ulloa and Carbó 2003; Moreno and Escobar-Lemmon 2008
Dominican Republic 1998 WVS 2004–6 LB	until '02: closed-list avg. DM = 4.9 *low* after '02: preference vote, electoral districts *high*	national party leaders *low*	party or faction loyalist[b] *low*	party network *limited*	coalition needed *competitive*	Hartlyn 1994, 1998; Sagás 1997, 1999, 2003; Agosto and Cuelo Villamán 2001

Case survey years	Electoral rules[a]	Nomination procedures	Type of candidates parties recruit	Party clientele or market	Access to state resources[d]	Coding sources
Mexico 1996 WVS 2001–6 LB	mixed-member closed list DM = 40 300 single member districts (SMDs) *medium*	PRI—national party leaders (also governors and surveys after '97) PAN—state party PRD—factions *before '97: low* *after '97: low/medium*	PRI—party loyalist / group delegate[c] PAN—party loyalist / constituent servant PRD—constituent servant *before '97: low* *after '97: low/medium*	party network *limited*	before '97: no coalition *limited* after '97: coalition needed *competitive*	Coppedge 1993; Fox 1994; Gibson 1997; Langston 2006, 2008
Peru 1996 WVS 2001–6 LB	1996: open-list DM = 120 *high* 2001–6: Lima = 35, avg. DM for 24 other districts = 3.5 *medium*	national party leaders *low*	before '01: party, loyalist[b] *low* post-Fujimori entrepreneurs[b] *high*	party network *limited*	1996–2001: no coalition *limited* after '01: coalition needed *competitive*	Schady 2000; Conaghan 2001; García Montero and Freidenberg 2001; Schmidt 2003, 2007
Uruguay 1996 WVS 2001–6 LB	factional list DM = 99 *medium*	virtual self-nomination faction leaders *medium*	faction loyalist *low*	market *competitive*	before '04 coalition needed *competitive* after '04: no coalition/unruly parties *intermediate*	Espíndola 2001; Altman and Castiglioni 2006; Moraes 2008

Case survey years	Electoral rules[a]	Nomination procedures	Type of candidates parties recruit[b]	Party clientele or market	Access to state resources[d]	Coding sources
Venezuela 1996 WVS 2001–6 LB	mixed-member closed list avg. DM = 13.3 94 single member districts (SMDs) *medium*	national party leaders *low*	AD, COPEI— party loyalist[b] *weak* Chavéz's movement— constituent servants[b] *high*	party network *limited*	1996–99: coalition (but not in past) *intermediate* after '99: no coalition *limited*	Becker 1988; Coppedge 1993, 1994; Crisp 1997, 2000; Crisp and Rey, 2001; Molina and Perez 1998; Roberts 2003

NOTE: (1) Low/medium/high indicate the degree to which an electoral or nomination institution affects the sanctioning capacity of poor people (the categories for the rows in tables 3.2 and 3.3). (2) Limited/intermediate/competitive indicate how competitive clientelism is based on whether a poor patron can easily find a new patron or if switching patrons is likely to be difficult and costly for the poor person (the categories for the columns in tables 3.2 and 3.3). (3) "Mode" indicates the predominant type of candidate recruited by parties (party acronyms are listed in the List of Abbreviations).

[a] Data from Otero and Pérez-Liñan (2005) and Sagás (2003).

[b] Represents my own coding based on reading of secondary literature on the case. All other cases are coded from Siavelis and Morgenstern (2008a).

[c] When the PRI was dominant legislators were often group delegates. After the PRI lost its dominance, local connections became more important for winning nomination (Langston 2006).

[d] Determined based on national election results.

FOUR

~~≫≫≫❮❮❮~~

EVOLUTION OF INSTITUTIONS:
AN OVERVIEW OF HONDURAS'S POLITICAL HISTORY

This chapter has a dual purpose: to trace the development that led to Honduras's current democratic institutions, and to dispel myths. Outlining the country's history demonstrates how political parties and clientelism are major themes of Honduran politics, rather than the violence that has characterized its better-known neighbors, El Salvador, Guatemala, and Nicaragua. It also reveals the path-dependent development of the country's current democratic institutions. Chapter 5 explains how these institutions operate in the current democratic regime.

Honduras is different from its neighbors in several ways that are key to understanding the present democratic regime and the consolidation challenges it faces. One, unlike in many Latin American countries that have fragmented or volatile party systems, Honduran politics has been dominated for one hundred years by the Liberal (Partido Liberal de Honduras, PLH) and National (Partido Nacional de Honduras, PNH) parties. Two, while Honduras has experienced dictatorship and military rule, elections have also been a means of competition between the traditional parties. Three, Honduras has always been poor, but unlike in neighboring countries where repression controlled the poor majority, in Honduras clientele networks connected the poor to politics, and scarcity promoted clientelism rather than repression. Four, Honduran governments have not routinely repressed attempts by labor or the peasantry to organize. Labor leaders and north coast progressive businesses often worked together to try to influence government policy, generally supporting the social democratic faction in the Liberal Party, and governments often worked with peasant unions (albeit in ways that produced clientelistic benefits) rather than using force to repress demands for land.

The important ways in which Honduras differs from its neighbors help explain why it did not experience a serious revolutionary movement during the twentieth century, even though it "shares many of the problems of poverty, inequality, dependency, and authoritarian tradition that are associated with its neighbors" (Ruhl 1984, 33). As Sieder (1995, 99) so aptly writes, "In so far as there is a mould of Central American politics, Honduras does not fit it."

Path Dependence

According to Levi (1997, 28), "Path dependence has to mean, if it is to mean anything, that once a country or region has started down a track, the costs of reversal are very high. There will be other choice points, but the entrenchments of certain institutional arrangements obstruct an easy reversal of the initial choice." Path dependence helps explain the apparently limited consideration of new institutions or of institutional modifications when a country under-goes regime change; "new institutions are created or adopted in a world already replete with institutions," and those "institutions are resistant to redesign ultimately because they structure the very choices about reform that the individual is likely to make" (Hall and Taylor 1996, 953, 940). Such a pattern of typically minor revisions can be seen in Honduras's many constitu-tions (see Moncada Silva 1986). If institutions "serve some function (e.g., integration, adaptation, survival) for larger systems within which they are embedded," those institutions are often maintained. Institutions will also persist "provided that a powerful elite that benefits from existing arrangements has sufficient strength to resist their transformation" (Mahoney 2001, 9). Both reasons for the persistence of vertically organized traditional parties—clien-telism and nomination institutions—are found in Honduras. Honduras's history explains the origin of key institutions and their supporters. It also helps explain why Honduran institutions operate the way they do today, and informs predic-tions about how those institutions will affect the representation behavior of elected officials.

Clientelism is arguably the oldest institution in Honduran politics. It was a necessity in a poor country where the government lacked the resources to take care of people's needs. Economic and political elites took on the role of provider, and they used it to win supporters for their elections and for civil wars when election outcomes were not accepted by the loser. Domestic elites were patrons to peasant clients, and international banana companies were patrons to client politicians. Patronage, rather than ideology, was the basis of competition (Ruhl 1996, 35; Ajenjo Fresno 2001, 188; Bowman 2002, 144).[1]

In Honduras, clientelism and vertically controlled parties are how party leaders have always controlled lower-level politicians and party activists. Electoral competition is centered on personalism, with political aspirants rallying around their leader and building a loyal clientele (Taylor 1996; Ajenjo Fresno 2001, 188). Parties avoided the development of internal democratic organizations.[2] Party leaders are patrons at the top of a clientelistic pyramid, and positions on party slates are one of the resources they distribute to loyal followers. Top-down control of parties developed in the early twentieth century, when constituent assemblies often selected the president, and the caudillo would purge the assembly of opposition parties and disloyal party members to ensure his victory was unquestioned.

Honduran society has changed dramatically over the past one hundred years, developing a domestic oligarchy as well as active labor, peasant, and student organizations (Euraque 1996; Bowman 2002, chapter 5). Yet traditional parties, clientelism, and nomination institutions persisted, in large part because clientelism has proven a successful political formula for both parties, and because vertically organized parties have allowed caudillos to retain political control. These institutions work together in the present democratic regime to constrain and shape elected officials' behavior. They also create only a limited incentive to attend to the policy and service interests of the poor, but create stronger incentives to attend to poor people in ways that promote clientelistic linkages with parties.

This chapter will provide an overview of Honduran history, explaining the development of the traditional parties and their continued reliance on clientelism, as well as the evolution of the military, business groups, organized labor, and peasants as political actors. The final section discusses the path-dependent development of electoral and nomination rules: why they were chosen, how and why they evolved, and which political interests supported maintenance or change in these institutions.

---

1. Today the traditional parties still compete on the basis of providing services to their loyal clients/partisans, rather than on a platform of policy proposals (Ajenjo Fresno 2007; Cuesta 2007).

2. In the 1990s, the traditional parties began choosing their presidential candidates through competitive primaries, but negotiations among national faction leaders still selected other candidates (Del Cid 1991, 5; Posas 1992, 17). In 2005, for the first time parties used open-list primaries to select their candidates for Congress, and open lists were also used for the general election.

Geographic and Socioeconomic Overview

Honduras shares borders with Guatemala, El Salvador, and Nicaragua. The country is mountainous, with the exception of the swampy eastern region, La Mosquitia. The largest cities are the capital, Tegucigalpa, in the south, and the industrial center, San Pedro Sula, in the north. The urban population is growing, but much of the population is still rural. Honduras has always had a unitary government. Eighteen departments are divided into numerous municipalities with limited policymaking power and access to few funds except those dispersed by the central government (Nickson 1995).

Nearly 90 percent of the people are mestizo, so ethnic cleavages have not been a political issue, though there is an Afro-Honduran minority on the north coast, and there are small indigenous communities as well. Arab immigrants, who arrived in the first half of the twentieth century, are important in the business community and are starting to play an important role in politics. Linguistic cleavages do not divide Hondurans because, with the exception of Bay Islanders who speak English, all Hondurans speak Spanish. Hondurans are overwhelmingly Roman Catholic, though there is a growing minority of evangelicals, and the Roman Catholic Church, led by Cardinal Óscar Rodríguez, is an important player in national politics.

Honduras's population is overwhelmingly poor, and education levels are low. Approximately 17 percent of Hondurans are illiterate, and in the 2001 census the average length of schooling reported was 6.2 years (8.1 for urban people, 4.5 in rural areas).[3] Poverty has decreased, however, from 75 percent in 1991 to 63 percent in 2002 and 59 percent in 2008, and extreme poverty decreased from 54 percent to 45 percent to 36 percent. In 1990, the UN Human Development Index (HDI) score for Honduras was 0.472. By 1998, before Hurricane Mitch destroyed large amounts of infrastructure and property, the HDI had increased to 0.653. After Mitch, the HDI fell to 0.634, but in 2008 Honduras ranked 115th out of 177 countries, with an HDI of 0.700. Despite improvements, poverty is still endemic throughout Honduras, but its extent varies across the national territory, and is greater in rural than in urban areas: "In rural areas nearly three out of four (72.2 percent) live in poverty, while one in four individuals in urban areas (27.6 percent) is poor" (World Bank 2006, 2; see also Cruz, Seligson, and Baviskar 2004, 5; UNDP 2006).

---

3. The literacy statistic is from UNDP (2008).

A prosperity index reflecting the percentage of households with plumbing, electricity, and TV reveals a dramatic difference across departments.[4] Most people lacked these amenities in 1988 in Gracias a Diós, Intibucá, and Lempira, while more than half of households had these amenities in Cortes and Francisco Morazan (see table 4.1). HDI scores in 1998, 2002, and 2004 also show departmental variation, ranging from a low in 1988 of 0.453 in Lempira to a high of 0.787 in the Bay Islands. HDI scores in 2002 ranged from 0.447 to 0.791 and in 2004 from 0.554 to 0.732, with a few departments moving up or down a bit in relative rank but little change overall. The prosperity index calculated from data in the 2001 census also shows that few departments changed much in their relative ranking from 1988.[5]

It is interesting that the department with the biggest improvement in relative ranking based on the prosperity index is Colón. This department may have benefited from its consistent and strong backing of the Liberal Party (see table 4.1). In 1981, the Liberals beat the Nationals in Colón by 23 percent—almost twice the national-level margin of victory of 12 percent. In 1985, the Liberals received 15 percent more votes than the National Party in Colón—almost three times the margin of victory at the national level. In 1993, the Liberal Party outpolled the National Party in Colón by 20 percent. In 1997, the Liberal Party again outpolled the Nationals in Colón by a wide margin (16 percent for president and 14 percent for Congress in the first unfused election, when separate votes were cast for Congress and president).[6] Two other departments consistently gave the Liberal Party wide margins of victory: Yoro, with the fifth-highest prosperity index scores in both 1988 and 2001, and Cortes, which moved from the second-highest score in 1988 to the highest score in 2001. It is also noteworthy that the three poorest departments (based on the

4. Prosperity index = (% households with access to plumbing + % households with electricity + % households with TV)/3. Honduran census data is used to calculate the prosperity indexes for 1988 and 2001. Changes in values over time should not be construed as absolute increases in service provision, as data collected across the two censuses are not identical (e.g., what type of plumbing a house has access to).

5. The two prosperity indexes have a correlation of 0.94 (p = 0.000); the correlation for the 1998 and 2002 HDI scores is 0.99 (p = 0.000) and for the 2002 and 2004 HDI scores, 0.94 (p = 0.000). The HDI and prosperity indexes have a lower correlation (0.67) for the 1988 prosperity index and the 1998 HDI, and correlation of 0.73 for the 2001 prosperity index and the 2002 HDI. This correlation increases to 0.84 and 0.91, respectively, if Gracias a Diós is omitted. The reason for removing Gracias a Diós is that the high HDI scores for the department are suspect, given that they rank the area as the fourteenth-highest-scored department in the country when it lacks most basic infrastructure.

6. Before 1997, elections for president and Congress were "fused," which meant people cast one vote that elected both the president and the congressional deputies for their department.

Table 4.1 Poverty and voting behavior by department

Department	1981 election Winning party	% victory	1985 election Winning party	% victory	1988 prosperity index	1989 election Winning party	% victory	1993 election Winning party	% victory	1997 election Winner pres./Cong.	% victory pres.	% victory Cong.
Gracias a Diós	*National*	*6.2*	*National*	*25.8*	3.7	National	20.0	Liberal	4.2	*N/N*	*5.0*	*6.6*
Intibucá	*National*	*19.7*	*National*	*8.4*	6.5	National	17.1	*National*	*16.0*	*N/N*	*10.9*	*10.6*
Lempira	*National*	*21.8*	*National*	*9.6*	7.2	National	18.7	*National*	*19.9*	*N/N*	*12.7*	*11.4*
Olancho	Liberal	7.8	Liberal	4.5	12.4	National	9.8	Liberal	7.9	L/L	8.3	6.8
La Paz	Liberal	9.3	Liberal	15.6	13.9	National	3.3	Liberal	7.8	L/L	9.5	9.5
Colón	Liberal	23.3	Liberal	15.5	14.2	National	1.6	Liberal	20.4	L/L	15.8	13.9
Copán	*National*	*1.3*	*National*	*2.1*	14.2	National	9.3	*National*	*4.9*	L/L	1.0	0.2
Sta. Bárbara	Liberal	6.0	Liberal	5.0	14.8	National	2.4	Liberal	6.6	L/L	5.5	5.3
Choluteca	Liberal	0.8	*National*	*5.3*	15.1	National	15.6	*National*	*3.7*	*N/L*	*4.6*	1.0
El Paraíso	Liberal	22.6	Liberal	21.3	15.4	National	8.8	Liberal	16.9	L/L	16.6	15.4
Valle	Liberal	4.0	*National*	*1.4*	16.5	*Liberal*	*5.6*	*National*	*1.1*	*N/L*	*1.0*	1.2
Ocotepeque	Liberal	5.7	Liberal	9.6	20.8	*Liberal*	*1.4*	Liberal	7.4	L/L	10.1	9.2
Comayagua	Liberal	9.1	Liberal	6.3	25.6	National	5.1	Liberal	11.4	L/L	10.7	10.7
Yoro	Liberal	23.7	Liberal	14.5	28.7	National	0.8	Liberal	22.3	L/L	19.1	16.7
Atlántida	Liberal	20.5	Liberal	10.2	36.3	National	7.6	Liberal	17.7	L/L	13.7	8.0
Bay Islands	Liberal	7.5	*National*	*3.6*	41.9	National	8.2	Liberal	2.6	L/L	14.8	16.3
Cortes	Liberal	34.9	Liberal	12.1	55.2	National	1.2	Liberal	28.7	L/L	23.4	19.0
Francisco M.	Liberal	15.1	Liberal	1.5	56.2	National	16.9	Liberal	10.2	L/L	9.7	5.0
HONDURAS	Liberal	12.3	Liberal	5.5	22.2	National	8.0	Liberal	10.0	L/L	10.0	8.0

Department	1998 HDI	2001 prosperity index	2001 election Winner pres./Cong.	2001 % victory pres.	2001 % victory Cong.	2002 HDI	2004 HDI	2005 election Winner pres./Cong.	2005 % victory pres.	2005 % victory Cong.
Gracias a Diós	0.669	18.9	*L/L*	*3.7*	*7.4*	0.679	0.635	L/L	23.5	9.5
Intibucá	0.499	30.5	N/N	16.5	20.7	0.491	0.582	*N/N*	*5.2*	*20.5*
Lempira	0.453	23.6	N/N	12.3	11.6	0.447	0.554	*N/N*	*4.0*	*14.6*
Olancho	0.612	41.6	N/N	1.8	1.9	0.608	0.608	L/L	5.1	1.4
La Paz	0.546	38.8	*N/L*	1.7	*1.3*	0.548	0.610	L/L	7.9	1.0
Colón	0.651	51.6	N/N	1.8	2.3	0.647	0.636	L/L	14.9	11.1
Copán	0.510	42.1	N/N	3.0	2.4	0.519	0.578	L/L	4.6	2.6
Sta. Bárbara	0.521	44.7	N/N	1.7	2.7	0.516	0.597	L/tie	6.0	0
Choluteca	0.614	45.4	N/N	13.2	12.4	0.619	0.627	*N/N*	*4.2*	*3.4*
El Paraíso	0.594	45.3	*L/L*	*7.7*	*8.2*	0.592	0.619	L/L	14.1	13.8
Valle	0.638	48.7	N/N	8.0	8.3	0.628	0.649	L/L	4.1	4.2
Ocotepeque	0.564	43.0	*L/L*	*7.2*	*3.8*	0.554	0.600	L/L	10.2	0.7
Comayagua	0.617	54.6	*N/L*	0.2	*3.0*	0.604	0.629	L/L	6.8	8.1
Yoro	0.634	61.2	N/N	4.0	1.2	0.636	0.651	L/L	10.8	15.3
Atlántida	0.678	70.6	N/N	11.0	4.0	0.687	0.687	L/L	2.0	1.3
Bay Islands	0.787	81.4	N/N	14.6	7.0	0.791	0.726	L/L	0.8	15.4
Cortés	0.697	85.7	N/N	14.9	9.3	0.705	0.709	L/L	8.7	9.7
Francisco M.	0.727	82.8	N/N	13.9	10.6	0.737	0.732	*N/L*	*4.6*	2.5
HONDURAS	0.634	61.9	N/N	7.9	5.6	0.638	0.664	L/L	3.7	10.9

NOTE: (1) Bold-italics indicate an election in which the department vote went against the national outcome. (2) Departments are listed in order of their ranking on the 1988 prosperity index from the least prosperous to the most prosperous.

prosperity index) and the two departments with the lowest HDI scores in 1998 and 2002 typically voted for the National Party when the Liberal Party won the elections (often giving the PNH a strong margin of victory in the department), and that their HDI scores increased during the National Party government. We must interpret these trends cautiously due to lack of systematic data for ranking relative prosperity before the installation of the democratic regime. They would suggest, however, that the clientelistic traditional parties reward longtime supporters when they win control of government.

Bananas, coffee, cocoa, and beef are the traditional exports, and "nontraditional" exports such as shrimp and melons developed more recently in the 1980s (Brockett 1988). A dynamic maquiladora sector employs much of the urban workforce centered in the north coast region near San Pedro Sula (Goldfrank and Schrank 2006, 4–5). The small size of the road and rail network hampers economic development, and other infrastructure has been limited (see Bowman 2002, 141–42, for assessments of how the banana industry affected Honduran development).[7] Schools and hospitals are concentrated in major cities and towns. Hurricane Mitch destroyed much of Honduras's infrastructure in October 1998, though extensive international aid funded a good deal of rebuilding.

It is not surprising for a country where politics has always relied on clientele networks that corruption is a problem. In 2002, Transparency International scored Honduras 2.7 on a ten-point scale for corruption (low scores indicate a high level of corruption). India, Russia, Tanzania, and Zimbabwe also scored 2.7. In 2007, Honduras's Corruption Perceptions Index score dropped to 2.5 (the same as Burundi, Iran, Libya, Nepal, the Philippines, and Yemen). In Latin America, only Ecuador, Paraguay, and Venezuela received a worse score (Lambsdorff 2003, 264; Transparency International Corruption Perceptions Index 2006).

Development of Modern Honduran Politics

Founding the Dominant Parties

Before the end of the nineteenth century, there were no organized political parties in Honduras (Moncada Silva 1986; McDonald and Ruhl 1989; Vallejo

7. Not surprisingly, Hondurans consider this lack of services to be a problem that government should address. A 2004 survey asked, "In your opinion, what is the most serious problem in this municipality at present?" Lack of street repair was the answer for 20.5 percent of respondents, 17.5 percent said the economic situation, 15.7 percent said lack of water, 14.0 percent said lack of security, and 12.5 percent said lack of services (Cruz, Seligson, and Baviskar 2004, 143–44).

Hernández 1990). The institutions that generate incentives for politicians today began to take shape during the "liberal reform" period, started by President Marco Aurelio Soto (1876–83).[8] Soto's plans to modernize the economy led to the creation of the banana enclave on the north coast, and competition between political caudillos, supported by funds from competing banana companies, led to the development of lasting political parties.

Foreign capital became important in Honduran politics in the last two decades of the nineteenth century. President Soto invited foreign capitalists to invest in Honduras to fund economic development. Foreign investment initially played a prominent role in reviving the mining industry, which domestic elites lacked the funds to do on their own (Arancibia Córdova 1991, 35). This practice then spread to the north coast, where the government granted concessions to companies to build railroads and other infrastructure.[9] In return, the companies received lands around their projects that they developed into banana plantations. Soto's liberal policies included agricultural reform intended to create a commercial agricultural economy dominated by small-scale family plots,[10] and a labor policy that focused on the government playing a regulatory role in worker-employer relations. This policy differs noticeably from the forced labor program adopted for peasants in Guatemala (Gleijeses 1991; Euraque 1996; Mahoney 2001, 169–70). But the liberal reform strategy and development of a class of yeoman farmers did not work out as planned, and the foreign banana companies became stronger than the government (Arancibia Córdova 1991, 40; Mahoney 2001, 176).[11] Many people of economic means left agriculture and moved to San Pedro Sula to become involved in commerce and industry, often working with or in support of the banana companies. Consequently, Honduran elites did not need to develop a strong state that

8. See Mahoney (2001) for a thorough discussion of the instability and weakness of the Honduran state during the nineteenth and first half of the twentieth centuries, and also for a discussion of the liberal reform period, its policies, and the aborted development of these reforms as foreign companies gained control over export agriculture.

9. The banana companies also received concessions in exchange for building or expanding docks, ports, and electricity plants (Euraque 1990, 90; Mahoney 2001, 176). The state had little capacity to enforce these arrangements, so the companies only built railroads and utilities within the banana zone and to connect their plantations to the north coast ports (Munro 1967, 134; Arancibia Córdova 1991, 47).

10. Land reform did not face elite opposition because at the time there was a land surplus in Honduras.

11. Investment by U.S.-based companies in the banana sector took off after 1908 and reached its peak right before the world depression in 1930. Samuel Zemurray, the director of the Cuyamel Fruit Company, is described as the most powerful person in Honduras by the end of the 1910s (Mahoney 2001, 169–78).

would give them the means to repress and control labor (Euraque 1996). The liberal reform period came to an end by the 1910s because of government dependence on the banana companies.

In this context of growing foreign investment and control of Honduras's economy, Dr. Policarpo Bonilla founded the Liberal Party (PLH) in 1891. Bonilla ran for president in 1891, and when he lost due to fraud he took up arms, finally bringing the PLH to power in 1893. Following the established pattern of electing a Constituent Assembly to write a new constitution to legitimize the government, the Assembly wrote the Constitution of 1894. Unlike previous constitutions, the 1894 document contained some new progressive elements: secret voting, representation of minorities, and a requirement that municipalities update voter roles annually so names could be viewed and checked in advance (Moncada Silva 1986; Bendel 1993). These changes were valued by the first real political party in Honduras since it had been denied election by an incumbent using time-honored methods of election fraud. A disgruntled faction of the PLH organized the National Party in 1902, and its ability to compete in elections was also advantaged by these rules (Moncada Silva 1986, 211; McDonald and Ruhl 1989, 112; Euraque 2000, 138, 140; Ajenjo Fresno 2001, 181). Progressive institutions were maintained when they were of use to the governing party. The 1904 Constitution did not contain the provision for representation of minorities, but the 1924 Constitution did. The 1936 Constitution, which supported the 1932–49 dictatorship of Tibúrcio Carías of the National Party, again dropped the provision.[12]

Both parties had vertical organizations led by caudillos competing for access to the political spoils that came with controlling the government. They were elite parties, lacking ideological identities, and party caudillos could appoint their cronies and supporters to run under their banner. The popular sectors were co-opted by one or the other party without gaining the opportunity to construct their own ideology or party (Arancibia Córdova 1991, 45), so no left-leaning party like Peru's APRA (Alianza Popular Revolucionaria Americana) or Nicaragua's Sandinismo developed in Honduras in the early twentieth century.[13] By the 1923 election, both parties had established electoral clubs all

12. Representation of minorities in Congress was not reestablished until the 1957 Constitution, which adopted proportional representation elections (Moncada Silva 1986, 188–89).

13. Forming such a party would have been legally difficult. Rules for founding parties were not clear until the 1957 Constitution stated the right of Hondurans to do so (Article 36), and the law prohibited parties with ideological programs or international connections contrary to the sovereignty of the state, a provision intended to prevent formation of Marxist parties (Moncada Silva 1986, 205–6, 212–13; Fernández 1988).

over the country, and the clubs were beginning to create popular political affiliations to the parties that extended beyond mere loyalty to the current party leader (Euraque 2000, 147). The two parties competed in a series of elections under the 1924 Constitution that provided for minority representation. The United Fruit and Cuyamel banana companies backed different political parties, making large donations to their political campaigns and "their candidates" in civil wars, as they sought new land concessions, tax breaks, and a government that would create obstacles for their competitors (McDonald and Ruhl 1989, 112; Arancibia Córdova 1991, 41; Euraque 2000; Mahoney 2001, 227–28).

Instability slowed development of the Honduran state, and because the state had yet to develop a real role in the society (it did not provide social services or a repressive military apparatus), the bureaucracy was small. Regular changes of the party in power and an extensive spoils system—where political loyalty and partisan affiliation, rather than skill, were the means for advancement—limited the bureaucracy's expertise and the administration's competence (Posas and Del Cid 1983, 88–92; Mahoney 2001, 178–79).

With the arrival of political parties, caudillismo "was transformed into a new kind of clientelism dependent on company patronage" and working through vertically organized parties (Sieder 1995, 106; see also Arancibia Córdova 1991, 41; Euraque 1996; Mahoney 2001, 226). Clientelism and funds from banana companies were the basis of political competition; further, no *national* elite identity developed, nor did the elite elaborate its own programs for developing the economy (Arancibia Córdova 1991, 44).[14]

The End of Banana Company Competition

Competition between Cuyamel and United Fruit ended in 1929 when United bought Cuyamel and Cuyamel's owner, Samuel Zemurray, became chairman of the board. By that time the two parties were well established because of the competing clientele networks they represented, so they sustained themselves without financing from the competing companies, instead using state resources to reward their supporters. Still, the National Party's long alliance with United

14. An entrepreneurial class developed on the north coast, in part due to seed money from the banana companies. Bowman (2002, 147) describes them as "in many ways reformists who supported a modernized economy and democratic openings." Euraque (1996) explores how the progressive business elites of the north coast, along with local organized labor, later became a progressive force in the country's politics, supporting and nurturing the social democratic faction of the PLH.

Fruit put the PNH in an advantaged position (Sieder 1995, 106; Euraque 2000, 150).

According to Euraque (2000, 135–36), the way Honduras was integrated into the world economy, and its factionalized elite, caused the nation's problems. Yet the lack of a domestic agriculture-based elite meant that Honduras's upper class did not need a strong military to protect their interests from rebellion by oppressed peasants. This makes a striking contrast to El Salvador and Guatemala, where the coffee oligarchy needed repressive institutions to protect them from the exploited masses (Karl 1995). Several factors may account for the more peaceful relations between the elites and the masses in Honduras than in the other Central American countries (with the exception of Costa Rica). As alluded to above, one reason is the lack of a local coffee oligarchy (Ruhl 1984, 36; Euraque 1996; Mahoney 2001; Bowman 2002, 142–43).[15] Local elites made their money in cattle ranching,[16] small-scale mining operations or banana production, or in commerce supporting the foreign banana companies— the last becoming an important progressive force (Sieder 1995, 103; Euraque 1996; Mahoney 2001, 179–80). A second factor could be the constant divisions within the political-economic elite, as large landowners backed different parties as they vied for a share of the political spoils. As a result, the government represented the interests of the banana companies and the political faction dominant at any particular time (Ruhl 1984, 37), rather than defending the interests of a united domestic oligarchy against the peasantry. A third factor is the availability of land due to the country's low population density, at least until the 1930s (Ruhl 1984), so the peasantry had little reason to rebel to demand land (Euraque 1996). In addition, the only way to obtain assistance or land was through a patron's connection to a political party, since the state was still too weak and poor to provide many services. Thus the utility for poor people of staying connected to a clientele network outweighed the potential utility of organizing a left-leaning party or an uprising.[17]

---

15. Coffee did not become an important export product for Honduras until the 1950s. Small- and medium-sized farms grow coffee in Honduras, so the country still does not have a coffee oligarchy, though a small group of elites does control coffee processing and marketing.

16. Until the 1950s, the "largest domestic landowners continued to be the technologically backward cattlemen who constituted the economically poorest and politically weakest rural oligarchy in Central America" (Ruhl 1984, 37). Starting in the 1950s, cattle ranching grew in economic importance, the industry modernized, and the ranchers became a strong and conservative lobbying organization. Large-scale cotton farmers were another conservative force that became strong at the time (Euraque 1996).

17. This party loyalty still exists, as illustrated by the very low level of electoral volatility, which indicates little crossover voting between the two traditional parties (Ajenjo Fresno 2001,

The traditional parties' interest in patron-client relations, rather than policy, is still true. They are described as "nonprogrammatic, patron-client political machines primarily organized to capture state jobs and resources" (Ruhl 2000, 519; see also Rosenberg 1987, 202; Ajenjo Fresno 2001, 187–88). Poor voters identify with the traditional party of their family or village, which is an obstacle for third parties (McDonald and Ruhl 1989, 111; Ajenjo Fresno 2001, 187).[18] It also impedes formula-based government welfare programs that would provide development assistance to all people. Welfare and redistributive programs exist (explained below and in chapter 8), but they have a clientelistic dimension that determines which people or communities get the benefits. The shortage of state resources directly reinforces clientelism: because there are not enough resources to provide services to everyone, attachment to a party clientele network is the way to gain access to state resources.[19]

The National Party Dictatorship of Tibúrcio Carías

In the 1932 presidential election, Tibúrcio Carías Andino, the leader of the National Party, defeated the PLH candidate, Angel Zúñiga Huete. Zúñiga was backed by north coast business and by banana workers who began organizing in the 1920s, but his party held the presidency during the onset of the world depression[20] and Carías easily won the election (Argueta 1989; Euraque 1996,

---

190; 2007). In addition, as noted above, before 1957 rules for forming new parties were not clearly codified, and the 1957 law made leftist parties illegal.

18. It is worth noting, however, that surveys show that members of Congress perceive that voter identification with traditional parties is decreasing. In 1997, only 23.9 percent of 71 deputies interviewed from the 1994–97 Congress agreed that "the majority of citizens identify with parties and parties have strong attachments with society." The statement "There is a growing distance between society and parties, although parties continue to be important referents for the majority of citizens" was selected by 59.2 percent of deputies. The balance of deputies (16.9 percent) agreed with the statement "Few people truly identify with parties." Perceptions of party attachment had improved by 2001 (1998–2001 Congress), with 51.8 percent of 102 deputies indicating that the majority of people identify with parties, 39.0 percent saying that there is a growing distance, and only 9.2 percent saying few people truly identify with parties (Datos de opinión 2005).

19. Mexico's PRI used a similar system (Rothstein 1979), though benefits were channeled through one party, while in Honduras the traditional parties sustain two-party competition for state resources. In Chile before the 1973 military coup, multiple parties competed for resources for their clients, and Arturo Valenzuela (1977) argued that scarcity and a unitary centralized government helped sustain this system.

20. The Liberal Party's Vicente Mejía Colindres won the 1928 presidential elections, which were described as free and democratic, under the banner of the Liberal Republican Party, while from 1928 to 1932 the National Party controlled Congress and the Supreme Court (Posas and Del Cid 1983, 97–98).

50, 57–59; 2000, 143–44, 153–54; Mahoney 2001, 229–30). Zúñiga's liberal ideology (viewed as leftist by the archly conservative banana companies) made
ideology a means to differentiate the parties for the first time. United Fruit was
concerned that if elected, the Liberals, and in particular Zúñiga Huete, would
make it difficult to continue the exploitative business situation the company
enjoyed (Euraque 1996, 51–52; 2000, 150; González 2001a, 106). Carías managed
to stay in power until 1949 by manipulating the Constitution.

While the Liberal Party was out of power, its social democratic faction continued to develop. This wing, which included the future president Ramón
Villeda Morales, was part of Latin America's "democratic Left," which included
José Figueres of Costa Rica and Venezuela's Rómulo Betancourt, and was a
source of concern for Latin American conservative dictators and anticommunist leaders in the United States (Euraque 1996). This group of reformers
would prove important in the 1950s when workers went on strike to demand
the right to organize, strike, and receive a minimum wage. But while Carías
was president, the National Party consolidated its power.[21] As noted above,
the 1936 Constitution dropped the provision for representation of minorities.
Carías repressed the Liberal Party, even taking over municipal governments it
won so that the PLH lost all access to state clientelistic resources, threatening
the party with extinction (Euraque 1996). Many Liberals were exiled or fled the
country.[22] New presidential elections did not occur because the 1936 Constitution extended Carías's presidency until 1949 (Argueta 1989, 89–97, 102;
Euraque 1994, 239).

Carías's government benefited United Fruit, his cronies, and their clientele
networks. Bowman (2002, 146) describes Carías as "a caudillo and a dictator
who exiled his enemies, massacred protestors, and clamped down on the press,"
though he "was much less repressive and violent than his counterparts in
Guatemala and El Salvador" (146n8). United Fruit supported Carías because
he repressed strikes and labor organization,[23] and granted the company's requests
for land concessions and tax exemptions. Carías had the backing of the domestic landed elite who wanted to avoid structural changes in Honduran society,

21. Carías became the "main military and political caudillo" of the National Party in the
1920s, and maintained this leadership position until 1963 (Euraque 1994, 239).

22. Carías also persecuted a dissident faction of the National Party that challenged his control
of the party (Argueta 1989, 90–91; Euraque 1994, 243–44).

23. After the recurring labor unrest in the banana zones in the 1920s and 1930s, Carías viewed
organized labor as a threat, and he moved, often violently, to eliminate the labor unions (Posas
1981; Acker 1988; Euraque 1996, 36–38; Mahoney 2001, 249).

but the north coast business and industrial elite did not support him. Military officers, particularly from the air force (which he strengthened), supported Carías because he granted them autonomy and tolerated officers enriching themselves. Top-level bureaucrats wanted Carías to remain in power because he accepted their illicit enrichment. The Franklin Roosevelt administration supported Carías because he backed the United States in the war effort.

Before the Carías dictatorship, Honduras experienced little economic development outside the banana zone as state resources went to paying debts from civil wars that erupted over contested election results (Posas and Del Cid 1983, 88; Sieder 1995, 103; Euraque 2000, 134).[24] Farmers and small entrepreneurs had little incentive to invest as the repeated wars often destroyed their investments, and it was easier to improve one's social and economic standing by gaining access to public resources (Munro 1967, 126–32). Few ministries or government agencies were established, and the government invested little in infrastructure. The stability produced by Carías's long tenure encouraged economic development, particularly in the cities and northern ports. San Pedro Sula, in the north, became the country's industrial center. Tegucigalpa, in the southern mountains, remained the political center but had little industry, due in part to the difficulty of access to the northern ports. The political elites in Tegucigalpa were also accused of being interested only in politics and in expanding their clientele networks.

Protests led by groups of students, professionals, and prominent liberal dissidents caused a crisis in 1944. Excited by the democratic ideals spawned by World War II, these groups pressured Carías to establish a democratic regime. Carías's supporters responded with heavy-handed repression, including a massacre at a July 6, 1944, demonstration in San Pedro Sula (Euraque 1996, 69; 2000, 115). Such tactics kept Carías in power for a few more years, but they eroded popular support for him and for the National Party (Mahoney 2001, 250–52; Bowman 2002, 146). In 1949, Carías handed the presidency to his handpicked successor, Juan Manuel Gálvez (1949–54). During the "Cariato," Honduras did not appear so different from its neighbors, with no presidential elections, a controlled congress, and constrained freedom to organize as Carías eliminated labor organizations, closed newspapers, and outlawed demonstrations (Acker 1988, 82; Euraque 1994, 242). Yet the Cariato maintained the

24. A merchant class began to develop on the north coast and soon became the leader of the region's commerce and industry; through involvement in the social democratic faction of the PLH, as well as from outside politics, it promoted economic development ideas that would be compatible with U.S. president John Kennedy's Alliance for Progress (Euraque 1996).

institution of clientelism. Along with oppressing opponents, Carías used state patronage (e.g., government jobs, scholarships, land grants) to buy the support, or tolerance, of the Honduran population (Argueta 1989, 104–7).

Return to Partisan Competition and the Creation of the Military

Though handpicked by Carías, Gálvez was a moderate reformer whom Carías did not control (Euraque 1994, 248; Mahoney 2001, 251; Bowman 2002, 147). Changes over the course of the 1950s in the economy, political institutions, and society made Honduras a very different country by the 1960s. A more diverse and capitalist economy finally started to develop, even producing a local bourgeoisie (Euraque 1996). A modern state also started to take form: in 1950 the Central Bank and a state development bank were established, the Ministry of Agriculture was created in 1955, and in 1957 the state electric company was formed and an income tax established. State growth helped form a middle class with the professional government jobs it created (Arancibia Córdova 1991, 51, 54–55; Ajenjo Fresno 2001, 196).

Workers tried again to organize after Carías stepped down, and Honduras's "critical juncture" with regard to labor occurred in the 1950s (Euraque 1996, 52). In 1954, workers staged a strike that proved to be a watershed. The strike began at Puerto Cortes and spread to United Fruit plantations. Workers at the Rosario Mining Company, the Honduran Brewery, and the British American Tobacco Company joined the movement. Ultimately, fifty thousand workers went on strike. Peasants helped feed the strikers and their families, and teachers, tradespeople, and north coast business elites contributed to the strike fund (Euraque 1996, 97; Bowman 2002, 148). What was most significant about this strike in the Central American context was that President Gálvez negotiated a settlement with the strikers, rather than using repression. Workers won the right to organize, strike, and demand a minimum wage, though unions were not legalized completely until the first labor code was passed in 1959. Banana workers obtained a 10–15 percent wage increase, medical care for their families, and a promise of paid vacations. The labor organization that resulted after the strike gave Honduras the largest organized labor force in Central America (Acker 1988, 82, 84–85; Karl 1995; Sieder 1995, 107; Euraque 1996, 95–98; Ruhl 2000, 515; Bowman 2002, chapter 5).[25]

25. The strike's results were moderated somewhat in the end. The U.S. government strategy of funding "passive alternative unions" undermined organized labor's power (Acker 1988, 83), though

The 1954 strike was important for organized labor, but also for reformist actors in general. The Liberal Party, now led by the social democratic Ramón Villeda Morales, had been out of power and repressed since the beginning of the Cariato. The progressive north coast business elite had also lacked political power. Thus, when Carías was forced to step down in 1949 and the banana workers went on strike in 1954, there appeared to be an opportunity for change. This change was delayed for two years by the de facto government of Julio Lozano Díaz (PNH, 1954–56), which engaged in election fraud and repressed the PLH and other factions in the PNH. When he was ousted by the military in 1956, it was the first time the military acted as an independent institution. A Constituent Assembly was elected in 1957 in elections that were viewed as free and fair (Bowman 2002, 161), producing a PLH majority, and the Assembly elected Villeda Morales president.[26] Several important changes ensued in the 1957 Constitution and election law:[27] women's suffrage, proportional representation elections, elimination of all restrictions on suffrage, the right of citizens to form political parties, and sectoral representation on the National Election Council (representatives for the PLH and PNH; a representative for the commercial, industrial, and agricultural business chambers; and representatives for

---

the United States also rewarded moderate unions with loans to build low-cost housing for workers in the early 1960s (Euraque 1996, 101). The banana companies modernized their operations so that they needed fewer workers, thereby cutting their workforce by half (Arancibia Córdova 1991, 59).

26. The means by which Villeda became president were problematic for developing democracy. He was elected by the Constituent Assembly, even though with his wide popular support he could have expected to win a popular election. Why Villeda accepted this indirect election that limited his legitimacy is shrouded in mystery, but Bowman (2002, 161–65) argues it was due to pressure from the now powerful military, and part of the quid pro quo that codified military autonomy in the Constitution. Euraque (1996, 73) attributes Villeda's decision to the PLH's need to gain "access to government spoils from which Carías and Gálvez had excluded them for decades."

27. There is disagreement about how to describe Honduran politics in the period after the end of the Cariato in 1949 until the first of a series of military governments in 1972. Bethell (1991, 54) lists Honduras as one of the countries where dictatorship managed to survive after World War II, and where "promises of liberalization that had been made were withdrawn or overturned." Euraque (1994, 247–48) objects to this interpretation as placing too much emphasis on the two-year interim government of Julio Lozano Díaz (1954–66) and ignoring the moderate presidency of Juan Manuel Gálvez (1949–54) that ushered in the transition away from dictatorship. Bowman (2002, 147) describes Gálvez as urbane, progressive, and willing to allow Honduras to become more pluralistic, though he argues that Honduras squandered its chance to democratize in the 1950s (see his chapter 5). According to Mahoney (2001, 248), "A series of dictators controlled the Honduran government in a relatively non-institutionalized manner." Whether the political system of that time was semi-democratic or a "dictablanda," clientelism and the two vertically organized traditional parties still dominated Honduran politics (Rosenberg 1989, 41–42).

professionals, women's groups, university students, teachers, and labor organizations).[28] Sectoral representation on the Election Council would benefit the social democratic faction of the PLH, as they had the support of north coast business, organized labor, and urban professional groups (Fernández 1988, 21). Expanded suffrage could benefit both parties—the PLH with its organized labor links, and the PNH with its links to traditional rural landowners. The suffrage expansion was large, since as late as 1948 only 18 percent of the population could vote (Fernández 1988, 24).

The 1957 Constitution and 1959 Labor Code showed that elites had decided to incorporate labor into politics (Arancibia Córdova 1991, 57–58).[29] For President Villeda, the leader of the PLH social democratic faction, it was logical to reach out to labor. He also reached out to the organized peasant movement that was pressuring for land reform, by establishing the National Agrarian Institute in 1961 and by approving an agrarian reform law in 1962 (Sullivan 1995, 187; Brockett 1988, 125). With this strategy the PLH was expected to win the 1963 election (Moncada Silva 1986, 222). This was a very different way of dealing with the "social question" of how to handle labor organizing (Collier and Collier 1991) than was seen in El Salvador or Nicaragua, which were both ruled by undeniably authoritarian and repressive governments. Labor was briefly incorporated in Guatemala during the 1944–54 revolutionary period, but progressive policies ended in 1954 with the ouster of President Jacobo Árbenz (Euraque 1996).

The 1954 strike and the Villeda Morales administration attracted the attention of the United States. U.S. officials had begun to distrust the Liberal Party in the 1920s, but in the 1950s the threat in Honduras became more concrete.[30] The number of independent rural organizations grew—partly due to the massive layoffs from the banana plantations (in response to the 1954 strike), and also prompted by a hurricane that destroyed the banana plantations (which

28. The electoral laws in 1960, 1964, and 1966 retained these rules, but the 1981 electoral law replaced the sectoral representatives with a representative of the Supreme Court (Moncada Silva 1986, 202, 214).

29. Acker (1988, 88) closes her chapter on "The Rise of Labour" by writing, "Despite labour repression, it is still true that no Honduran president acts without testing what the workers will say. He may defy them, placate them, bribe them, repress them, but he cannot afford to ignore them."

30. In the 1920s, the U.S. ambassador, Walker Smith, became concerned about PLH leader Vicente Mejía Colindres's attitude about the U.S. anti-Sandino policy in Nicaragua. He described Mejía Colindres as a socialist who enjoyed the support of certain elements of the younger generation within the party who were only a little less radical than the communists in the Soviet Union. While these charges were likely exaggerated, they underscored an important difference between the Liberal and National parties as far back as the 1920s (Euraque 2000, 142–43, 152–55).

forced the former banana plantation workers into subsistence agriculture and increased demands for land). Campesino organizations radicalized due to these changes in the banana zone, and a second social question, now concerning how to handle peasant organizing, became important in Honduras (Sieder 1995, 108–9; Euraque 1996, 102–3, 159). In 1954, Honduran territory was the staging point for the Guatemalan invasion force to overthrow President Árbenz in Guatemala.[31] To counter the perceived threats growing in Honduras, the U.S. government promoted development of a modern Honduran military (Bowman 2002, chapter 5). Before the 1950s, Honduras had no real military. Armies existed as instruments of competing caudillos, but the military lacked an institutional identity (Ropp 1974; Arancibia Córdova 1991, 59; Funes 1995; Sieder 1995, 106; Ruhl 1996, 35; Euraque 2000, 115).[32] In 1954, the United States signed a military assistance treaty with Honduras, and the new military institution was developed to be independent of civilian control so that it could move with ease if it needed to oust a government that was "soft on the Left" (Arancibia Córdova 1991, 59; Bowman 2002).[33]

In the 1957 Constitution, the new institutional military demanded concessions to guarantee military autonomy. The president could neither give orders directly to the military nor choose or dismiss the chief of the armed forces (Arancibia Córdova 1991, 61; Sieder 1995, 107; Ruhl 1996; 2000, 515; Bowman 2002, 163–64).[34]

President Villeda's reformist policy agenda angered the National Party. PLH relations with organized labor and peasants in the context of the now universal suffrage created an obstacle for the PNH, in the 1963 presidential elections. The broad popular support of the PLH, and its ability to win almost all local elections and to appoint local officials, threatened the PNH with extinction. Villeda's policies also angered conservative rural bosses in the Liberal

31. Part of the reason for the United Fruit Company's concerns about Árbenz was that his policy of supporting unions and labor reforms could spread to other Central American countries, such as Honduras. The Árbenz government was accused of being behind the 1954 banana workers' strike in Honduras (Arancibia Córdova 1991, 56–57). See Schlesinger and Kinzer (1982), Gleijeses (1991), and Taylor-Robinson and Redd (2002) for details of United Fruit's concerns about the leftist threat spreading throughout the region.

32. Carías began modernizing the military when he built up the air force in the 1940s, but his strategy was similar to earlier political caudillos who were rewarding loyalists and building networks of supporters.

33. See Bowman (2002, 150–55) for the debate in Honduras at the time concerning whether it was advisable for Honduras to have a military, or whether it should follow the Costa Rican model and abolish its military.

34. Military independence continued in the 1982 Constitution, until it was amended in the 1990s.

Party, and domestic agricultural elites in the rapidly growing beef, cotton, and sugar industries (Fernández 1988, 23; Brockett 1988, 126). When Villeda created a national guard to balance the military, the military turned against him (Ruhl 1996). The National Party formed an alliance with the new institutional military to oppose the Liberals in the 1963 election. The military then staged a preemptive coup that brought Colonel Oswaldo López Arellano to power and a "reentrenchment of traditional Tegucigalpa-based caudillo politics," which was a "slap to the regional identification of San Pedro Sula elites with the Villeda Morales presidency" (Euraque 1996, 75).[35] López led a military government from 1963 to 1965, at which point the PNH-dominated Constituent Assembly elected him president for a term ending in 1971 (Posas 1989, 66; Sieder 1995, 107).[36] His conservative, civil-military government rigged the 1965 and 1968 national and local elections to insure PNH victories, and opposed the reformist agenda of the north coast business elite and organized labor (McDonald and Ruhl 1989, 113; Arancibia Córdova 1991, 68–69; Euraque 1996, 123, 130, 160).

Population growth and the development of commercial agriculture after World War II made land scarce for the first time in Honduras, and peasants organized to demand their share (Ruhl 1984; Brockett 1988). Initially, López tried to repress the demands, but the campesino movement regained strength and land conflicts sharpened (Sieder 1995, 109).[37] Banana workers unions and reformist elements in the Catholic Church assisted the peasants. López switched tactics, permitting some land invasions and evicting about eight thousand Salvadoran peasants to free up land for Hondurans.[38] He also increased the power of the National Agrarian Institute, laying the groundwork for a major land reform when he returned to power in 1972 (Ruhl 1984, 51–52; 2000, 515).

By the 1960s, there were more players in domestic politics than in the past and the military had become the most important political actor (Bowman

35. United Fruit was also rumored to be involved in the movement to overthrow President Villeda (Sieder 1995, 107).

36. Interestingly, the 1965 Constitution expanded proportional representation to municipal elections and maintained it for congressional elections (Moncada Silva 1986, 190).

37. Recall that Honduran peasant groups had gained important organizational resources in the late 1950s when laid-off banana workers with strike experience were forced to become peasant farmers (Sieder 1995, 108–9; Euraque 1996, 102–3, 159).

38. Land scarcity had plagued El Salvador for decades, and immigration to Honduras helped alleviate pressure, so the new policy to oust illegal Salvadorans created a serious problem for El Salvador. Concerns in Honduras's fledgling manufacturing community about cheap Salvadoran products entering Honduras under the Central American Common Market contributed to the tension between the countries. In 1969, these pressures flared into a brief but bloody war.

2002). Despite these changes, caudillismo did not disappear: military leaders constructed clientelistic power bases, and the traditional parties still were built on clientele networks (Arancibia Córdova 1991, 63). López started building links to peasant clients during this 1965–71 presidency (Ruhl 1984, 52). This strategy was feasible in the aftermath of the 1969 war with El Salvador as he capitalized on backing from the younger, reformist generation in the military, and used the ineptitude of the military's commanders in the war as an excuse to purge conservative senior officers (Sieder 1995, 112).

The Military Regimes of the 1970s

In 1971, Ramón Ernesto Cruz of the National Party was elected president to lead a government based on a national unity pact signed by the PLH and PNH. Patterned after the Colombian National Front, the pact provided for the parties to share power and patronage and to cooperate on a common reform program. Pressure from the COHEP (Consejo Hondureño de la Empresa Privada) and the CTH (Confederación de Trabajadores de Honduras) prompted this power-sharing arrangement as business and labor were frustrated by the inability of traditional caudillo politics to address the country's policy needs (Euraque 1996). But the power-sharing government did not meet demands for reform, so in December 1972 López Arellano led a military coup (McDonald and Ruhl 1989, 113; Arancibia Córdova 1991, 71–72, 85; Posas 1992, 2–4; Sieder 1995, 112).

The 1969 war spurred the north coast business community, peasants, and organized labor to rally around the military, which induced López to ally with those groups and break his union with the PNH (Arancibia Córdova 1991, 69, 72, 85; Sieder 1995, 109, 111; Ruhl 2000, 515–16). That these interests would turn to the military for help seems odd, given the military's conservative tradition of alliance with the PNH and the reformist reputation of the PLH social democratic faction. But the Liberal Party was deeply divided and unable to take advantage of these groups' frustrations, so business and popular sector groups turned to "more corporate forms of representation in order to voice their dissent" (Sieder 1995, 110; see also Euraque 1996). López followed the example of Peru's General Velasco Alvarado (1968–75) and established a reformist-style military regime pursuing state-sponsored economic development (Arancibia Córdova 1991, 76–79; Del Cid 1991, 3; Sieder 1995, 101; Euraque 1996; Ruhl 1996; Bowman 2002, 176). He was "anxious to defuse peasant discontent and to remold it into political support for himself" (Ruhl 1984, 52), and he said land reform was his fundamental reason for taking over the government (Arancibia Córdova 1991, 77).[39] The land reform program redistributed land to about one-fifth of the landless and land-poor peasant population, and reasserted municipal control over traditional *ejidal* lands and government lands that had been illegally fenced by large landowners (Ruhl 1984; Sieder 1995, 101; Mahoney 2001, 253).[40] While critics have said that it did not go far enough, they concede that the land reform defused unrest in the countryside because it co-opted the families who benefited from the program. It was "very important symbolically because the program demonstrated the continued flexibility and reform potential of the Honduran government and fostered an 'incrementalist' policy orientation among the peasant organizations" (Ruhl 1984, 55). López also established the first minimum wage and many new government agencies, increasing the government's role in the economy and creating new middle- and lower-class employment opportunities with the government (Posas 1992, 4; Ruhl 2000, 516).

Clientelism continued to be important. According to Sieder (1995, 113), "Between 1972 and 1978, patron-client relationships were restructured, recreated and selectively extended in an attempt to incorporate emergent social actors on the terms of those controlling the balance of power within the reformist state, providing the latter with a limited but nonetheless significant degree of legitimacy." Peasant unions were also clientelistic, especially in how they controlled access to obtaining land and credit (Sieder 1995, 121–23). López transformed the Congress into a corporatist body representing labor, peasant organizations, business groups, and political parties. The progressive north coast business elite and organized labor supported López (Euraque 1996, 161). The major change was that both the PNH and PLH were out of power and excluded from state clientelistic resources. The traditional parties, landed oligarchy, agro-export bourgeoisie, and banana companies rebelled, but their opposition did not bear fruit until they united.[41] Again according to Sieder

39. Euraque (1994, 246) writes, "In my view, the fact that the leadership of the Honduran armed forces in the 1960s and 1970s was found in the modernizing officer corps of the air force meant the exclusion of traditional landowning interests from personal influence within the policy-making circles of the armed forces high command. Colonel López Arellano's attentiveness to local and Latin American progressive forces in Honduras after 1968 must be understood in this broader context."

40. Lands used for agro-export crops were exempt from expropriation, so the banana companies did not oppose López's land reform, though domestic landed elites did oppose it (Sieder 1995, 115–16; Euraque 1996).

41. Part of the reason for conflict was that the peasant discontent and militancy that some of Lopez's reforms were intended to address had surfaced in the 1960s "in the areas where agrarian

(1995, 118), "One notable effect of the reformist process was to transform the nature of the dominant class in Honduras: galvanised by the threat of expropriation, a rural elite previously dominated by an intense regionalism became a formidable power block which employed anti-reformist discourse to considerable unifying effect. Those sectors of the private sector initially favouring reform increasingly turned against the government's agrarian programme after 1975, subsequently reaccommodating themselves within the anti-reform camp." When the "Bananagate" scandal broke in 1975, charging that López received a bribe to reduce the banana export tax, he was ousted by a coup (Arancibia Córdova 1991, 86; Sieder 1995, 116–17; Ruhl 1996, 37).

López's successor, General Juan Melgar Castro, was a conservative who had never supported the military's reformist sector. The military was not united behind the reformist banner, even in 1972, though the faction that was ascendant at that time was willing to try the strategy to achieve national security and unity. Officers were more concerned with professionalizing the military and with individual advancement than with a reformist economic development program. Melgar's government dragged its feet on further land reform, though it did not officially end the program, prompting campesino protests that the government repressed. It also adopted an antilabor stance and intervened in the most militant unions (Ruhl 1984; Brockett 1988, 133; Arancibia Córdova 1991, 90–91, 95–96; Posas 1992, 6; Sieder 1995, 114, 117–19).

Both traditional parties joined forces with commercial and landowning elites to pressure the military to return power to civilians. General Melgar announced that he would return power to an elected government, but his lobbying for the PNH presidential nomination alienated the rest of the officer corps. That alienation, combined with a lack of progress on the transition and frequent reports of corruption in the officer corps, led to another coup in August 1978 (Arancibia Córdova 1991, 97; Posas 1992, 5–6; Sieder 1995, 117, 119).

Melgar's successor, General Policarpo Paz García, understood that he could not govern on his own, so he began a "national dialogue" to discuss transition. He renewed military ties with the National Party and large landowners, and repressed popular organizations (Posas 1992, 13). Yet some land redistribution continued, and unions were still political players. Due to the past record of reforms, the popular sectors pressed their demands through established political channels. They demonstrated in support of democracy, and turned

---

capitalism had been registering its greatest success, in the southern departments of Choluteca and Valle" (Euraque 1996, 161).

out in large numbers for the elections that installed the new regime. Honduras avoided revolution during this turbulent period in part because Honduran peasants and workers still had reason to believe that maintaining links to government actors (traditional parties and military leaders) was the best strategy for getting benefits from a resource-constrained government. Joining rebel groups and taking up arms would not produce any rewards in the short term, if ever, so it was too costly a strategy for most poor people in Honduras to pursue, particularly compared to the probable benefits of a more conventional strategy when the PLH and PNH needed to reach out to their traditional clients to win the 1980 Constituent Assembly elections and the 1981 founding elections for the new regime (Brockett 1988, 133–34; McDonald and Ruhl 1989, 114; Del Cid 1991, 4; Mahoney 2001, 256).

Negotiating Democracy

General Paz's national dialogue was timely. The economy was not prospering and corruption charges were growing, so it was an auspicious time for the military to step down. The U.S. embassy also pressured for elections as part of President Jimmy Carter's pro-democracy policy. On April 20, 1980, a Constituent Assembly was elected. The military was expected to deliver a fraudulent victory to the PNH, but to everyone's surprise the elections were fair and the Liberal Party won the most seats.[42] Still, the transition was uncertain. General Paz liked being president, and it was not certain if he would hold elections. To ease the transition, the Liberal and National parties asked that Paz serve as president until a civilian president could be elected and inaugurated, and that he choose his own cabinet, though some members came from the two parties (Posas 1989, 65–66; 1992, 15; Del Cid 1991, 4; Casper and Taylor 1996; Ruhl 1996; Binns 2000).

The 1979 Sandinista overthrow of Nicaragua's dictator heated up the cold war in Central America, of course drawing U.S. attention. As the FMLN (Frente Farabundo Martí para la Liberación Nacional) became a threat to the Salvadoran government, the Central American conflict grew even more intense. Leftist-guerrilla insurgency in Guatemala was the third bloody conflict in the region. U.S. president Ronald Reagan engaged in intense military operations to oust the Sandinista government in Nicaragua and to prevent the FMLN

---

42. The elections were not perfect, however, as the National Elections Tribunal under PNH leadership did not allow the Christian Democratic Party to register (Posas 1989, 65; Del Cid 1991, 11).

from taking power in El Salvador, and these operations were often based in Honduras, including extensive funding for the Honduran military.[43] The United States still put pressure on the military for a transition, however, as the U.S. Congress did not want to approve anticommunist aid unless Honduras had a civilian government.

In this context, the military and the traditional parties negotiated the transition (Casper and Taylor 1996). As in 1957, the military wanted constitutional guarantees. In the cold war atmosphere of the Central American conflict, the military could justify its need for a national security doctrine and independence in order to defend the country from communist threats on its borders (Salomón 1982; 1992, 58–62; Schulz and Schulz 1994; Ruhl 1996). Both traditional parties wanted to regain control over government resources for clientelism, so they agreed to the military's demands. The 1982 Constitution created the essential trappings of democracy—a popularly elected president and legislature, essentially maintaining the election rules from the 1957 Constitution and election law—but the president lacked commander-in-chief powers; in fact, during the 1980s the military chief negotiated defense policy directly with the U.S. government and then informed the Honduran president of what was decided (Posas 1989, 85–86; Salomón 1992, 68).

Founding elections were held in 1981. The election was seen as fair because the Liberal Party won by a large margin, demonstrating that any attempts at PNH-military collusion had not marred the election (Posas 1989, 81). President Roberto Suazo Córdova was inaugurated on January 27, 1982, along with a PLH majority in Congress. The traditional political parties—led by caudillos running vertical organizations with support based on clientele networks, rather than ideology or competing policy platforms—returned to power (Ajenjo Fresno 2001, 188).

Assessment of Democracy in Honduras

A democratically elected government was installed in Honduras in 1982, but the 1982 Constitution contained perverse elements such as military autonomy from civilian control. Would Honduras's installed democracy be able to remove

43. Funding continued throughout the 1980s and facilitated military independence (Ruhl 1996, 38–41). See Bowman (2002, chapter 7) for discussion of how military aid deflected Honduran government attention from addressing the country's economic crisis.

those perverse elements and make progress toward consolidating? (Casper and Taylor 1996).

Like many who study democratization, I apply a minimal procedural definition to categorize a country as having *installed* a democratic regime. The necessary attributes to meet this minimalist concept of democracy are "fully contested elections with full suffrage and the absence of massive fraud, combined with effective guarantees of civil liberties, including freedom of speech, assembly, and association" (Collier and Levitsky 1997, 433). I assess removal of "perverse elements" (Valenzuela 1992) and the broader functioning of citizenship, particularly for poor people, in the context of *consolidating* democracy. A minimal procedural definition of democracy is useful because it has a deliberate "focus on the smallest possible number of attributes that are still seen as producing a viable standard for [installed] democracy" (Collier and Levitsky 1997, 433). I focus on "political features of the regime" (ibid.) instead of on substantive policies the government adopts because I view the type of policy a government adopts as an outcome of the political features of the regime.

Like the 1957 Constitution, the 1982 Constitution guarantees the right (in fact the duty) of all Honduras to vote, and also the right to form parties and associations and the right to freedom of speech. Since 1982, elections for all national and local offices have been held every four years.[44] But installing democratic institutions does not guarantee that the regime always meets all minimal procedural attributes of an installed democracy, nor does it mean the regime is free of perverse elements.

Removing perverse elements fits most appropriately, I believe, as work an installed democracy must do in order to make progress toward consolidation according to a "positive conception" of consolidation (Casper and Taylor 1996; Schedler 2001). Other problems faced by Honduras's democracy in the first decade raise questions about whether and when the regime qualified as "democratic" rather than a "protected democracy" or "democradura." I address the latter question first because it pertains to whether Honduras in the 1980s met a minimal procedural concept of democracy.

With the exception of the constitutional crisis precipitated by President Suazo in 1985 that led to the one-time use of a double-simultaneous vote, free and fair elections have been held every four years without major violations,

---

44. Thus Honduras's regime meets a "subminimal procedural" definition of democracy—one that only requires free and fair elections and allows for an alternation in power, which is the definition used by Przeworski et al. (2000).

and suffrage is universal. Throughout the 1980s it was common for election losers to claim fraud, though the claims typically lacked concrete evidence. Even in the early 1990s coup rumors were regularly floated in the press, creating anxiety that democratic rules of the game were not yet secure (Ruhl 1996; Schedler 2001). By the mid-1990s, however, claims of fraud diminished and, perhaps of greater import, the traditional parties have peacefully handed over power to each other multiple times (Ruhl 1997; Taylor-Robinson 2006b). In 2001 and 2005, international observers certified the elections were fair, though they did urge that the Elections Tribunal be made apolitical (OEA recomienda 2001; Taylor-Robinson 2003; Organization of American States 2005). Three small parties, including one leftist party, now win seats in municipal governments and Congress. Thus, on the procedural dimension of "fully contested elections with full suffrage and the absence of fraud" (Collier and Levitsky 1997, 433), Honduras was a democracy by the 1990s.

On the dimension of "effective guarantees of civil liberties, including freedom of speech, assembly, and association" (ibid.), there were serious questions in the 1980s. Concurrent with the transition to democratically elected government, the military began fighting the cold war, aiding the Reagan administration in supporting the Nicaraguan Contras, opposing the Salvadoran FMLN, and confronting small leftist groups in Honduras. Particularly notorious was the military's Battalion 3-16 death squad, whose hit list threatened some of the nation's more liberal-minded elites as well as activists and supporters of leftist groups. Though the number of victims was small compared to atrocities committed in other Latin American countries,[45] they were committed under a putatively democratic government, calling into question guarantees of civil liberties (Ruhl 1996, 37–39). On that count alone, Honduras merited the "partly free" rating of Freedom House from 1981 to 1984 and the "semidemocracy" coding for the 1980s from Mainwaring, Brinks, and Pérez-Liñán (2001) and Bowman, Lehoucq, and Mahoney (2005).[46] In 1992, a National Commissioner

45. Fifty-four disappearances occurred during the period of the 1980–81 Constituent Assembly, and eighty-two during Suazo's presidency. Disappearances continued throughout the 1980s, though they became less frequent, with thirty-eight documented disappearances from 1986 to 1990 (Posas 1989, 97; Del Cid 1991, 7; Salomón 1992, 64–66; Human Rights Watch 1994). A much smaller number of cases of political repression occurred in the early 1990s; by then public opinion had turned strongly against the military, however, and those cases were widely discussed in the press and some military officers even went to prison for their crimes (Salomón 1994, 77–78).

46. Honduras's combined Freedom House score for 1984/85 through 1992/93 is five, moving it to the "free" category. Before the 1990s, however, Freedom House scores were often more lenient. Further, Freedom House lacks explicit coding rules, making it difficult to know the reason for changes in scores. Mainwaring, Brinks, and Pérez-Liñán (2001, 53–55) provide a useful discussion

Table 4.2 Comparison of regime evaluation scores

Year	Freedom House Political rights	Freedom House Civil liberties	Group	Bowman et al. (2005) index	Mainwaring et al. (2001) index
1982	3	3	PF	0.5	S
1983	3	3	PF	0.5	S
1984	2	3	F	0.5	S
1985	2	3	F	0.5	S
1986	2	3	F	0.5	S
1987	2	3	F	0.5	S
1988	2	3	F	0.5	S
1989	2	3	F	0.5	S
1990	2	3	F	0.5	S
1991	2	3	F	0.5	S
1992	2	3	F	0.5	S
1993	3	3	PF	0.5	S
1994	3	3	PF	0.5	D
1995	3	3	PF	0.5	D
1996	3	3	PF	0.5	D
1997	2	3	F	1	D
1998	2	3	F	1	D
1999	3	3	PF	1	D
2000	3	3	PF	—	—
2001/2	3	3	PF	—	—
2003	3	3	PF	—	—
2004	3	3	PF	—	—
2005	3	3	PF	—	—
2006	3	3	PF	—	—
2007	3	3	PF	—	—
2008	3	3	PF	—	—

NOTE: (1) Freedom House scores countries from one to seven on a political rights and a civil liberties dimension, and low scores are more democratic. Free (F) and Partly Free (PF) indicate the status Freedom House designates for a particular year based on the combined political rights and civil liberties ratings. (2) Bowman et al. (2005) code countries on five dimensions constituting a minimal procedural definition of democracy, with scores of 0, 0.5, or 1. The aggregate score for a year is the highest score that a case receives on *all* dimensions, so one rating of 0.5 and ratings on the other four dimensions of 1 yield an aggregate score for the year of 0.5. (3) Mainwaring et al. (2001, 41) code countries on four dimensions constituting a minimal but complete procedural definition of democracy, meaning "all four criteria are necessary components of democracy, without which a regime should be not considered democratic." Thus S indicates a semidemocratic category that has competitive elections but does not meet all the other necessary criteria, while D indicates a democratic regime.

for Protection of Human Rights was established, and it investigated the human rights violations of the 1980s (Ruhl 1996, 1997). Politically motivated violations of human rights ended and Battalion 3-16 was disbanded.[47] Table 4.2 shows several regime evaluation scores for Honduras.

Another major question about democracy in Honduras pertains to an "expanded procedural minimum" definition, where an additional attribute is added to the earlier list: "elected governments must have effective power to govern" (Collier and Levitsky 1997, 433). I follow Valenzuela (1992) and Collier and Levitsky (1997) and view civilian supremacy over the military as part of consolidating democracy, whereas Mainwaring, Brinks, and Pérez-Liñán (2001) and Bowman, Lehoucq, and Mahoney (2005) include this dimension in their procedural minimum scorings.[48] Regardless of the stage in the democratization process where this dimension falls, there is no question that lack of civilian control of the military is a problem for democracy. In the cold war context of the 1980s Central American conflict, it was a huge impediment to consolidation and even the stability of Honduras's fledgling democracy. Karl (1995, 80) referred to the democracies installed in Central America in the 1980s as "hybrid" regimes that "are not merely reconstitutions of previous authoritarian coalitions; rather, they are a hybrid form that has the potential to mobilize mass pressures for increased political contestation and inclusion." But when the Central American conflict ended (after the Sandinistas in Nicaragua stepped down in 1990 when they were defeated in elections, and the FMLN and the Salvadoran government successfully negotiated a peace treaty in 1990/91), Honduras's military became vulnerable.[49] Hondurans were weary of the draft,

---

of the utility and shortcomings of Freedom House rankings. During the 1980s, Bowman, Lehoucq, and Mahoney (2005) scored Honduras 0.5 out of 1 on national sovereignty and civilian supremacy in addition to respect for civil rights.

47. Common and organized crime rose in the later 1990s, leading presidents to adopt a heavy-handed antigang policy. Though detrimental to popular evaluations of democracy (Ruhl 1997; Cruz, Seligson, and Baviskar 2004), such problems are not generally considered part of the political and civil liberties dimension central to the concept of an installed democracy.

48. Bowman, Lehoucq, and Mahoney (2005, 950) also add a "national sovereignty" dimension, coded based on whether "the national government [is] a self-governing polity" and if "elected officials implement policy without direct obstruction from foreign actors." Karl (1995) cautioned that the role of the U.S. government in the politics of Central American countries presented an additional challenge for consolidating democracy not present in South American cases. For Honduras specifically, she explained that the long-enduring, strong U.S. influence has left domestic forces "unaccustomed to defining their own interests or developing the leadership credentials that are essential during periods of transition" (Karl 1995, 77; see also Ruhl 1996, 40).

49. Guatemala's civil war was formally ended in 1996 with a peace accord between the URNG (Unidad Revolucionaria Nacional Guatemalteca) rebels and the government (Trudeau 2000, 507).

constitutions provided for some electoral reward for the smaller party, which comports with the predictions of Przeworski (1991) and Colomer (2004). In 1957, closed PR lists by department were adopted, and they had been maintained until the 2004 election law reform adopted open lists. Starting in 1971, fused presidential and congressional elections were used (Bendel 1993, 395), reinforcing the president's position as the chief of a vertical organization.[52] Since party clienteles were built by local elites delivering votes to their party in elections (and foot soldiers in a civil war when an election outcome was contested), majority elections fit the needs of strong local patrons and party leaders. The switch to PR came with the Liberal Party's social democratic faction leading the party in the 1950s and controlling the Assembly that wrote the 1957 and 1960 election laws. The social democratic faction had the backing of north coast business and organized labor, and PR lists would facilitate providing representation to those interests. Labor support had new importance with the adoption of universal suffrage in 1960. Representing north coast business mattered because the Tegucigalpa political business elite had dominated both parties in the past, and traditional party leaders had ignored north coast businessmen who had political aspirations. Even if the PLH was not concerned about power sharing with the PNH, President Villeda Morales still had to maintain unity in a divided party where his social democratic faction had ideological differences with rural conservative factions (Fernández 1988), and it was thought that PR might preserve party unity.[53]

Because only large parties had a chance of winning access to executive branch spoils, it would be political suicide for a disgruntled faction to leave its party. This was true even if the division had an ideological base, as with the social democratic faction of the PLH; while its position in the party has varied over time, the faction has only changed names and leaders, and has never left the party (see Fernández 1988; Vallejo Hernández 1990; Ajenjo Fresno 2001, 87–88). Another factor restraining party splits was that rules for forming new parties were not clearly defined prior to 1957, and the 1957 rules prohibited leftist parties. In addition, the traditional parties (particularly the PNH) used

---

52. No information exists about whether fused elections were used before 1971, but even if a fused ballot was the formal rule it would not have been applied often: the president and Congress were only elected at the same time in 1924, 1948, and 1954; even then, the 1948 election had only one presidential candidate, and the 1954 elections were extremely fraudulent (Morris 1984; Bendel 1993, 395).

53. Proportional representation did not unify the party, however, and the rural-conservative faction that opposed Villeda facilitated the military coup before the 1963 election, leading to a military-PNH government (Fernández 1988, 23–24).

technicalities to prevent new parties from registering. Thus the only viable strategy for ambitious politicians has always been to work within a traditional party, and that meant accepting the vertical organization.

Vertical party organization has always meant that national party faction leaders controlled nominations for congressional and municipal posts. This insured partisan support in Congress, enabling the president, whose constitutional powers are weak, to legislate and fulfill campaign promises to clients. When de facto presidents legitimized their rule through formal appointment by a Constituent Assembly, it was important for the leader to control backbenchers to ensure his "legitimate" election. Deputies continued to support or acquiesce to party leaders, instead of demanding internal party democracy for nominations, because they needed state resources for clientelism; in addition, they relied on presidential coattails to get elected, which cost less than running their own campaign. Even with primaries to select presidential nominees, starting in the 1990s deputy and municipal candidates continued to be nominated by faction leaders. Even the PLH's social democratic faction left nominations to the faction leader. This arrangement permitted politicians to build careers and local clientelistic networks, so there was no compelling incentive to democratize parties.

Party rules help maintain faction leader control over nominations by giving the faction leaders representation on the party's national executive committee. Before 1977 there was no legal requirement of competitive nominations or PR for factions. When PR rules for party posts were adopted in the 1977 election law, leaders of dominant factions claimed the party had no factions because it had united behind one candidate slate (Fernández 1988, 55, 57). The traditional parties finally adopted primaries to select their presidential candidates in the 1990s, after each party experienced a serious election defeat (the PLH in 1989, PNH in 1993) that prompted party faction leaders to view a primary as a better strategy for winning the presidential election. This reason for changing nomination procedures comports with the expectations of party change literature (see Harmel and Janda 1994). When presidential primaries were adopted, party statutes still gave faction leaders latitude to negotiate who would be nominated and list positions for both congressional and municipal elections to balance factional interests and maintain party unity. Dominant factions have an incentive to keep other factions within the party because an inclusive party would maintain the votes of clients of all its factions, thereby increasing its chances of coming in first in the elections. Even when election rules were modified to allow a separate vote for municipal

elections (1993), and then also for congressional elections (1997),[54] candidates
below the president did not have incentives to run independent campaigns
because they lacked funds to do so, and their names and pictures were not
on the closed-list ballots. Even though voters could now split their vote, politicians who wanted or needed access to executive branch resources to maintain
their clientele network had no incentive to buck the system. It was still easier to
get poor clients to vote for a party than it was to build a personal reputation,
and a united party was still needed to win the presidency (see Ajenjo Fresno
2001, 186–87).

Vertically organized traditional parties with clientelism linkages to voters
made it feasible to maintain for twenty years in a democratic regime election
and nomination institutions that did not give much real choice to the mass
public. The two parties connected poor people and political patrons to government though party-based patron-client networks in a way that produced a
likely clientelistic payoff when their party was in power. These institutions
persisted because they served a survival function in a resource-scarce environment. Party faction leaders and multinational banana companies both benefited
from these arrangements that gave them control over state resources—limited
though they were—which they needed to pursue their own political and
commercial goals, respectively. Even leaders of the social democratic faction
of the PLH played by these rules, because doing so was how they could win
office. The PLH social democratic faction and its progressive allies on the
north coast might have been able to break the power of traditional elites that
benefited from institutions that enhanced the role of clientelism, but they were
in power only briefly during the 1957–63 administration of President Villeda
Morales. During that time some significant democratizing changes were made
in government institutions (e.g., PR elections and universal suffrage), but
the military staged a coup before the 1963 election, so the opportunity for
institutional reform came to a halt. When civilians returned to power in 1982,
the faction that controlled the PLH was conservative, unwilling to share power
with other factions, and did not promote democratizing changes in institutions
(Moncada Silva 1986, 221; Fernández 1988; Ajenjo Fresno 2001, 225). Powerful elites benefited from old institutional arrangements, the social democratic
faction of the PLH was small at that time, and reform-oriented popular

---

54. The PLH, PINU (Partido Innovación y Unidad), and PDCH (Partido Democrata Cristiano
de Honduras) representatives on the National Elections Tribunal made the proposal to separate
ballots in April 1993 (Ajenjo Fresno 2001, 185), when those parties were all in opposition and closed
out of executive branch spoils, as the PNH held the presidency and a majority in Congress.

organizations did not have the political strength to force a change. Even the social democrats in the PLH worked to pursue their goals within the party, since if they split from the PLH they would lose access to the state's limited clientelism resources.

The persistence even in a democratic regime of election and nomination rules developed by party caudillos in an authoritarian milieu prompts the question of how it was possible to adopt open-list nominations and elections in the 2004 election law. The answer is behind-the-scenes pressure from the international aid organizations that gained much influence in Honduras after Hurricane Mitch in 1998, plus recognition by party leaders that the small parties were increasing their vote share and more voters were becoming disaffected with the traditional parties (Paz Aguilar 2008, 637–38). Before the 2001 election, the presidential candidates of all five parties signed a "Manifesto to the Honduran People" promising to pursue election reform. A Comisión Política with the support of the United Nations Development Programme evaluated reforms, including changing the National Elections Tribunal (TNE) to make it independent, separating the National Registry of Persons from the TNE, having the TNE hold party primaries, and changing the method of nominating and electing deputies to bring them closer to the voters. In the 2005 election, this last change appeared to benefit the traditional parties since the small parties did not increase their seats in Congress, but many party caudillos lost renomination or reelection bids when voters got to select their preferred candidates.

Election and nomination institutions have proven extremely "sticky" in Honduras, and even apparently important changes (adopting PR elections, unfusing ballots) did not reduce national party leaders' control over backbenchers. In large part this is due to the importance of clientelism for maintaining the support of poor people for traditional parties, and to the importance of maintaining party unity since large parties have the best chance of winning the all-important presidential election. These imperatives have persisted in both authoritarian and democratic regimes.

FIVE

INSTITUTIONS AND INCENTIVES IN HONDURAS'S
THIRD-WAVE DEMOCRACY

The arrangements made by key political actors during a regime transition establish new rules, roles, and behavioral patterns which may or may not represent an important rupture with the past. These, in turn, eventually become the institutions shaping the prospects for regime consolidation in the future.

— Terry Lynn Karl, "Dilemmas of Democratization in Latin America"

Many democracies have formal institutions like those found in Honduras, but how they function in Honduras is influenced by the country's history and the informal institutions that the Liberal and National parties brought into the new regime. Institutions need to be analyzed in concert, incorporating their path-dependent development, because the combination of institutions creates the institutional milieu shaping the capacity of poor and rich Hondurans to sanction their officials, and creating incentives that influence members of Congress about how to do their job and whom to represent.

Macro-level observable implications of the theory presented in chapter 2 concern the incentives created by multiple institutions that constrain and influence the strategies of citizens and elected officials. This chapter begins with a description of how the institutions that create incentives and constraints for legislators work in Honduras's third-wave democracy, examining constitutionally defined rules and informal institutions. After that I assess the monitoring capacity of poor and rich people, and then I apply the theory developed in chapter 2, assessing how Honduras's institutions affect the ability of poor and rich people to sanction, and whether members of the Congress have an incentive to represent poor people. This appraisal forms a basis for assessing if incentives for representation by elected officials may help explain the ongoing dominance of traditional parties, despite a poverty level that could be expected to have made Honduras ripe for the instability and revolutionary movements found in neighboring countries. Chapters 6 and 7 explore micro-level observable implications of the theory, examining whether and how legislators engage in efforts to represent poor constituents.

Institutions in the Democratic Regime

Electoral Rules

When the democratic regime was installed in 1982, the president, three presidential designates (equivalent to vice presidents),[1] departmental slates of representatives in the Congress, and municipal governments were all elected on a fused ballot. A slate of Parlamento Centroamericano (PARLACEN) delegates was later added to the fused ballot. Fused elections presented to voters a very simple ballot: each party had a column showing the party's name and banner, a picture of its presidential candidate, and the presidential candidate's name. Names of candidates for other offices were not listed. In 1993, municipal elections were unfused, allowing two separate votes to be cast, but votes for the municipal election and the still-fused presidential-congressional-PARLACEN election were both cast on one ballot paper. In 1997, congressional and presidential elections were unfused, but deputy candidates' names and pictures did not appear on the ballot, and again one ballot paper was used. In 2005, an open-list ballot was used for congressional elections, providing candidates' names and pictures (see chapter 4 for explanations of how and why these modifications were possible).[2]

The president is elected by simple majority and cannot be reelected (Articles 236 and 239 of the Honduran Constitution). Congressional seats are allocated proportionally to parties, using the largest remainder Hare formula,[3] and

---

1. The Constitution was amended in 2002 so that starting with the administration that took office in 2006 one vice president was elected on a slate with the president. In 2008 the Supreme Court overturned another part of this amendment, so that there are now three presidential designates selected once again.

2. Honduras's traditional parties have always maintained their base of electoral support with clientelism, so changing election laws may have been a logical and necessary, though somewhat slow, response to ongoing *democratic* partisan competition.

3. According to this method of seat allocation in PR elections, each party first receives the number of seats for which it won full quotas of votes. The "quota" is the total number of votes divided by the total number of seats. Any seats not allocated by full quota are distributed to parties in the order determined by which party has the "largest remainder" of votes (votes left over after seats have been allocated by full quota), then to the party with the second largest remainder, and so on.

Table 5.1 Seat breakdown of congresses since the installation of democracy

Term	President's Party	Number of seats held by:				
		PLH	PNH	PINU	PDCH	PUD
1982–85	PLH	44	34	3	1	—
1986–89	PLH	67	63	2	2	—
1990–93	PNH	55	71	2	—	—
1994–97	PLH	71	55	2	—	—
1998–2001[a]	PLH	67	55	3	2	1
2002–5	PNH	55	61	3	4	5
2006–10	PLH	62	55	2	4	5
2010–14	PNH	45	71	3	5	4

SOURCE: Data compiled from election results obtained from the National Elections Tribunal.

NOTE: For the 1982–85 term, the Congress had 82 members. For the 1986–89 term the number was increased to 134 as part of the Act of Compromise to resolve the crisis caused by President Suazo's maneuvers to hold on to power. Since the 1990–93 term, the number of deputies has been fixed at 128.

[a] Elections in 1997 for the 1998–2001 term were the first time separate votes were cast for president and Congress.

deputies (*propietarios*) are each paired with a substitute (*suplente*). Until 2005, deputies were elected from party-presented closed and blocked lists. Congressional district magnitude (the number of representatives elected per department) in Honduras ranges from one to twenty-three. Municipal councils are elected by closed-list PR, and the leader of the list that wins the most votes is the mayor. All officials serve four-year terms. Voting is obligatory for citizens over eighteen (Article 44), but this is not enforced.

Plurality elections for president gave voters an incentive to vote for the traditional parties rather than waste their vote on a party with little chance of winning the presidency and the access to resources for clientelism it provides. Plurality elections for president, combined with fused elections or unfused elections on one ballot paper, created strong party discipline in Congress. When municipal and then congressional elections were unfused from presidential elections, most voters still voted for a traditional party.[4]

4. In recent elections, abstention has increased dramatically, reaching 45 percent in 2005, but Honduran analysts suggest the traditional parties may view this as beneficial because those most likely to abstain are independents. Poor, particularly rural voters, on the other hand, are less likely to abstain or to split their ballot, and are most likely to continue to support the traditional parties (Abstencionismo electoral 2005; 63 por ciento 2005; Taylor-Robinson 2006b).

Table 5.2 Effective number of parties in the Honduran Congress

Election	1981	1985	1989	1993	1997[a]	2001	2005	2009	Average
Effective # of parties:	2.17	2.12	2.00	2.03	2.18	2.41	2.37	2.30	2.18

SOURCE: Data compiled from election results obtained from the National Elections Tribunal.
[a] Elections in 1997 were the first time separate votes were cast for president and Congress.

Vote splitting does occur, and it helps the three small parties to win seats in Congress, municipal councils, and a few mayoral posts, but in 2005 their upward trajectory stopped (Taylor-Robinson 2006b; Booth and Aubone 2007). The traditional parties still dominate elections (Ajenjo Fresno 2001, 190), and the effective number of parties is still close to two (see tables 5.1 and 5.2).[5]

The logical strategy for ambitious politicians is to work with a traditional party, as that maximizes their chances of being elected and having access to state resources for clientelism. Along with the rootedness of the parties within the population, this has undoubtedly helped limit the number of parties in Honduras. The clientelistic nature of politics has meant that parties win national elections by combining strengths across elections for president, Congress, and municipalities. Presidential candidates help attract voters to the party's slates, and deputy and municipal candidates mobilize local clients to vote for the party. The strategy of campaigning at all three levels gives factions an incentive to stay within one of the traditional parties. New parties are disadvantaged, not because of fraud, but because they lack access to state resources for patronage and clientelism, which makes it hard for them to attract voters who value clientelistic benefits.

Nominations

Party leaders at the national level controlled nominations for party slates until 2005, and the presidential candidate was the most important party leader.[6] The ability of the presidential candidate to select candidates for party lists

5. "Effective number of parties" is a method for counting the number of parties in the party system or represented in the Congress. It weights the parties by their relative strength (in popular votes or in seats in the legislature). Unless all parties have equal strength, the effective number of parties is lower than the actual number of parties (Lijphart 1999).

6. In 2005, deputy candidates were chosen by open-list PR primaries. This new nomination system may produce changes in deputy behavior, as many party stalwarts (referred to as dinosaurs by the press) lost their reelection bid in the primaries or the general election. The two traditional parties won as many seats as they had in 2001, but there was higher turnover among their representatives. It is notable that the Congress elected via these new nomination and election

(and safe positions) produced strong loyalty to the president. Many deputies explained in my interviews that they were elected in the shadow of their presidential candidate, as people voted based on party ID or preference for a presidential candidate. Executive branch control over state resources for clientelism creates another incentive for loyalty to the president (McDonald and Ruhl 1989, 117; Taylor 1996; Ajenjo Fresno 2001, 186), and chapter 4 showed how that incentive survived through changes in regimes and election rules.

The Electoral Code (Article 19) specifies that parties with internal factions must hold primaries and proportionally represent factions when filling party posts and selecting candidates. Both traditional parties have factions, but until 2005 neither held primaries to select candidates for Congress or municipal lists.[7] Faction leaders traded "electable" *propietario* slots for "safe" *suplente* slots, and some deputies said in interviews that the presidential candidate held an electable slot open for them on the list until the deadline for submitting lists to the National Elections Tribunal.

Many deputies have built careers in the Congress or other posts. Reelection rates have risen (see table 5.3), though sometimes there is a gap in a deputy's career. Gaps often appear voluntary—as when a deputy with a safe slot on the party's list does not return to the Congress in the next term, during which time that deputy's party loses the presidency, only to return in a later election once again with a safe slot on the list. This may be a strategic decision to attend to personal business during a term when the deputy will not have access to executive branch resources and their bills are less likely to pass. Though many deputies serve only one term, 34 percent of deputies have served two terms, 14 percent have served three terms, 4 percent have served four terms, and 3 percent have served between five and seven terms. Before or after serving in the Congress, some deputies are mayors, hold executive branch offices, or serve in the PARLACEN. The percentage of deputies with two or more terms in elected or appointed office has increased dramatically over time, reaching 90 percent in the 1998–2001 Congress.

---

rules was the first one that was willing to check the president. But President Zelaya balked at the Congress (and also the Court) trying to check his autonomy, which eventually led to the Court issuing a warrant for his arrest. When the military and police went to detain him on June 28, 2009, instead of simply bringing him into custody to stand trial they flew him to Costa Rica (which violated the Constitution), thereby producing the political crisis that beset Honduras and garnered it international attention for the rest of the year.

7. In the 1985 election, as a response to the constitutional crises precipitated by President Suazo, who wanted to remain in power or at least control selection of the 1985 presidential candidates, a double simultaneous vote was used, so multiple factions ran presidential and deputy candidates in the general election (Posas 1989, 104–22; Del Cid 1991; Schulz and Schulz 1994).

Table 5.3 Career statistics of Honduran deputies (percentage of deputies elected in a term)

Term elected as propietario	Reelected immediately	Reelected after break	Total reelected	Held prior post	Career continued immediately	Career continued w/break	Total with a career
1982–85	27.1	9.4	36.5	—	29.4	14.4	43.5
1986–89	33.6	5.2	38.8	29.1	28.4	11.2	55.2
1990–93	33.6	10.2	43.8	45.3	46.9	10.2	74.2
1994–97	43.0	7.8	50.8	47.7	67.2	6.3	85.2
1998–2001	36.7	3.9	40.6	75.0	45.3	3.9	90.6
2002–5	29.7	3.9	33.6	73.4	32.0	5.5	91.4
2006–9	39.0	—	—	39.0	42.8	—	61.9

NOTE: (1) A deputy is counted as reelected if reelected as either a *propietario* or a *suplente*. (2) A *propietario* is counted as having a "career" if reelected at least once to the Congress, elected to another post (e.g., municipal government or PARLACEN), or received an appointed post as a cabinet minister or head of an executive agency. (3) Prior posts include all the posts listed in note 2 plus election to the 1965 or 1981 Constituent Assemblies. (4) Complete historical data were not available for prior posts before the 1982 term.

Clientelism

As chapter 4 showed, clientelism is a venerable institution in Honduran politics. Traditional parties still bind supporters to the party with clientele networks (Ajenjo Fresno 2001, 186). They are the way to gain access to the state's scarce resources, whether for elites who want government contracts, or for poor people who need a political patron to get them a job or welfare assistance.

Systematic evidence about the need for clientelistic connections to get access to state services (e.g., doctor's appointment or a school scholarship) or to get things done (e.g., register a business, obtain a gun permit) is not available. Deputies often mentioned in interviews that they help people with such requests, and I observed people waiting for deputies to give them letters for jobs in January 1994, when the Liberal Party came back into power after four years of National Party government. A 2004 survey question concerning encounters with corruption provides possible evidence of the need for connections. The survey reported that 11 percent of respondents who had children enrolled in school said that they had been asked to make a payment greater than that required by law, 10 percent of respondents who had done business with their municipality said they were asked to pay a bribe, and 7.2 percent who used public medical services said that they were asked to pay fees above those stipulated by law. While the number of people who reported direct encounters with corruption is low, 73.6 percent said they think corruption is common or very common, which may indicate the need for connections (Cruz, Seligson, and Baviskar 2004, 67, 73–74).

The need for connections to gain access to even basic government services (e.g., schooling, health care, cash transfers) makes it very costly for poor people to leave a traditional party if they are frustrated by its platform not representing their policy interests. They can switch parties, but doing so severs their relationship with their party-based clientele network. Small parties, due to their inability to win the presidency and their very limited success winning mayoral elections, are unlikely to give their activists access to state resources. A client who switched to the other traditional party should—in theory—have access to state resources when that party wins the election. In the severely constrained resource environment faced by the Honduran state, however, parties reward longtime activists and supporters to retain their loyalty before they share clientelistic resources with new supporters. Thus a poor person who switches parties will need to demonstrate loyalty to and activism for the new party before reaping rewards. Indirect evidence of the importance of party activism for creating a person's connection to a party-based clientele network can be found in Booth and Aubone's (2007) analysis of survey data from Honduras. Socioeconomic, urban/rural, and community size variables are not significant predictors of political participation, which indicates that Hondurans from all classes and walks of life are equally likely to participate in politics. They find that party activism increases as standard of living decreases. Although these relationships were not strongly significant, it was consistent with anecdotal observations, and Booth and Aubone (2007, 18) propose that this result is possibly the most interesting in their study: "The poor take part in campaigns and party activities more than those who are better off."

A frustrated partisan could protest by privately defecting from their party in the voting booth. If the traditional party still won the election, the defector then would still have access to party-channeled government largesse. But the traditional party would not be punished effectively unless many voters in the community acted in the same fashion, and then, if the party still won the national election, it would punish the community by not providing it with state funds. Small precincts of about 350 registered voters help local party leaders to keep an eye on the behavior of purported party supporters.

Congress

Based on the powers granted in the Constitution, the Honduran Congress should be strong. It can make and reform laws, and must approve the nation's budget, loans, taxes, and treaties. It appoints the Supreme Court and the comptroller. It can interpolate ministers and other executive branch officials. It can extend its ordinary sessions, and call special sessions (Articles 189, 190, 205). Yet the Congress historically has not made full use of its constitutional powers, due to the tradition of presidential dominance[8] and the president's partisan powers. For government posts appointed by the Congress, typically the president has sent a list of nominees whom the Congress then appoints. Congress rarely calls in executive branch officials to answer questions in person or writing, and if questioned they do not feel compelled to answer. Presidential vetoes have been rare, but congressional overrides are even more rare. In sum, the president's partisan powers in Honduras outweigh the Congress's constitutional powers.[9] The president's party had a majority in every term until 2002, and since then was only a few seats shy of a majority and formed a majority coalition (see table 5.1).

The Congress has not organized itself to aid in developing policy expertise or constituency service. Deputies do not have staff, and only congressional leaders have offices. The number of committees has expanded from eighteen to over fifty, and deputies on average serve on three committees, but sometimes many more. There are no seniority norms for committee assignments or selecting committee presidents. Committees lack offices, staff, or the power

8. Historical literature makes little mention of the Congress, but what it does say indicates that the Congress deferred to the president. Between 1896 and 1941, the Congress usually approved the executive's bills. The president's legislative success rate ranged from 63 percent in 1931 (the year before the Carías dictatorship began) to 100 percent in 1896–98, 1901–2, 1906–7, 1909, 1915, 1919, and 1938–39. William Stokes (1950, 280) described the Congress as a curtain behind which the executive carries out the real work of government. Munro (1967, 125), writing in 1918, described the government as one "where all branches of the administration are under the absolute control of the president." Argueta (1989, 97–100) describes the Congress as willingly giving up power to the executive in the 1936 Constitution. An exception to the subservient Congress occurred during the administration of President Mejía Colindres (PLH, 1928–32), when the National Party controlled the Congress and a divided government allowed the legislature to develop and temporarily assert its independence (Posas and Del Cid 1983, 98).

9. The 1982 Constitution grants the president few proactive or reactive legislative powers (Shugart and Mainwaring 1997). The president can veto legislation, though it is not a line-item veto, and Congress needs a two-thirds vote to override. The president has no decree powers and no exclusive rights to initiate specific types of legislation, but the executive can and does initiate bills on a wide range of topics (Taylor-Robinson and Diaz 1999).

to subpoena witnesses. Rational choice theory predicts that institutions are endogenous (Hall and Taylor 1996; Carey 2000), so deputies would be expected to organize the Congress to give themselves the capacity to gain policy expertise or to serve constituents if it would help them to achieve their political career goals. If they do not, it is because such resources are not useful to deputies. Historical institutionalists might also expect that most deputies in Honduras would not think to empower their institution to take on the president, given the history of executive dominance of politics. The executive controls access to state resources for clientelism, and "the overriding purpose of traditional party politics has remained the provision of *chamba*, or patronage, to party bosses and their followers" (McDonald and Ruhl 1989, 115). Vertical clientele networks are important for deputies to gain political access to ministers and agency directors for services (Rosenberg 1987; interviews with deputies). In Honduras, bucking the system is likely to lead to loss of access to clientelistic resources, hurt a deputy's career chances, and cause independent deputies to conclude that politics is not a fruitful way to pursue community development goals.

Monitoring and Sanctioning Capacity of Voters and Incentives for Elected Officials

This section applies the theory of institutional incentives developed in chapter 2 to Honduras. The first part defines the actors in the Honduran version of the strategic decision game. The next part assesses the monitoring capacity and sanctioning resources of rich and poor people. The final part considers how institutions affect deputies' strategies, whether deputies have an incentive to represent poor people, and what form representation takes.

Actors

The rich actor is a member of the elite, such as a business owner with funds to make significant campaign contributions or a member of the local traditional oligarchy. These elites have business interest organizations that facilitate communication with government regardless of which party is in power. The poor actor is from the lower class and is likely to work in the informal sector (if he or she lives in a city) or is a peasant in a rural community. Backbench deputies from the two traditional parties are the elected officials who are the focus for this analysis about incentives to represent poor people.

Monitoring and Sanctioning Ability of Poor and Rich People

The first challenge that poor people in Honduras face in holding their elected officials accountable is obtaining information about what officials are doing. Media coverage is limited and tends toward the politically sensationalist and biased, as some newspapers are known to be affiliated with one of the traditional parties and journalists are reputed to be in the employ of the government. Still, if one reads beyond the headlines, it is possible to get news about some legislative initiatives by specific deputies. Poor people are unlikely to have ready access to the Internet, but even if they did, government Web pages are not set up to provide much detailed information. The congressional Web site has pictures of deputies and now includes e-mail addresses and phone numbers, but it does not provide links to deputies' personal pages, and before 2007 it did not provide any information about the bills and amendments offered by the deputies. Deputies are not required to file reports with the Congress about their work, and they do not have a budget for mailings or trips to their district to keep in touch with constituents. People can come to the Congress to make requests or pressure officials—and they do, individually and in groups—but such trips are costly in terms of transportation and time away from work, and do not guarantee that they will get to meet with the official. Thus the capacity of poor people to monitor is largely limited to what they can observe in their community and to whether they have received a promised personal benefit.

Rich people are limited like poor people in the quality of the information they can obtain from the media or the Internet. But they can get information from personal meetings with officials in the Congress and executive branch, as well as via their interest organizations, which also meet with officials. Like poor people, rich people can observe whether they received promised particularistic benefits, but they can also go to the Congress to check on the progress of a bill that is important to them (e.g., to import goods duty-free).[10] In sum, rich people have access to more extensive resources for monitoring.

Closed-list PR elections and party leaders' control of nominations made it difficult for poor people to sanction deputies, but gave rich people a strong sanction if they exercised influence with party leaders. National-level party leaders have been able to control ballot access, list position, and executive branch appointments, which made them able to virtually guarantee a politician a long career.[11] The

10. While collecting data in the Congress Archive, I frequently saw businesspeople checking on the progress of a bill or getting a copy of a recently passed law, and the staff always attended to them promptly and respectfully.

11. Even with open-list primaries to select deputy nominees starting in 2005, national party leaders still control ballot access for the primaries and appointments to executive branch posts.

only way poor people can thwart this control is by defeating the party at the polls so that it loses the presidency, wins few seats in Congress, and wins few municipalities, which requires many frustrated people voting against the party. Low electoral volatility shows that Hondurans have not engaged in this type of mass sanction; instead, they have tended to demonstrate their frustration by not voting. Since the majority of Hondurans are poor, and abstention rates are lower among the poor, it seems that poor people have not reached the point where large numbers think it is worth incurring the individual cost of trying to punish the traditional parties.

The step return ratio discussed in chapter 2, NV/n^*c (Croson and Marks 2000; Goeree and Holt 2005), predicts that poor people will be unlikely to sanction. The number of people (n^*) who would have to vote against the party to harm a deputy's career chances is very large, and the number of other people who are dissatisfied (N) is difficult for poor people to assess. The personal cost (c) that the poor person is likely to pay for a sanction attempt is high, as they risk severing their link to the party clientele network. Until very recently, a poor person could not sanction a deputy directly because closed-list PR elections have required voting for a party's entire slate. The poor person could not transfer support directly to a new patron, because the poor person could only vote for another party's entire slate. Losing one vote would not hurt the deputy, and simply voting for another party would not connect the poor person to a new party clientele network.[12] To become attached to a party's clientele network a poor person must establish a relationship with a broker, which includes voting for the broker's faction in presidential primaries and the party in elections, attending campaign rallies, organizing party supporters, and repeatedly demonstrating militancy for the party or faction. If a poor person's party wins the executive branch at the national or local level, a poor person can expect to receive clientelistic benefits, but a poor person who switches parties will be at the end of the line to receive clientelistic benefits from their new party.[13] Since the Honduran government's budget is very limited, competition for patronage and local infrastructure projects is fierce, and a person, group, or community needs a reputation of party loyalty

12. A frustrated poor person could split his or her ticket. But this sanction can be costly if enough people in their precinct vote against their clientele party that the party will not want to target scarce resources to that precinct. Small precincts give the parties finely grained estimates about whether their clients voted loyally.

13. If longtime party supporters do not receive what they consider their due, they may sanction the party in the next election, as happened to the incumbent National Party when it was badly defeated in 1993. Analysts explained the election outcome as largely due to the dissatisfaction of PNH supporters, who chose to abstain rather than to vote for the Liberal Party.

to receive benefits. Communities receive projects (e.g., a school or a paved road) if the community is known to be loyal to the governing party.[14] If many people in a community attempt to sanction by voting against the deputy's party but the party wins the election, the entire community will be passed over in the allocation of resources for the next four years.[15] In sum, the sanction is likely to be personally costly and unlikely to be successful, so the poor person is unlikely to sanction. In addition, the improvement in policy/service (V) the poor person would likely obtain by changing representatives is small due to the similarity of the two traditional parties.

Party alternation in power in Honduras reinforces the party allegiances of poor people. Although a poor person whose party loses the presidency or municipal elections will not likely receive clientelistic benefits from government for four years, they have an incentive to continue to back their party because if it wins the next election, they will be in line to receive benefits from the new government. Rich people, by contrast, can use connections to party leaders in both parties to influence nominations and reward or sanction. Connections come from campaign contributions, family and friendship networks, and leadership positions in both parties. The century-long dominance of the Liberal and National parties has taught economic elites the value of building connections in both camps (Amaya Banegas 1997, 2000). Campaign contributions are very important to the traditional parties, particularly to pay for presidential primaries, which receive no government financing (Ajenjo Fresno 2001, 193–94, 230, 267–68). Until 2005, backroom deals decided candidate slates, so a rich person's connections were a direct threat to a deputy.[16]

How the Probability of Sanction Affects Deputy Strategy

Under closed-list elections, a deputy wanting a political career could not afford a sanction from rich people who had influence with party leaders. This meant it was important that policy initiatives and service not attract negative attention from rich people. Poor people might lose faith in a deputy working against

---

14. It is possible to insure that party clients are the actual beneficiaries of a project that on the surface appears to be a public good if a connection to the governing party is needed to actually use the service (e.g., a letter from a deputy to get an appointment with a health clinic doctor).

15. Several deputies explained in interviews that if they bring an infrastructure request for a community or local development organization (*patronato*) that supported the party that lost the national election, the request will not be funded.

16. Rich people should continue to have influence over deputies with open-list elections, as deputies now need funds to run personal campaigns.

their interests, but they would be unlikely to observe the deputy's work on national policy due to their limited monitoring resources. If a deputy delivered particularistic benefits to poor persons or a development project to their community, it would be easy for the community to observe and should win their support for the deputy and the party. Since the partisan nature of access to resources has long been widely known, poor persons should understand a deputy's failure to deliver benefits when his or her party was in opposition, and they should delay judgment until that party is in power. In the case where a deputy from the governing party failed to deliver on promised personal or community benefits, closed-list elections, particularly with large district magnitude, made it virtually impossible for poor people (even acting in concert) to sanction the deputy; further, the cost of trying to sanction the deputy's party was too high to justify incurring, since the poor people affected might hope to receive benefits (from a different deputy or party broker) during the next administration, should their party win.

Based on this assessment of the low likelihood that poor people could monitor or sanction a deputy under closed-list elections in Honduras, a deputy with political career aspirations should represent rich people to insure his or her own political future. The deputy should represent poor peoples' policy preferences only if they do not conflict with the interests of rich people. It is unlikely that providing particularistic benefits to poor people and infrastructure projects to their communities would conflict with the preferences of rich people if enough funds were available, and poor people have had the capacity to monitor this type of representation, though some deputies got away with not providing such benefits because the poor had such weak sanctioning ability. Clientele networks have long been the base for both traditional parties in Honduras, and party members in the Congress and municipal government (especially mayoral candidates) have been expected to mobilize the party's clientele base in support of the party and its presidential candidates. Yet the informal institutions that have controlled nominations for Congress and municipal slates did not screen candidates primarily based on their connections to the party base. Honduran party leaders conduct local soundings to determine which political aspirants have local backing when there is competition for a slot on the party's list, but parties lack funds to conduct formal polls for these slots, and political aspirants with funds (or who have backers with funds) are known to buy a safe slot on the party's list. Thus, providing clientelistic representation to poor people has been and remains an option for deputies, but does not appear to have been a requirement for building a political career.

Conclusion: What Does This Imply for Representation of the Poor?

Poor people in Honduras have been unlikely to receive representation in national policy when their preferences conflict with the interests of rich people. Additionally, while poor people can monitor clientelistic representation, it is difficult and costly for poor persons to sanction should they receive less clientelistic representation than they had hoped for. It appears that a deputy *can* provide clientelistic representation to poor people without losing the backing of party leaders, but such work is not required of all backbenchers in order to build a career.

The possibility of a person receiving clientelistic representation by staying with a traditional party appears to have given poor people in Honduras an incentive to not desert the traditional parties. The PLH and PNH still dominate politics, even with unfused elections and the new open-list elections for Congress, and poor people are considered to be the strongest supporters of the traditional parties and the least likely to split their vote.

System support is also higher among poor people than other groups. Cruz, Seligson, and Baviskar (2004) used five questions from their 2004 survey to develop a composite measure of diffuse system support:[17]

> To what extent do you believe the courts in Honduras guarantee a fair trial?
> To what extent do you respect the political institutions in Honduras?
> To what extent do you believe that basic citizen rights are well protected by the Honduran political system?
> To what extent are you proud to live under the Honduran political system?
> To what extent do you think one should support the Honduran political system?

The mean score for system support in Honduras is 53.7,[18] but support was higher in rural than in urban areas (mean 55.0 vs. 49.0, sig. < 0.001), and poverty is higher in rural areas. System support was also highest among respondents with less education, ranging from a mean of 60.0 for people with no education

17. Responses to each question ranged from "not at all" to "a lot" on a seven-point scale. This was converted to a 0–100 range, and responses to all questions were averaged to construct the measure of system support.

18. Mean scores for the other countries included in the "Political Culture of Democracy" study conducted under the direction of Mitchell Seligson at Vanderbilt University are: Costa Rica 67.6, Mexico 58.5, El Salvador 57.9, Panama 56.0, Colombia 53.3, Nicaragua 50.7, and Guatemala 48.6 (Cruz, Seligson, and Baviskar 2004, 26).

to 46.0 for people with a university education (sig. < 0.001). System support was higher among people with lower incomes, ranging from a mean of 54.0 for low-income respondents to 49.5 for middle-income and 50.5 for high-income respondents (sig. < 0.01) (Cruz, Seligson, and Baviskar 2004, 24–31).

Why have Honduras's traditional parties been able to maintain dominance? Part of the reason is undoubtedly rational behavior by poor people, who stay with their party to avoid losing a link with their clientele network and the benefits it may provide them in the future. In addition, institutions also shape deputies' views about their job. As the next chapter will show, some deputies see themselves as local development agents or local patrons. This identity can be compatible with Honduras's institutions, and comports with the historical and sociological institutionalism view that institutions not only create incentives for and constraints on behavior of strategic politicians, but also affect "the very identities, self-images and preferences of the actors" (Hall and Taylor 1996, 939). For a poor person who values personal services and local infrastructure, which they can monitor more effectively than national policy, deputies who see themselves as local development agents or patrons may reinforce party loyalty.

The next two chapters, based on interviews and surveys with deputies, explore deputy roles and what they mean for the representation of poor people. As will be seen, deputies who want to develop their community or build a personal reputation as a local patron can try to pursue these goals within Honduras's institutions. Those deputies want to provide at least clientelistic representation to poor people, and their actions may be part of the explanation for Honduras's stability in spite of its poverty, and for why poor voters have not defected from the traditional parties.

SIX

INSTITUTIONS, INCENTIVES, AND ROLES:
LEGISLATORS' IDENTITIES ABOUT THEIR JOB

Institutions constrain the strategies legislators adopt to achieve career goals, and they also shape legislators' identities about their job. The institutional milieu of a country's politics should draw certain types of people into politics. Katznelson and Weingast (2005, 10) argue that "individuals often have preferences by virtue of being in an institutional and political environment with determinate characteristics. . . . Indeed, members without these preferences soon would cease to be members." Institutions constrain Honduran deputies, but there is still room for choice about how they will do their job, and legislators are unlikely to be a homogeneous group.[1] Roles or identities are the product

---

1. By exploring their patterns of party switching, Desposato (2006b) demonstrates that Brazilian legislators are not homogeneous. He finds that deputies "use parties for electoral, ideological and distributive ends, but not for institutional advancement," and that "the roles parties play for politicians are not static within a political system but can vary with electorate preferences. More simply, legislators with different kinds of constituents use parties to very different ends" (77). Hagopian (2001, 11) surveyed legislators in Argentina, Chile, and Brazil (in 1997, 1998, and 1999/2001, respectively) to find out how "*they* view their roles as elected representatives" and which role they prioritize. She asked legislators to select and rank order three roles from a list of six: "fulfilling party program; representing those without voice in the political system; working to realize the objectives of social groups; securing resources for the district; resolving pragmatically people's problems; and promoting policy or legislation according to public opinion" (13). In Argentina, the most commonly selected role was promoting policy or legislation according to public opinion, and second was pragmatically solving people's problems. In Chile, these were again the two most common choices, but their order was reversed. In Brazil, the most common role was promoting policy according to public opinion, and the second most common was securing resources for the district (13). She argues that this "observed variation in role definition," as well as the differences she finds in how legislators allocate their time and staff resources, indicate that while electoral laws constrain legislators (by giving voters or party leaders power over their career futures), such a simple, rational-choice-based explanation for behavior is theoretically incomplete because institutions do not create a single national pattern of political representation (2). She calls for research into the nature of legislators' constituencies as a possible explanation for the different roles legislators adopt, and to explain why the opinions and behaviors of legislators differ from what would be expected from a purely rational choice analysis of the constraints legislators face from electoral and nomination institutions (35).

of the institutional milieu that over time helps "establish the identities and
categories of actors and their range of possibilities" (ibid., 4; see also Hall and
Taylor 1996, 939).

This chapter adds a historical institutionalist perspective to what so far has
been a largely rational choice type of examination of institutions and incentives.
Both approaches "acknowledge that a good deal of behaviour is goal-oriented
or strategic but that the range of options canvassed by a strategic actor is likely
to be circumscribed by a culturally-specific sense of appropriate action" (Hall
and Taylor 1996, 956). Chapter 5 assessed the capacity of poor and rich people
in Honduras to monitor government officials, and used the theory about institutions and incentives to assess both their capacity to sanction as well as the
strategy a deputy needs to adopt in order to build a political career. This
chapter and chapter 7 examine micro-level observable implications of the
theory of incentives to represent poor people—in other words, the roles
deputies adopt within the constraints created by institutions. Deputies decide
how they will do their job, whether that includes focusing on legislation, party
work, or constituency service. Politicians bring their own identities and preferences to their job in the Congress, though the range of preferences is influenced
by the institutional milieu of the country, and those preferences then influence
whether a deputy will benefit from representing poor people—and if so, how
a deputy will work for poor constituents.

The first step to studying this micro-level observable implication of the theory
is to conduct a role analysis of a group of elected officials to determine their
identities—the ways they see their job opportunities within a set of institutional
constraints. This is the subject of this chapter, which presents three distinct
roles adopted by most members of the Honduran Congress. The second step,
which is the subject of chapter 7, is to examine whether deputies who adopt
different roles behave differently, particularly with respect to poor constituents.
The Honduran Congress provides many cases for analysis, as I explore in-depth
how seventy-one deputies interpret their jobs. This analysis illustrates in
high relief the possibilities for representation within a context of poverty.

Identifying the Roles Legislators Adopt Within Constraining Institutions

What legislators choose to do with their time in office is constrained by the
institutional context in which they operate as politicians, but also by their
identities, self-images, and preferences (the interests that draw a person into

politics). They are also influenced by the roles they see exhibited by their colleagues. Some deputies may be drawn into politics out of a concern about particular policy issues or to promote better policy in general; others may want to gain access to patronage or resources to develop their community; other deputies may want prestige in their party. Institutions constrain legislators and make it rational for legislators with certain types of goals to adopt particular roles (Strom 1997). Informal roles become part of the legislature as an institution, fulfilling different needs of the Congress as well as other institutions in the political system.[2] Some roles may even develop names, like the "constituency member" in the British House of Commons (Searing 1985, 1994). Motivational role analysis offers an indirect yet systematic way to view how identities differ across deputies: "The motivational approach defines roles as patterns of goals, attitudes, and behaviors that are characteristic of people in particular positions" (Searing 1994, 412).[3] Motivational role analysis does not predetermine roles; rather, it asks legislators how they view their job, what their duties are, and what it is about their job that gives them satisfaction. Analyzing answers to these questions produces a typology of roles in a legislature, and chapter 7 will show that behaviors vary systematically with those roles.[4]

Both motivational role analysis and institutional analysis of legislator behavior view legislators as rational actors constrained by institutions. Motivational role analysis takes the institutional setting as a starting point and examines how legislators' identities differ. Different roles are linked to different goals of the legislature or other institutions in the deputies' institutional milieu. In his study of informal roles in the British Parliament, Searing (1994) explains that the Parliament has several goals, and MPs who adopt different roles focus on those different goals, causing MPs to view their job differently from one another. After determining the informal roles or identities found in the Honduran Congress, I consider how they fit within the constraints imposed on

2. Legislatures also have formal roles, such as Speaker in the U.S. House, or president, vice presidents, and secretary in the Honduran Congress. The Constitution or chamber rules define the duties of legislators who hold these formal roles.

3. Strom (1997, 158) defines roles from a rational choice institutional perspective as "routines, driven by reasons (preferences), and constrained by rules." Historical and sociological institutionalists view roles as constrained by institutions (i.e., institutions that allow a politician to make strategic calculations about the likely strategies of others), and also "by reference to a familiar set of moral or cognitive templates, each of which may depend on the configuration of existing institutions. . . . Strategies induced by a given institutional setting may ossify over time into worldviews, which are propagated by formal organizations and ultimately shape even the self-images and basic preferences of the actors involved in them" (Hall and Taylor 1996, 955, 940).

4. Motivational role analyses conducted for legislators in developed countries with consolidated democracies in western Europe and Australia found that behavior differs across informal roles (Searing 1994; Studlar and McAllister 1996; Müller and Saalfeld 1997).

Table 6.1 Descriptive characteristics of Honduran deputies by role type (percentages)

	Role type				
	Congress Advocates (n = 12)	Party Deputies (n = 21)	Constituency Servers (n = 30)	No role[a] (n = 8)	All propietarios (n = 128)
Party					
PLH (governing party)	58.3	47.6	63.3	12.5	55.5
PNH (opposition party)	33.3	52.4	33.3	87.5	43.0
PINU (minority party)	8.3	0.0	3.3	0.0	1.6
Type of department[b]					
Center	58.3	42.9	30.0	37.5	33.6
Periphery	41.7	57.1	70.0	62.5	66.4
Average prosperity index of deputies' departments	42.6	34.9	27.9	28.9	31.1
Gender					
Male	83.3	95.2	70.0	100.0	93.0
Female	16.7	4.8	30.0	0.0	7.0
Experience in Congress[c]					
First term	50.0	71.4	70.0	62.5	56.3
Second term	25.0	23.8	23.3	37.5	28.1
Third term	8.3	4.8	6.7	0.0	9.4
Four or more terms	16.7	0.0	0.0	0.0	6.3
Currently elected as					
Propietario	83.3	76.2	76.7	75.0	100.0
Suplente	16.7	23.8	23.3	25.0	—
List position					
Safe	100.0	57.1	43.3	62.5	60.9
Marginal	0.0	42.9	56.7	37.5	39.1
Average DM	16.1	12.8	10.9	12.5	11.0

[a] Deputies who participated in the study but did not fit any of the three roles.
[b] Center departments are Francisco Morazan, where the capital is located, and Cortes, which includes the major industrial city, San Pedro Sula.
[c] Experience can be as either a *propietario* or a *suplente*.

deputies by the institutions of Honduran politics. I then explore how different roles or identities affect incentives to represent poor people.

Deputy Roles in the Honduran Congress

Interviews and surveys with 71 members of the 1994–97 Honduran Congress form the basis for the analysis of deputy roles. The Congress has 128 members (*propietarios*) and 128 substitutes (*suplentes*). The study includes deputies from all parties and fifteen of eighteen departments, new deputies and deputies with experience, men and women, *propietarios* and *suplentes* (see table 6.1).

I asked deputies questions ranging from how they view their job, constituents, and committee work, to their future career plans. Responses to three questions were analyzed to determine their roles or identities in the Honduran Congress:

(1) Thinking broadly about your role as a deputy, what are the most important duties and responsibilities involved?

(2) Thinking for a moment very broadly about Honduran society, how important is your work as a deputy to the functioning of society as a whole?

(3) Thinking about your political activity, what do you personally find most satisfying about it? What would you miss most if you left politics?

Question 1 allows the deputy to *describe* how they view their job. Question 2 asks the deputy to *evaluate* the importance of the job. Question 3 explores the deputy's *motivations* for wanting the office.[5]

The book's appendix explains the method used to uncover the typology of roles or identities in the Honduran Congress. Briefly, preliminary expectations about roles and their motivational themes came from fieldwork over several years in the Congress. Based on their answers to the questions above, each deputy received a cumulative score for the motivational themes associated with each role or identity. Confirmatory factor analysis indicated that the roles structure the data and are reasonably distinct. The role or identity in which a deputy received the highest cumulative score is the deputy's role type.

A role reflects a strategy to achieve career goals (Strom 1997) or preferences within institutions (Katznelson and Weingast 2005), and each role or identity is linked to different goals of the Congress, parties, or clientele networks (Searing 1994; Patzelt 1997). Backbench roles illustrate how deputies operating within the same institutional constraints mold their job to fit their goals (Hagopian 2001). Descriptive information in table 6.1 indicates that deputies with different backgrounds tend to adopt different roles. Deputies from periphery departments where communities are even more impoverished than the Honduran average are likely to adopt a Constituency Server role. Congress Advocates, in contrast, typically reside in Honduras's major urban areas (even if they are elected from the province where they were born), which may contribute

5. Searing (1994, 412–13) developed these questions for his motivational role analysis of the British Parliament.

to their quite different view of the country's needs and the duties of a member of Congress.

Members of the Honduran Congress have few formal duties, which gives them latitude to adopt different roles or identities. Explaining British MP roles, Searing (1994, 33) wrote, "Because there are so few duties and responsibilities that *must* be done, there are so many that *might* be done." Honduras's 1982 Constitution says only that deputies must attend congressional sessions (Article 197), and that they are representatives of the people (Article 202).[6] Searing (1994, 33) explains that backbenchers' roles are "constrained by responsibilities associated with the position of the backbencher, particularly responsibilities related to the principal goals of the House of Commons." Patzelt (1997) argues that several institutions influence the roles adopted by German deputies.[7] In Honduras, responsibilities associated with the goals of the Congress, political parties, and clientele networks shape deputy role options. The roles or identities identified in the Honduran Congress are *Congress Advocate*, *Party Deputy*, and *Constituency Server*.

Congress Advocate

The identity and self-image of deputies who adopt the Congress Advocate role is based on a preference to build the Congress as an institution, increasing both congressional independence from the executive and backbenchers' independence from party leaders. Their aim is to improve the quality of the laws passed by the Congress (i.e., to consider implications of new projects, to make sure laws do not conflict, or to learn from legislation passed by other legislatures). They also want to strengthen Honduras's democracy, including promoting checks and balances.

Congress Advocates see themselves as legislators, but mentioned that they must attend to constituent requests if they want to be reelected. Because of their interest in legislating, they would rather not provide particularistic benefits and development projects that only solve the problems of an individual voter or a single community. They prefer to develop a policy to address a problem that affects a sector of society (e.g., assistance for banana workers with health

---

6. The Constitution lists forty-five duties of the Congress (Article 205), but these are jobs the Congress as an institution performs, not individual deputies.

7. "The overall structure of the political system and the functional cohesion of its individual parts constitute the casting mould within which the roles of the MPs are formed" (Patzelt 1997, 55).

problems from pesticides, or regulating discriminatory hiring practices prejudi-
cial to older women). They view particularistic service as a distraction from
legislative work, and one of their goals is to educate people that the job of
deputies is to legislate. They believe voters' expectation that a deputy is a welfare
agent who owes jobs and favors to supporters makes the Congress weak. Some
Congress Advocates suggested the institution of a bicameral Congress, with
the lower house handling constituency service and an upper house working
full-time on legislation, with staff to support their work and to conduct
research for committees.

Congress Advocates construct their role around the Congress's constitutionally defined duty to legislate and check the executive. This can cause conflict
with the president's desire to defend his partisan powers, which allow him to
dominate policymaking (Shugart and Mainwaring 1997).[8]

Adopting a Congress Advocate role is a rational strategy for an ambitious
deputy who wants to have an impact on national policy. Deputies in this role
want to strengthen the Congress, and doing so creates better political career
opportunities; after all, there are more opportunities to win reelection to the
Congress than to receive a top executive branch appointment.[9] A stronger,
independent Congress would also provide a venue where politicians from
opposition parties could influence policy. It is noteworthy that all the deputies
who adopt this role were elected from "safe" list positions (see table 6.1).[10]
Congress Advocates also had more experience than the norm in the Honduran Congress: only half were serving their first term, and more deputies in
this role had experience than was the case with the other roles.

Many deputies who adopt the Congress Advocate role are lawyers (see table
6.2), and they are better educated than other deputies.[11] Their advanced
education and law training prepare these deputies to write legislation that
will be compatible with existing legal codes, and is commensurate with their
interest in strengthening the legislative capacity of the Congress. Most Congress
Advocates are elected from "center" departments (where the capital or the

8. For the origin of the Honduran president's partisan powers, see chapter 4 and Taylor (1996).

9. Fewer than 5 percent of deputies have moved on to become cabinet ministers or agency directors.

10. Congress Advocates are significantly more likely than their colleagues to have been elected from a "safe" position on their party's list (p = 0.001).

11. Congress Advocates are significantly more likely than their colleagues to be lawyers (p = 0.000). No central source has information about the education of members of the Honduran Congress. I did not feel it was appropriate to ask deputies how much education they had, as some had only an elementary education and this could cause embarrassment. Thus I provide education information for deputies who volunteered this information (many did) and for cases where I could infer education from occupation.

Table 6.2 Deputy occupation by role type (percentages)

	Role type			
	Congress Advocates (n = 12)	Party Deputies (n = 21)	Constituency Servers (n = 30)	No role[a] (n = 8)
Occupation				
Agriculture	8.3	28.6	50.0	37.5
Business	16.7	42.9	36.7	37.5
Education	8.3	9.5	6.7	0.0
Engineer	16.7	4.8	3.3	0.0
Journalist	8.3	4.8	3.3	12.5
Lawyer	50.0	9.5	0.0	37.5
Medical	16.7	9.5	3.3	12.5
Social work	0.0	0.0	6.7	0.0
Other[b]	8.3	4.8	16.7	0.0

NOTE: Totals in role columns may sum to more than 100 percent as deputies listed more than one type of occupation.

[a] Deputies who participated in the study but did not fit any of the three roles.

[b] Other occupations include government jobs (e.g., regional manager for a government agency, employee of municipal government), secretary, housewife, and one case where no occupation was given.

major industrial city is located), and those who were elected from periphery departments tend to be longtime residents of the major urban areas. For the twelve deputies who obtained their highest cumulative score on the motivational themes associated with the Congress Advocate role, their identity appears to be connected to their personal background and the urban, industrialized, nationally oriented districts or constituencies they represent.

Party Deputy

Legislators who adopt the Party Deputy role display an identity as agents of their party or faction. They define their job in terms of party-oriented political activities such as campaigning and attending to the needs of party supporters (for government jobs or personal needs). When in the opposition, Party Deputies focus on oversight of the executive—not because they expect oversight will change the executive's behavior, but to alert party supporters to the partisan behavior of the governing party so they will turn out in large numbers in the next election. Party Deputies do not view obtaining development projects for their district as a major part of their job, but their motivation is different from Congress Advocates, who see such work as a distraction from legislating. Party Deputies see themselves as agents of their party, not of the people.[12]

Party Deputies say legislating is a deputy's duty, but they did not elaborate or show interest in increasing the legislative capacity of the Congress. They do not mind taking voting cues from party leaders, nor do they complain about the use of *mayorías mecánicas* to pass legislation.[13]

Party Deputies construct their role around two elements: their party's goal to win the presidency so it will control the state's patronage resources, and the Congress's oversight duty. Party Deputies from the governing party support executive dominance of policymaking, which gives the president his partisan power, and in return they get access to patronage resources. Party Deputies in the opposition are waiting for their party to be in power so they will have access to the state's patronage resources.[14]

Adopting a Party Deputy role is a rational strategy for a deputy who wants to build a political career through a party. Until the adoption of open-list primary elections in 2005, party leaders controlled candidate list position, and they still control access to executive branch posts. Politicians who define their role as working for their party or faction leader choose their role and career strategy "from culturally-specific repertoires" that fit neatly into the path-dependent development of Honduran institutions (Hall and Taylor 1996, 951).

Party Deputies display intense loyalty to their faction leader. They hitch their career wagon to a powerful politician and risk a career setback if they attach themselves to the wrong one. No Party Deputies expressed frustration with their experience in the Congress, and none said he or she did *not* want to return to the Congress because being a deputy was not what they had expected. Party Deputies from the opposition accepted that they could not do much while their party was out of power, and they did not view the intense partisanship of the Congress as a reason to leave government. One Party Deputy even referred to being in Congress while their party was in the opposition as a vacation (PNH, Cortes).

Party Deputies' occupations are diverse, which is understandable as many jobs can benefit from political connections in this clientelistic system. Over

12. Hondurans may have noticed Party Deputies' views. A 2004 survey asked, "Politicians seek power for their own benefit and don't care about helping the people. To what extent do you agree or disagree?" A mean score of 63.6 shows a high degree of agreement with this unflattering statement about politicians (not necessarily deputies) (Cruz, Seligson, and Baviskar 2004, 159).

13. *Mayorías mecánicas* is a derogatory term for Congress leaders passing bills, motions, and amendments by asking deputies to say "aye" rather than counting the votes.

14. It is noteworthy that no deputies from the small, opposition PINU adopted a Party Deputy role.

40 percent of Party Deputies are in business, and fewer than 10 percent are lawyers (see table 6.2).[15]

Twenty-one deputies who participated in this study have a Party Deputy identity. The majority is from "periphery" departments, indicating that the Party Deputy role is most common for deputies from departments that are more rural and traditional in their expectations of politics, which makes sense given that it is arguably the most traditional deputy role. Most are freshmen, 24 percent are *suplentes,* and 43 percent were elected from "marginal" positions on their party's slates. That many Party Deputies appear to be in a weak political position (elected from a marginal list position) could be part of their reason for adopting this traditional role, yet more Constituency Servers than Party Deputies were elected from marginal positions on the party list, so political insecurity alone does not explain why a deputy adopts this role.

Constituency Server

The identity and self-image of Constituency Servers is based on acquiring infrastructure projects for communities in their department and helping individuals. Many said that though a deputy's job is to legislate, they are more concerned with development projects. Several said they lack the education to legislate, but they know the people and try to attend to their needs. Some said they do not have time to work on congressional committees because they are busy addressing people's needs.

Constituency Servers take pride in delivering results, not just words. They say that if you make promises during the campaign and do not deliver, people think you lied and just wanted to be a deputy for the immunity.[16] Opposition party Constituency Servers complained of their frustration that they could only help people with their personal resources or by working with international organizations; they said they explain to people that they cannot do much for them now, but that if their party wins the next election, they will be able to do much more. Several governing party Constituency Servers explained that

15. Congress Advocates are significantly less likely than Party Deputies to be in business (p = 0.038).

16. Until 2004, deputies and other officials had immunity from prosecution unless Congress lifted the protection (Article 200.1). To my knowledge, the Congress has never lifted a deputy's immunity. Immunity is the subject of much debate and is lampooned in the press, and people accuse politicians of using government office to protect themselves from crimes ranging from corruption to murder.

part of their job was keeping people calm by explaining delays in delivering services (e.g., before a road can be built, surveys must be conducted, legislation passed, and funds secured). Constituency Servers made a point of explaining that they did not move to the capital and lose contact with their department, as many deputies do. They live at home, close to the people, and travel to the capital for Congress sessions.

Constituency Servers construct their role around the Congress's responsibility to represent the people, which they interpret to mean local development projects and assistance for individuals, rather than representing constituents' views on national policy. The Congress's subordinate role to the executive in policymaking is convenient for these deputies; if they had to spend their time developing bills and working on committees, they would not be able to attend to constituent needs since deputies lack staff to do constituency service work.

For deputies who view themselves as local patrons, adopting a role that focuses on providing local development projects and services to individuals is a logical strategy. Yet the success of this strategy depends on both the deputy's party winning control of the executive branch and the deputy being a member of a faction allied with the president. An opposition deputy or one from an out-of-favor faction will not have access to state resources to deliver infrastructure projects. Consequently, some Constituency Servers are frustrated; some even say they could have accomplished more for their community from outside of government. Their role is compatible with the importance of clientelism in Honduran politics, and their work should contribute to keeping voters loyal to the traditional parties. But the intensely partisan nature of Honduran politics (exacerbated by the state's very constrained resources) and the factional rivalries within the traditional parties jeopardize the ability of Constituency Server deputies to achieve their goals while in Congress. Their role and preferences might be expected to mesh with *parts* of their institutional and political environment but clash with others. Katznelson and Weingast (2005, 10) expect that deputies whose preferences do not fit their institutional and political environment will cease to be members, and the frustration expressed in my study by opposition and out-of-favor faction Constituency Servers—four of whom said they did not intend to run again—supports this expectation.

Constituency Servers are locally oriented, and few want to move up in national politics (see table 6.3).[17] Most want to be reelected to the Congress because it

17. The Constituency Servers who would like to move up the political ladder want to do so in ways that will allow them to continue their local development work: three aspire to posts in the executive branch, one wants to be the director of the FHIS (Fondo Hondureño de Inversión Social),

can help them provide services to their departments. Others plan to retire, saying that they are worn out from the long hours involved in attending to people's needs, though helping people is the part of their job they will miss most. For locally oriented deputies, a Constituency Server role is a rational way to achieve their personal and career goals. Being a deputy allows them to work for the people of their community, and their days in the capital allow them to pursue solutions to the needs of their communities.

Thirty deputies in this study adopted the Constituency Server role. They are generally from the poorest departments (see table 6.1), and those who were elected from better-off departments identify themselves as representatives of specific municipalities that are poor.[18] Women are overrepresented in this role.[19] Most Constituency Servers are freshmen, 23 percent are *suplentes,* and 57 percent were elected from "marginal" list positions. Half the Constituency Servers are involved in agriculture, and a third own local businesses (see table 6.2).[20] They have attachments to the communities they represent, and few have occupations that require a college education, which supports their frequent statements that they are unprepared to legislate but that they know the needs of the people.

The Constituency Server is a well-known role in the Honduran Congress, and many refer to themselves as "Los Rangers." There is a *Local Organizer* sub-type in this role, with six deputies who emphasized their work helping groups (unions, cooperatives, women, agricultural workers) organize to help themselves. Like other Constituency Servers, Local Organizers have a preference to work on local development projects rather than legislate on national policy, but they are distinguished by their aspiration to help groups help themselves so

---

which is responsible for distributing small development projects throughout the country, and one wants to be minister of agriculture, which makes policy on many of the issues that are of concern to his department. One Constituency Server wants a post in the congressional leadership because it gives greater access to state resources. One would like to move on to PARLACEN or be appointed governor of his department. A PARLACEN seat is unlikely to be useful for getting local development projects for his department, but serving as governor would.

18. The prosperity index is a composite of the percentage of households in a department with electricity, plumbing, and television. The average prosperity index for Constituency Servers is lower than for the other role types, but the difference of means is not statistically significant ($p = 0.152$). Constituency Servers are significantly more likely than Congress Advocates are to be elected from "periphery" departments ($p = 0.088$), but the difference between Constituency Servers and Party Deputies is not significant ($p = 0.344$).

19. Women are significantly more likely to have adopted the Constituency Server role than either of the other roles ($p = 0.035$).

20. Constituency Servers are significantly more likely to have an occupation in agriculture than are deputies who adopt the other two roles ($p = 0.017$).

Table 6.3 Political ambitions by role type (percentages)

	Role type			
	Congress Advocates (n = 12)	Party Deputies (n = 21)	Constituency Servers (n = 30)	No role[a] (n = 8)
Want to continue political career	66.7	85.7	70.0	75.0
% of *all* deputies in role type who have continued their political career	58.3	66.7	66.7	62.5
% in role type who *wanted to continue* in politics who have continued their career	87.5	77.8	90.9	71.4
Specific political career aspiration				
Reelection to Congress	58.3	71.4	63.3	50.0
Congress leadership post	16.7	0.0	6.7	25.0
Executive post[b]	16.7	23.8	10.0	12.5
President	8.3	9.5	0.0	12.5
Supreme Court	8.3	0.0	0.0	0.0
Mayor/city council	16.7	9.5	10.0	25.0
PARLACEN	0.0	4.8	3.3	0.0
Do *not* plan to continue in politics				
Retire	25.0	9.5	16.7	12.5
No reelection[c]	0.0	4.8	13.0	0.0
Unknown	8.3	0.0	0.0	12.5

NOTE: Totals in role columns may sum to more than 100 percent as some deputies listed more than one post they desire in the future.

[a] Deputies who participated in the study but did not fit any of the three roles.

[b] Executive posts include the following: for Congress Advocates, one minister, one unspecified; for Party Deputies, three ministers, one agency director, one vice president; for Constituency Servers, one minister, one unspecified, one deputy who wants to be the director of the FHIS.

[c] Deputies who explicitly stated they did not want to return to the Congress because it had not turned out to be what they had expected.

they will be less reliant on government, unlike a patron who wants to bind clients in a dependent role.

Deputy Roles and Their Implications for Representation of the Poor

This role analysis highlights that Honduran deputies are not all the same; they have different identities and self-images that fit within the institutional and political environment of Honduran politics, though some roles make a more comfortable fit for deputies than others. All Honduran deputies were elected under the same institutions, but the different roles indicate that deputies' preferences for their time in office are most strongly related to different parts of their institutional milieu. Party Deputies want to build their career within their party and are working within the institutions that historically allowed traditional parties to control their militants and made executive-legislative relations lopsided. Congress Advocates want to improve policy, prove their worth to their party as policy leaders, and strengthen checks and balances, though they run a risk of alienating party leaders. Constituency Servers want to develop their communities and help constituents. They help to maintain their party's links to local people (*los bases*), and many are responding to the strong history of clientelism in Honduran politics.

Do any of these roles and the strategic choices they prompt promote the representation of poor people? We can use the preferences of deputies who adopt different roles and the constraints imposed by Honduras's institutions to gauge when and how the poor are likely to count in Honduran politics.

First we need to confirm that deputies have political ambitions. A majority of the deputies in each role type wanted to be reelected, and others wanted to continue their career elsewhere in government. Most deputies thus confront the problem of how to achieve their preferences for their time in office while working within the constraints imposed by institutions for how to pursue a political career. Many apparently have succeeded at this balancing act, as most deputies who wanted to continue a career in politics have succeeded in doing so (see table 6.3).

Deputies face several institutional constraints on their strategy for simultaneously achieving a political career and satisfying their other preferences. Closed-list PR elections made it difficult for voters both to reward individual deputies for representing them well and to sanction a deputy who did not fulfill expectations. Vertically organized parties and centralized nominations gave party leaders, rather than voters, control over a deputy's opportunity to continue in politics.[21] Clientele networks are attached to parties, not individual politicians, and only two parties have a real chance of having access to state resources for clientelism. The Congress provides deputies almost no resources for developing legislation, so if a deputy wants to pursue specific policy goals

---

21. Party leaders still control who gets to run in primaries, but with open-list primary elections since 2005 they no longer control who will be nominated, nor can they give out "safe" list positions. But party leaders still control access to positions in the executive branch.

they must use their own expertise or research resources to do so.[22] If a deputy's legislative agenda conflicts with the president's, the president can first marshal congressional leaders to defeat the bill and then punish the deputy by denying him or her access to executive branch resources for clientelism. Some Congress Advocate deputies from the governing party complained that they had been victims of such retaliation, for advocating a policy to defend artisanal fisherman whose livelihood was being destroyed by the development of the shrimp industry as a nontraditional export product.

Given the institutional constraints, an obvious strategy for a deputy whose only goal was to build a political career would be to follow the cues of party leaders. But deputies' identities indicate that they have other interests in addition to building a career that should also influence their strategy choices and affect representation.

Congress Advocates oppose executive domination of policy and the legislature, but to act on their preference to strengthen the legislature without destroying their future career chances they must offer something of value to party leaders.[23] What they offer is good policy for which their party can take credit. Better national policy should help the party appeal to independent voters who do not have a clientelistic attachment to a party (many of whom are from the urban middle class and have greater capacity than poor people to monitor policy if they choose to do so), to the business elites they rely on for large campaign contributors, and to international lending agencies—support parties cannot buy cheaply with particularistic benefits and local development projects. Congress Advocates work to position themselves as advisers to the Congress, offering their legal or other professional knowledge to make themselves opinion leaders in the chamber. They try to influence party leaders on technical grounds so that the leaders, with the support of the rest of the backbenchers, will take policy in the direction the Congress Advocate desires.

Because poor people are unlikely to be aware of the work of Congress Advocates—since these deputies spend their time working on national legislation, which is hard for poor people to monitor—they are unlikely to want

22. An example would be a deputy who is a member of a business chamber working with the chamber to develop a bill.

23. Strom (1997, 169–71) argues that few MPs pursue party or chamber leadership posts because doing so is risky and may jeopardize the legislator's chances of renomination and reelection. Similarly, we would only expect career-seeking deputies to adopt the risky role of Congress Advocate if they believe their reelection chances are good.

to reward or sanction legislators of this role type.[24] Rich people have the capacity to monitor what Congress Advocates are doing, particularly if the deputy works with an interest group with connections to elite sectors, or develops legislation that major interest groups oppose. If rich people are aware of the Congress Advocate's work, they could use their campaign contributions and connections to party leaders to influence whether the deputy is renominated to a safe slot on the party's list.[25] Congress Advocates must not push party leaders too far or their political career will end. Because they spend their time on national policy, they will not have local party activists arguing that they should receive a safe position on the party list.[26] A Congress Advocate who wanted to continue a political career would need the backing of the leader of a strong faction in their party to obtain a "safe" or "electable" position on the list. Therefore, a Congress Advocate deputy should work on policy issues supported by their faction leader, using those policy initiatives to improve the quality of legislation and strengthen Congress's role in the policy process. Before the adoption of open-list elections in 2005, Congress Advocates were only likely to suffer from sanctions by poor people if they first ran into conflict with party leaders and then were put in a "marginal" position on the party list in an election where poor party supporters showed their frustration by abstaining. Since 87.5 percent of Congress Advocates who were not planning to retire have continued their political career (see table 6.3), they appear to know how to balance party leaders' interests with their desire to improve policy and strengthen the Congress. The question is, do party leaders reward work on issues that benefit the poor? Some Congress Advocates promoted legislation targeted at poor people, such as benefits for banana industry workers who have been injured by contact with pesticides, or regulation of the shrimping industry to protect artisanal fisherman. Both of these bills would benefit poor people, but the first would primarily harm foreign banana companies, while the second would harm Honduran businesses. The author of the first bill wanted to return to the private sector, and the other bill's author did not run for reelection.

Along with having a political career, Party Deputies want to move up in their party, and institutional constraints made their strategy clear: ingratiate

24. They may want to sanction a Congress Advocate who does not deliver expected particularistic benefits. Recall that Congress Advocates complained that people expect deputies to be local welfare agents.

25. Even with open-list elections, rich people can use campaign contributions to sanction deputies because candidates now need to finance their own campaigns.

26. Some deputies mentioned that they were moved up the party list due to local pressure.

themselves to party leaders by doing their bidding. The use of *mayorías mecánicas* in the chamber indicates that party leaders want backbenchers to vote as a block. Parties need funds to organize campaigns and primaries and to maintain party headquarters (Ajenjo Fresno 2001, 193–94, 230, 267–68), so a Party Deputy with enough money could "buy" a safe seat on the party's list with campaign contributions to their party's presidential candidate.[27] They should also work for their party faction by campaigning and organizing local party activists (Dalton 1994).[28]

Poor people cannot monitor how Party Deputies vote on national policy bills because votes are taken by *mayorías mecánicas,* but also because poor people lack the monitoring resources to observe what is going on in congressional policy debates. They can observe if a deputy moves to the capital and does not visit the district or respond to constituents' requests for help, but poor people lack efficient means to sanction a deputy who ignores the district. As individuals, poor people can deny their party their vote, but a single vote is a small sanction and is potentially costly to the poor person because it can weaken their link with their party clientele network. If many poor people sanction, their party will not win the presidency, so the party will not have access to state resources for the next four years. But this is costly to the party's poor clients as well, because they will not receive government resources. Voting against their party is also likely to be costly for poor people at the local level, since "voters know that municipalities headed by the opposition party are likely to be penalized in intergovernmental transfers and special projects funding" (Dalton 1994, 14). While the poor person and the community may pay a cost for attempting to sanction, before open lists were adopted the deputy could be insulated from poor people's ire by having the backing of a party leader and thereby receiving a safe slot on the party's list. In sum, party leaders can monitor and reward or sanction Party Deputies, but it is hard for poor people to do so. Because they are not concerned with developing a community, Party Deputies do not need their party to win the presidency in order to achieve their preferences, further insulating them from popular sanction.

---

27. Deputies frequently mentioned this in interviews, but campaign contribution records are not available to determine if there is a correlation between campaign contributions and list position.

28. Eighty-six percent of Party Deputies said that they were involved in the local or departmental party organization (often as a local leader), compared to 80 percent of Constituency Servers and 33 percent of Congress Advocates. Forty-three percent of Party Deputies have been involved in their party's campaigns, compared to 37 percent of Constituency Servers and 25 percent of Congress Advocates.

The challenge Party Deputies face in achieving their preferences for a political career and in moving up within their party is competition from other Party Deputies as well as party militants who aspire to be Party Deputies. They need to demonstrate to national party leaders that they deserve a slot on the list, another government post, or a party leadership position. Part of doing this is voting with party leaders on national policy bills. If party leaders indicated that a requirement for moving up in the party is working to maintain poor people's support for the party, Party Deputies would actively represent poor people. If such a signal were sent, I would expect Party Deputies to "claim credit" for their activities for poor people to make sure party leaders were aware of their actions. Contrary to this expectation, chapter 7 presents data that indicate Party Deputies did not "claim credit" for working on projects for poor people or communities, which indicates that party leaders do not make representing poor people a requirement for receiving a safe position on the party's list.

Constituency Servers want to bring development projects to their communities and build a political career. Their challenge is how to achieve their goal of developing their communities. If their party wins the presidency, thereby giving them access to executive branch resources, Constituency Servers are busy meeting with local groups and carrying their needs to the appropriate offices to obtain state resources. If their party is in opposition, however, or their faction does not have a good relationship with the president, they do not have access to executive branch resources. Given the strong party discipline provided by *mayorías mecánicas*, Constituency Servers cannot cut deals with the executive by exchanging resources for votes on the president's legislation, as deputies do in Brazil and Ecuador (Ames 2001; Desposato 2001; Mejía Acosta 2002).

Poor people can easily monitor whether Constituency Servers delivered on their promises to work for the community and help people, and since developing their community is a preference of Constituency Servers, poor people should want to reward these deputies. But closed-list PR elections and party leaders' control of nominations made it hard for poor people to reward Constituency Servers.[29] Constituency Servers think they are doing important work to develop communities and keep their party in touch with *los bases*, but they often expressed frustration at their inability to provide the

---

29. Since open-list primaries and general elections were adopted in 2005, a poor person can now cast a vote directly for a specific deputy running for reelection, so they can use their vote to reward a Constituency Server if that deputy was placed on the ballot for the primary.

projects their communities need.[30] Party leaders want to target state resources to partisans, without slippage to clients of the other party, so party leaders may prefer using resources for particularistic benefits instead of for infrastructure projects, unless the community that receives a development project is known to back the party. A Constituency Server who complains about the partisan allocation of state resources can be marginalized by party leaders, which causes the deputy to lose opportunities to provide development projects to his or her community. Despite Constituency Servers' *desire* to represent poor people, they may not always be able to do so.[31] One Constituency Server deputy from an out-of-favor faction of the governing party said that he had been trying to get three local development projects built in his municipalities (a road, a grain silo, and a rural bank). He had gotten the endorsement of the president for the projects and an endorsement from the minister in charge of building roads, but by the third year of his term the projects were still not being built. A deputy from the opposition explained that it can be harmful for a local development group if an opposition deputy tries to help them organize, because it will cause the group to be viewed as supporters of the opposition party, making it more difficult for the group to obtain government support. Because of these problems, this deputy tried to help groups in small ways by putting them in contact with people who could get them supplies, such as a blackboard for a school.

If poor people are frustrated by what appear to be broken promises, they may not want to reward the Constituency Server. Constituency Servers from the opposition party said that they work to explain to their constituents that there is little they can do for them from the opposition, but if their party wins the presidency in the next election they will be able to do much more. In sum, Constituency Servers' preference for community development and

30. Their concerns may be justified, as respondents in a 2004 survey did not indicate that they trusted political parties, garnering a mean trust score of 31.63 out of 100.00 (Cruz, Seligson, and Baviskar 2004, 159). Deputies in the 1997–2001 term surveyed by the University of Salamanca also indicated their concern about the growing gap between traditional parties and the electorate. Only 24 percent of 71 deputies surveyed thought that most people identify with parties and that parties have strong connections with society. A growing distance between society and parties was cited by 59 percent of deputies. In the 2001–5 Congress, deputies were more positive, with 52 percent of 102 deputies saying parties have a strong connection with society, and only 39 percent saying there is a growing party-society distance (Datos de opinión 2005).

31. The demands of partisan politics are even more constraining for the Local Organizer subtype of the Constituency Server role. They want to help groups to help themselves, which would ultimately end people's need for ties to a party, so party leaders do not support the Local Organizers' work. Two of six Local Organizers did not want to return to the Congress, arguing they can work to help groups organize from outside of politics.

helping individuals with their needs makes them want to provide clientelistic representation to poor people, particularly since most Constituency Servers' constituencies are poor communities. But the highly partisan nature of Honduran politics prompted by the harsh resource constraint faced by the government, along with the exigencies of party clientele networks, means that a Constituency Server may not be given the resources needed for community development even if the deputy is from the governing party.

Do Parties Give Deputies Incentives to Represent Poor People?

If they can gain access to resources, Constituency Servers provide clientelistic representation to poor people because doing so is part of their identity. For other deputies, particularly those who adopt the Party Deputy role, representing poor people is not part of their identity, so they only have an incentive to represent poor people if party leaders make it a requirement for building a political career.

Do party leaders signal to deputies that representing poor people will improve their chances of continuing their political career? They should if poor sectors of society can hold parties accountable, but experience has shown that poor Hondurans do not readily vote against their party. They are more likely to show their frustration by abstaining, which has facilitated party alternation in power as clients of the out-of-power party turn out expecting to benefit from government largesse if their party wins.

This party-based form of clientelism makes it costly for a poor person to sanction for insufficient representation. If a poor person is not observed supporting their party, they lose access to clientelistic benefits, and the party will be punished only if enough of its supporters turn against it so that it loses the election. Lyne (2007) calls this the "voter's dilemma" and argues that a voter will only turn away from clientelistic benefits (and vote based on national policy) if they view the benefit to have no value; for poor Hondurans, however, even small clientelistic benefits and connections have great value. Since the party will be punished if many poor people sanction, parties need to be careful to provide at least some benefits to clients. Poor people's votes can typically be bought cheaply with particularistic goods that can be targeted at party activists; for that reason, party leaders are unlikely to want to provide benefits to poor people in a less targetable form, such as a community development project, unless the community is known to support the party or the service can be rationed so that party activists are the only real beneficiaries (e.g., you need a connection to get an appointment with the doctor in the new health clinic). Clientelistic rationing of access to what appear to be public goods like schools is highly developed in Honduras because demands and needs exceed government resources (see chapter 8). For parties, "government jobs are a key resource for maintaining party cohesion and rewarding supporters" (Dalton 1994, 20). Parties also "get local party members who are professionals, e.g., doctors and lawyers, to provide services free of charge to supporters who are indigent" so they can provide immediate benefits to supporters during their campaigns (23). In contrast, rich people are in a better position to demand representation because they have a greater capacity to monitor policy development. As mentioned previously, rich people and their interest groups also often have ties to both traditional parties (Amaya Banegas 1997, 2000), so they do not risk losing their connection to government if they sanction the incumbent party.

Yet parties would be ill advised to ignore poor people, because they need their votes to win the presidential election and thereby obtain control over state resources to maintain their party clientele network. Even in the most prosperous department, poor people make up a large percentage of the eligible voters, and in poorer departments they are the majority. Voter turnout increases across departments as poverty statistics worsen (Petrovsky and Taylor-Robinson 2005). A 2004 survey (Cruz, Seligson, and Baviskar 2004, 151–53) asked people about their intention to vote, and found that 81 percent of people with no education planned to vote, while 65 percent of people with a secondary education intended to vote (voting intent increased to almost 80 percent for people with a university education) (sig. < 0.01). More rural people than urban expressed an intent to vote as well (sig. < 0.05). This indicates that parties that want to win the presidency have an electoral incentive to appeal to poor voters.

Given the historical importance of clientelism in Honduran politics, and the rationality for parties to use clientelistic methods to obtain the votes of poor people, it is surprising that all deputies do not view providing particularistic benefits and community projects as an important part of their job. Clearly clientelism is not the only institution that shapes deputy identities. Congress Advocates and Party Deputies did not talk much about their constituents when describing their vision of the duties of a deputy. Only Constituency Servers emphasized the provision of local development projects to their communities as the job of a deputy. This indicates that party leaders do not require deputies to do constituency service, though they accept such activity if it is targetable to party supporters. When paired with electoral rules that, until 2005, did not give deputies an incentive to seek a personal vote, it appears that deputies are only likely to have a strong incentive to represent poor people if doing so is an important part of their role or identity.

Party leaders appear to count on the high cost of party switching to keep clients loyal even if they receive only limited benefits. Poor people have little reason to switch their vote since the other traditional party will not make different policy, as both are oligarchy parties.[32] Interestingly, when open-list PR election rules were used in 2005, allowing voters to punish or reward particular deputies, voters made use of their new sanctioning ability. They continued to vote for the traditional parties, but they sanctioned specific incumbent deputies from those parties. Fifty-nine incumbent *propietarios* ran in November 2005 (several more lost their reelection bid during the open-list primary elections), and just thirty-two won. Only 25 percent of the deputies in the 2001–6 Congress returned for the 2006–10 term, which is a lower reelection rate than in recent terms (see table 5.3), and, as noted earlier, local commentators concluded that voters turned against political "dinosaurs."

Party-based clientelism creates many ways patrons can help poor clients. For example, obtaining an appointment with a doctor at a government hospital or a permit to own a gun requires connections, as does getting a government job or a scholarship. The need for clientelistic benefits outstrips available resources, particularly if most government resources go to policies representing elite interests or debt service, so elites have a strong interest in defending the clientelism system to allocate scarce resources. Deputies are influenced and constrained by their institutional environment, which shapes the roles they adopt. This part of the analysis indicates that the institutional milieu of Honduran politics did not create an imperative that deputies represent poor people or risk sanction that would end their political career, and that many deputies adopted a role or identity that clearly did not emphasize representing poor people.

---

32. In the 2005 election, both major parties had similar platforms (emphasizing fighting crime and boosting citizen participation) that largely ignored the concerns of the poor majority (Taylor-Robinson 2006b; Ajenjo Fresno 2007).

SEVEN

ROLES, ATTITUDES, AND ACTIONS:
DOES ANYONE REPRESENT POOR PEOPLE?

This chapter continues the examination of micro-level observable implications of the theory of incentives to represent poor people. Chapter 6 presented the three informal preference roles found in the Honduran Congress, and assessed which deputies have an incentive to represent poor people given the identity and preferences that led them to adopt their role, the capacity of poor people to monitor and sanction, and the constraints that institutions place on deputies. Here I examine whether deputies who adopt different roles behave differently, particularly with respect to poor constituents. Do they have different perspectives about whom they represent and how they should do so? Do legislative agendas differ across deputy roles, and if yes, does the legislation proposed by some types of deputies represent policy or service interests of poor sectors of society? This analysis provides a systematic basis for assessing whether the poor count, at least for some types of deputies, and how.

Roles and Constituents: Whom Do You Represent?

How do deputies who adopt different roles or identities define their constituents? The Honduran Constitution says only that deputies are to be representatives of the people.[1] What does that mean? Do they see themselves as representatives of all the people of the country, the people of the department from which they were elected, their party, an interest group or sector of society, a community, or some other group? These are interesting questions because in a PR electoral system, deputies share their district (department) with other deputies, and each deputy as a rule does not have a unique, geographically defined district for

---

1. "Los diputados serán representantes del pueblo" (Article 202).

which he or she is known to be responsible.[2] Eligibility requirements also prompt questions about who deputies will represent. A deputy can be elected in the department where they were born, or where the deputy lived for at least the last five years before the election (Article 198.5). If a deputy was born in a "periphery" department, for example Intibucá, moved to the capital years ago, but is elected on the slate for Intibucá, does that deputy know the needs and policy/service preferences of those people? How often will the deputy visit the department? Is the deputy more likely to represent the department where he or she now lives?[3] Since deputies are not required to live in the department they were elected to represent, and closed-list PR elections allowed party leaders to give an activist or important donor a "safe" position on the party's list, a deputy could win election and be reelected without knowing the people of the department.[4]

I asked deputies, "Please describe in some detail whom you consider the people you represent." Most deputies in all three roles identify their department as their constituency (see table 7.1).[5] Some said "I represent my department" and others "community X in my department," while a few answered "the municipalities assigned to me by my party." District magnitude appears to be the key to whether a deputy would define the entire department or specific

2. Gracias a Diós and the Bay Islands, with DMs of one, are exceptions. Ocotepeque, with a DM of two, and Intibucá and La Paz, with DMs of three, may also be exceptions, since there is likely to be only one deputy elected by each major party, and that deputy might consider him- or herself the representative of the entire department. Deputies can informally partition their department into districts. For example, in Costa Rica deputies elected from the same party in a province each take responsibility for particular cantons (Taylor 1992). Honduran deputies in some of the larger departments mentioned that their party divided the territory among the deputy candidates, at least for the campaign.

3. The reverse can also occur. A deputy elected from the capital explained that he was born in a periphery department where his mother still lives, and people from that department come to him for help with problems because they consider him their deputy.

4. Constituency Server deputies complained about this. Part of the identity of Constituency Servers is their work staying in contact with their department. To Constituency Servers it is important to not move to Tegucigalpa and forget about the department—something they accused many other deputies of doing.

5. Responses to the 2002 survey conducted by the University of Salamanca were similar. They asked deputies, "Of the following options please tell me who you think you represent in your parliamentary activity," and 72 percent of deputies selected "all the voters of my department" (other choices were the "supporters of my party" and "my political party"). The responses to Salamanca's 1998 survey look very different, as 76 percent selected "all Hondurans" and only 23 percent selected "all the voters of my department" (other choices were, again, the "supporters of my party" and "my political party"), but note that in 2002 the surveyors did not read "all Hondurans" as an option (PELA 1998, 2002). In my study the deputies were asked an open-ended question to which they could give more than one response; 76 percent said they represent their department and 25 percent volunteered that they represent all the people.

Table 7.1 Comparison by role type of responses to the question "Who are the people you represent?" (percentages)

	Role type				
	Congress Advocates (n = 12)	Party Deputies (n = 21)	Constituency Servers (n = 30)	Local Organizers[a] (n = 6)	No role[b] (n = 8)
Response					
My department or specific municipalities	83.3	76.2	86.7	66.7	25.0
All people	33.3	38.1	13.3	0.0	25.0
People from my party or my party faction	0.0	19.0	23.3	0.0	12.5
Humble people[c]	58.3	14.3	33.3	100.0	62.5
Middle class	16.7	4.8	16.7	33.3	25.0

NOTE: Columns may sum to more than 100 percent as many deputies used more than one characteristic to describe their constituents.

[a] Local Organizer is a subtype of the Constituency Server role. Along with the characteristics of the Constituency Server role, they expressed a concern for helping people to organize so that they would become less dependent on the government.

[b] Deputies who participated in the study but did not fit any of the three roles.

[c] This category includes peasants, workers, lower classes, "majority populations," and "humble people."

municipalities as his or her constituency. Many deputies clarified that though they represent their entire department, they have a strong preference for municipality *X*, which is their home. Several commented that deputies always come from the *cabecera* (the department capital), so they know its needs and problems, but they are less able, and less interested, to represent other municipalities. The problem becomes self-sustaining, as only the *cabecera* produces party activists with the experience and connections to become deputies. Some parts of a department might not be represented unless party leaders sanction deputies for not representing their department more broadly, and no such sanctions were mentioned in interviews.

Some deputies said they represent all Hondurans.[6] Most explained they represent "all people" when legislating but work on development projects for communities or benefits for individuals in their department. This is an interesting distinction in a Congress where many deputies initiate few or no bills, and legislation passes on voice votes by *mayorías mecánicas*. Presumably, voting with party leaders is how they represent the entire country when legislating. Constituency Servers are significantly less likely than are other types

6. Only two deputies who said that they represent "all people" did not also say that they represent their department (one Party Deputy and one deputy in the "no role" category).

of deputies to say "all people" are their constituents (p = 0.036), and no deputies in the Local Organizer subtype of the Constituency Server role said that they represent all people. This is consistent with the way Constituency Servers describe their role, as they emphasized that they are knowledgeable about the needs of their communities and are not interested in legislating.

Twelve deputies (17 percent of study participants) said they represent people from their party.[7] Some explained that they represent all people on policy issues but also help co-partisans obtain benefits, such as jobs. Representing people from your party may be a rational strategy for pursuing a political career in Honduras's clientelistic political system, where state resources are severely constrained and parties need to hoard the resources they can obtain from the government to take care of clients. Congress Advocates were less likely than other deputies to say they represent co-partisans (p = 0.077), but the percentages of Party Deputies and Constituency Servers offering a partisan answer are statistically equivalent (p = 0.714), which is surprising because Party Deputies are the ones who clearly have a party-oriented view of their job. No Local Organizers said that their constituents were people from their party, which is consistent with the defining trait of this subgroup of Constituency Servers—helping people to organize so they can help themselves and become less dependent on the government.

Thirty-five percent of deputies said that they represent "humble people" (some specified peasants, workers, or the lower classes).[8] In a country where poor people are the majority of eligible voters, it is noteworthy that so few deputies offered this type of answer.[9] All deputies in the Local Organizer subtype of the Constituency Server role said their constituents are humble people, which is consistent with the types of groups they said they are helping to organize.[10]

A small number of deputies in each role type identified the middle class as their constituency (often the answer was middle and lower classes). With

7. This is similar to the 2002 Salamanca study, where 16 percent of deputies selected "supporters of my party" and 8 percent selected "my political party." In their 1998 survey, however, only 1.4 percent of deputies selected "supporters of my party" and none selected "my political party" (PELA 1998, 2002). As discussed above, this could be because in 1998 "all Hondurans" was one of the options, and since deputies could only select one answer, most opted for "all Hondurans."

8. Most also said that they represent their department, but ten did not give a geographic definition of whom they represent (two Congress Advocates, one Party Deputy, three Constituency Servers [two in the Local Organizer subtype], and four deputies in the "no role" category).

9. Party Deputies were significantly less likely than other deputies to define their constituents as humble people (p = 0.035), though the difference between Party Deputies and Constituency Servers does not meet traditional levels of significance (p = 0.125).

10. Local Organizers are significantly more likely than even Congress Advocates to say they represent humble people (p = 0.063).

the small size of the middle class in Honduras, it is not surprising that elected officials do not indicate a strong identification with this group.

Most Honduran deputies have a local orientation to representation and interpret their constitutional duty to "represent the people" to mean the people of their department. For those who aspire to continue their political career in the Congress or local government, a local notion of their constituents is strategic because those people must elect them (or more accurately, elect their party). But national-level party leaders are the "nominating constituency" (akin to the "primary constituency" in Fenno 1978) because they control who gets to run for Congress and municipal elections, and until 2005 they also controlled which list position a deputy candidate received. This local focus may appeal to national party leaders, since one way to earn a faction leader's support is by building the faction's local campaign machine (Dalton 1994).

What does this mean for representation of poor people? More than half of Congress Advocates and all the Local Organizer subtype of Constituency Servers view humble people as their constituents. As a consequence, their activities in the Congress may attend to the policy/service preferences of poor people. Overall, only 35 percent of deputies said they represent humble people, implying that most deputies apparently do not define their constituents in a way that reflects the socioeconomic status of the majority of Hondurans. A department or party focus is consistent with the incentives produced by electoral rules and nomination procedures, yet the lack of focus on humble people is surprising given the importance of clientelism to Honduran politics.

Roles and Actions: What Do You Do for Your Constituents?

Different roles or identities are built around different preferences about what deputies will do while in Congress (e.g., Congress Advocates want to improve the quality of laws, Constituency Servers want to obtain infrastructure projects for communities). I asked deputies what activities they engage in for their constituents, and table 7.2 shows their answers organized by role type.

Fifty-six percent of the deputies listed working on local development projects (e.g., building a school, paving a road, providing electricity service) as something they do for their constituents. But not all types of deputies were equally likely to include such work in their answer. Only 38 percent of Party Deputies listed this type of work, significantly lower than for the other roles (p = 0.019), which fits with their party orientation. They want to work for their party or

Table 7.2 Comparison by role type of responses to the question "What types of activities do you engage in for your constituents?" (percentages)

	Role type				
	Congress Advocates (n = 12)	Party Deputies (n = 21)	Constituency Servers (n = 30)	Local Organizers[a] (n = 6)	No role[b] (n = 8)
Response					
Local development projects	58.3	38.1	73.3	83.3	37.5
Particularistic services	25.0	71.4	53.3	33.3	50.0
Legislative work[c]	75.0	23.8	26.7	33.0	50.0
Participation in organizations	50.0	28.6	33.3	83.3	37.5
Keeping in touch	8.3	33.3	26.7	0.0	0.0
Political activities	0.0	19.0	13.3	0.0	12.5

NOTE: Columns may sum to more than 100 percent as many deputies gave more than one response to the question.

[a] Local Organizer is a subtype of the Constituency Server role. Along with the characteristics of the Constituency Server role, they expressed a concern for helping people to organize so that they would become less dependent on the government.
[b] Deputies who participated in the study but did not fit any of the three roles.
[c] This category includes proposing bills, committee work, and making policy.

party faction and local development projects will benefit nonpartisans, as well as the party clientele, unless the project is built in a community known to be loyal to the party or designed so that a person needs a party connection to get to use the service. It is interesting that more than half of Congress Advocates list development projects as part of what they do for constituents, given their role's emphasis on improving the quality of laws the Congress produces and their frequent complaints that such work consumes time they should spend on legislating. But several Congress Advocates did say people care more about projects than legislation, and if all they do is legislate, they will not be reelected. Thus working to provide local public works may be part of their strategy to get to continue their political career so they can pursue their goal of strengthening the Congress and democracy. The high percentage of Constituency Servers (and even higher percentage for the Local Organizer subtype) who list local development projects is consistent with their local orientation. Most Constituency Servers are elected in poor departments, even by Honduran standards (see table 6.1), which may prompt them to represent poor people by bringing services to communities.

Fifty-four percent of deputies listed particularistic service as work they do for constituents (e.g., providing jobs and scholarships, driving a sick person to the hospital, helping someone who is in jail, assisting someone to obtain a business permit), but again the incidence is uneven across roles. Party Deputies are the most likely to list particularistic service as how they serve constituents (p = 0.049). This is consistent both with the importance of patronage to both traditional parties and with the desire to target resources to party supporters. Half of Constituency Servers said they provide particularistic services for constituents, which fits with their desire to help the people of their communities. That few Local Organizers mentioned particularistic service fits with their desire to help people help themselves so they cease to be dependent on government. Only a quarter of Congress Advocates listed particularistic service as work they do for constituents, consistent with their contention that the job of deputies is to legislate and that petitions for help with particularistic needs distract deputies from this task.

Congress Advocates are most likely to list legislative work as work they do for their constituents (p = 0.001). In fact, they are the most active legislators in the Congress (see table 7.3, below), adding credibility to their claim. Local Organizers are more likely than other deputies to list participation in organizations as part of their work for their constituents (p = 0.009), consistent with their desire to help people organize to help themselves.

Twenty-three percent of deputies said "keeping in touch" is something they do for their constituents (e.g., visiting communities, attending festivals, seeing to the needs of a municipality, being aware of what is happening in the department, meeting with *patronatos*). That only a quarter of deputies say they do this indicates that party leaders do not require deputies to maintain contact with their department. The way Congress has organized itself supports the notion that "keeping in touch" is optional: First, deputies do not receive a budget for travel around their district.[11] Second, only deputies in official congressional leadership positions have offices,[12] so if a constituent or community group comes to ask a deputy for help with a problem, they must wait outside

---

11. Deputies did vote to allow themselves to import a new car tax-free, and the justification for this privilege was that "the National Congress constitutes the genuine expression of representative democracy." But they can import the new car at any time during their term, or even within one year of *leaving* the Congress (Law 296-93, December 20, 1993).

12. The congressional president, four vice presidents, and two secretaries have offices. Each party has a suite for the party leader in the Congress (the *jefe de bancada*). Though other deputies also use those rooms for business, I conducted many interviews in the party *bancada* offices and I never saw a deputy meeting there with a constituent. Some standing committees have a small office that the president of the committee uses, but most do not have a secretary or waiting area; unless a constituent or community group were aware the deputy had a committee office, they would not know to find the deputy there.

during plenary sessions and send a message to request that the deputy come out to see them.[13] Lastly, deputies have no budget to hire staff (in the capital or the district) to serve as a contact point for constituents, though some said they hired an assistant with their own money, or that people could contact them at their business or leave messages with their family.

Thirteen percent of study participants listed political activities as something they do for their constituents. Given how politicized Honduras is, it is interesting that Congress Advocates and Local Organizers did not connect political work to constituency work. It is also notable that only 19 percent of Party Deputies listed political work, such as organizing their party in their department, since such activities create an opportunity to distribute small particularistic benefits (e.g., a T-shirt or a meal). When Constituency Servers listed political activities as constituency service, they referred to registering people to vote or making sure they have party credentials, which can be helpful to a person who needs access to a government service (see Dalton 1994).

What can we extrapolate about representation of poor people from the work deputies say they do for their constituents? With the exception of legislative work, done primarily by Congress Advocates, and working with organizations, which is primarily an activity of Local Organizers and Congress Advocates, deputies see their work for constituents in clientelistic terms. Party Deputies focus on particularistic service, which might lead a poor person to give a positive answer to the question "What has government done for me lately?" For Constituency Servers and Congress Advocates, obtaining local development projects for their district is constituency service, and this could induce people in beneficiary communities to think their officials represent them. Few deputies other than Congress Advocates see legislating as work for their constituents. Congress Advocates want to legislate and improve policy, which could be policy representing the interests of poor people. Other deputies are unlikely to address the policy side of the policy/services package desired by poor people. Public works projects and particularistic services do little to solve the needs of poor people as a sector of society, or to give poor people a voice in deliberation about policy (Mansbridge 2003), but they can address immediate, concrete needs and are easy for poor people to monitor.

---

13. Often there is a large crowd of people waiting to meet with deputies. A small staff of guards asks whom a person wishes to speak to and then gets the deputy, who can bring the individual or group into the large foyer area of the Congress meeting hall, where couches and tables are available for conversations. While conducting interviews there I observed many deputies meeting with people.

Roles and Legislation: Do Some Deputies Legislate for Poor People?

Legislative records offer a way to compare representation across roles. All deputies can initiate bills, including bills for local public works, benefits for an individual, or policy targeting a sector of society or the entire country. In Honduras, the national government controls most sources of revenue, creating many opportunities for deputies to bring local development projects and resources to communities (Nickson 1995). For example, the national government funds schools, electricity service, and flood control projects. If a municipal government buys road construction equipment, it pays import taxes on the machinery unless a law is passed to exempt the purchase from tax. Changing a school's curriculum to allow it to offer a technical degree requires a law authorizing the curriculum revision. If a ministry or agency owns a property in a town, a law is needed to transfer the property to the local government or an organization. Deputies can and do initiate bills on any topic, as the president has no exclusive initiation power (Taylor-Robinson and Diaz 1999). Thus deputies who want to represent poor people have the capacity to initiate legislation to attempt to realize those constituents' national policy preferences (or draw attention to the issues), or to provide local infrastructure projects and personalistic benefits.

In general, initiating a bill is not the only way for a deputy to obtain local development projects. Brazilian deputies, for example, amend the budget for infrastructure projects for their district (Ames 2001; Samuels 2003). Costa Rican deputies want to sit on the Finance Committee, where they can add local development projects to the national budget (interviews with Costa Rican legislators, 1988, 1989). In Honduras, deputies do not get to add amendments to the national budget, whether in the Budget Committee or from the floor (interviews with deputies). The executive branch prepares the budget and the Congress votes on it, typically on the last day of the annual session, when there is no time for discussion or amendments. Even the Budget Committee has no real opportunity to mark up the budget. Partisan powers (Shugart and Mainwaring 1997) and the norm of approving legislation by *mayorías mecánicas* give the president control over the budget. Deputies can request public works projects for their department from ministries and executive agencies, and many mentioned making such contacts, but no systematic source of information about them exists. Even if it were available, opposition deputies do not have access to executive branch resources, and even deputies from out-of-favor factions in the governing party complained about their lack of access. Finally, anecdotal evidence indicates that the executive does not share credit with deputies for local projects. The president makes many campaign promises and wants credit for local projects so people will see him delivering on his promises (Shepherd 1986; Rosenberg 1989; Taylor 1996). The FHIS is the executive agency that administers many local development projects (e.g., schools, roads, potable water). The FHIS Web page shows pictures of recently inaugurated projects, and the absence of deputies is notable. The president or a senior executive branch official is shown inaugurating projects, indicating that the executive branch is responsible.[14] Thus, while initiating a bill is not the only way a deputy can work to get development projects for his district, bills are the only systematic indicators of local development work, the only means available to all deputies, and something for which a deputy can claim credit.

Legislative effort differs across roles (see table 7.3). Congress Advocates are the most active in the number of bills they propose initiating significantly more bills than Constituency Servers (p = 0.005) and passing more laws than either Constituency Servers (p = 0.001) or Party Deputies (p = 0.003). They are also the most active participants in plenary sessions, in the number of speeches in general (p = 0.000), and in the speech subset known as *manifestaciones,* given specifically to draw attention to a problem (p = 0.002). This is consistent with their interest in strengthening the legislature and improving the quality of laws. Constituency Servers are the least active, which supports their claims that they are more interested in working on local development projects than legislating. Party Deputies vary; some are party spokespeople, and others are seen but not heard, presumably just voting with their party.[15]

14. FHIS is one of the social funds supported by the World Bank to compensate poor people for the hardships of economic structural adjustment. Studies of social funds indicate that they do target benefits to poor people and communities, but that they are also sources of clientelistic resources for presidents (Schady 2000; Tendler 2000).

15. We can only assume that silent deputies are following the cues of party leaders on votes, since the Congress does not take roll call votes. Legislation passes with *mayorías mecánicas* and party leaders are best able to wield that tool with voice votes. Deputies can justify their vote afterward, but they rarely claim their right to say they voted against a motion supported by their party. The only way to obtain information about vote justifications (*razonamientos*) is to read the transcripts of Congress debates, and I have that information for only the 1994–97 Congress. Nine deputies used this right—three from the governing PLH, five from the PNH, and one from the PINU, for a total of thirteen vote justifications (five PLH, seven PNH, and one PINU). Eight of these deputies participated in this study: five were Congress Advocates, one was a Party Deputy, one was in the Local Organizer subtype of the Constituency Server role, and one did not fit any role category. Given Congress Advocates' preference for improving the quality of legislation, it makes sense that they object to the Congress leadership using railroading techniques to silence opposition, which was often the reason for their *razonamientos.*

Table 7.3 Legislative work by role type, 1994–97 Congress (average [SD])

	Role type					
	Congress Advocates (n = 12)	Party Deputies (n = 21)	Constituency Servers (n = 30)	Local Organizers[a] (n = 6)	No role[b] (n = 8)	All propietarios (n = 128)
No. of bills proposed	7.2 (5.4)	3.7 (6.8)	1.5 (2.6)	0.5 (1.2)	4.6 (6.5)	4.1 (9.7)
No. of bills passed into law	3.7 (4.3)	0.9 (1.5)	0.7 (1.2)	0.0 (0.0)	2.0 (3.7)	2.2 (7.5)
No. of speeches in plenary sessions	256.4 (231.1)	50.4 (58.3)	29.6 (47.1)	30.2 (48.9)	100.1 (114.3)	85.3 (206.5)
No. of *manifestación* speeches	9.9 (12.7)	4.6 (5.9)	1.5 (2.5)	1.2 (2.0)	9.3 (9.5)	3.8 (6.5)
No. of national-level bills proposed	3.8 (2.9)	1.8 (4.8)	0.2 (0.8)	0.0 (0.0)	1.5 (2.1)	1.4 (3.6)
No. of local-level bills proposed	1.3 (1.9)	0.7 (1.1)	0.5 (0.9)	0.0 (0.0)	1.8 (3.2)	1.2 (2.7)
No. of individual-level bills proposed	1.3 (1.6)	0.4 (0.7)	0.3 (0.6)	0.0 (0.0)	0.3 (0.7)	0.6 (2.5)

NOTE: (1) National-level bills affect all people or the entire country (e.g., mandatory military service, narcotics traffic policy, delay of deadline to pay a tax). (2) Local bills target one or more municipalities or a single department. (3) Individual-level bills target a person, organization, or company (e.g., create a pension for a widow, allow an organization to import a bus without taxes, modify the organic law of the College of Journalists, approve a contract for an electricity-generating company).

[a] Deputies who participated in the study but did not fit any of the three roles.

[b] Local Organizer is a subtype of the Constituency Server role. Along with the characteristics of the Constituency Server role, they expressed a concern for helping people to organize so that they would become less dependent on the government.

To assess whether some types of deputies use legislation to represent poor people, I examine their legislation in more detail. In table 7.3, bills are broken down by the target of the legislation (national, local, or individual) (Taylor-Robinson and Diaz 1999). Several points stand out in these data. Congress Advocates are active legislators, while Constituency Servers initiate very few bills, and Local Organizers even fewer. This pattern holds for legislation with a national target, where Congress Advocates initiate significantly more bills than do Constituency Servers (p = 0.006). For legislation with a local target, however, differences across role types are not statistically significant (p = 0.110). We might expect Constituency Servers to be more active in local legislation than deputies who adopt other roles, but Constituency Servers actually initiate few bills. In all legislative categories, Congress Advocates initiate the most bills. When Constituency Servers do legislate, however, their bills frequently have a local target, which generally means that the bill concerns a development project or resources for a community. Bills with an individual-level target are particularistic service bills. We would expect Party Deputies to be the group who most often initiated individually targeted bills, since parties prefer to target services to party supporters and because Party Deputies did not express an interest in local development projects. Instead, Congress Advocates are once again the most active legislators, initiating significantly more individual-level bills than either Party Deputies (p = 0.017) or Constituency Servers (p = 0.004).

Since the number of bills most deputies initiate is small, I also examine legislative records over multiple terms. Combining records from more than one term helps control for the possibility that deputies initiate fewer bills when their party is in opposition, due to the lower chance that the measures will pass. Table 7.4 presents data from three terms.[16] Given their role's defining interest in obtaining development projects for their communities, Constituency Servers would be expected to initiate the most local public works bills (see table 7.5 for examples), but the average number of local public works bills initiated does not differ significantly across the roles (F value for Anova not significant). If we examine local public works bills as a proportion of all bills deputies initiate, differences across roles are significant (p = 0.077).[17] The

---

16. A majority of deputies in the study served more than one term between 1990 and 2001: 58.3 percent of Congress Advocates, 66.7 percent of Party Deputies, 66.7 percent of Constituency Servers (including 50.0 percent of the Local Organizers), and 63.5 percent of the "no role" deputies served two or three terms in this period.

17. Comparisons were made on proportion data after arcsine transformation.

Table 7.4 Legislative work for the poor by role type, 1990–93, 1994–97, and 1998–2001 Congresses (average [SD])

	Role type					
	Congress Advocates[a] (n = 12)	Party Deputies (n = 21)	Constituency Servers (n = 30)	Local Organizers[a] (n = 6)	No role[b] (n = 8)	All propietarios[c] (n = 128)
No. of bills proposed	14.7 (13.6)	6.3 (11.2)	3.7 (5.1)	1.5 (3.7)	13.6 (16.6)	4.1 (9.7)
No. of bills passed into law	6.9 (9.2)	2.8 (7.8)	1.4 (2.5)	0.0 (0.0)	7.1 (12.0)	2.2 (7.5)
No. of local public works bills proposed	2.6 (4.2)	0.9 (1.4)	1.5 (2.5)	0.0 (0.0)	2.9 (4.9)	0.9 (1.9)
Local public works bills as proportion of all bills[d]	0.18 (0.29)	0.23 (0.24)	0.41 (0.28)	0.0	0.17 (0.14)	0.33 (0.53)
No. of local public works bills passed into law	1.4 (3.4)	0.7 (1.1)	0.6 (1.2)	0.0 (0.0)	2.0 (4.6)	0.6 (1.6)
Local public works laws as proportion of all laws[e]	0.17 (0.31)	0.54 (0.40)	0.41 (0.33)	—	0.14 (0.11)	0.32 (0.36)
No. of bills beneficial to poor proposed	2.0 (2.0)	0.5 (1.2)	0.7 (1.3)	0.8 (2.0)	1.4 (1.9)	0.4 (0.9)
Bills for the poor as proportion of all bills[d]	0.15 (0.16)	0.06 (0.11)	0.20 (0.28)	0.55	0.12 (0.09)	0.12 (0.22)
No. of bills beneficial to poor passed into law	0.7 (0.9)	0.1 (0.3)	0.2 (0.6)	0.0 (0.0)	0.6 (1.1)	0.1 (0.4)
Laws for the poor as proportion of all laws[e]	0.16 (0.30)	0.02 (0.06)	0.15 (0.30)	—	0.11 (0.11)	0.07 (0.18)

NOTE: Most, but not all, deputies in the study served more than one term.

[a] Local Organizer is a subtype of the Constituency Server role. Along with the characteristics of the Constituency Server role, they expressed a concern for helping people to organize so that they would become less dependent on the government.

[b] Deputies who participated in the study but did not fit any of the three roles.

[c] Data about legislative records of all *propietarios* are from the 1994–97 Congress only.

[d] Means of proportions of bills introduced are based only on deputies who introduced at least one bill (twelve Congress Advocates, fifteen Party Deputies, seventeen Constituency Servers, one Local Organizer, four no role, seventy-six *propietarios*).

[e] Means of proportions of laws passed are based only on deputies who introduced at least one bill that was passed into law (ten Congress Advocates, nine Party Deputies, thirteen Constituency Servers, zero Local Organizers, four no role, fifty-six *propietarios*).

Scheffe's test paired comparison of the proportion of local public works bills to all bills for Constituency Servers versus Congress Advocates verges on significant (p = 0.128). Constituency Servers spend proportionally more of their legislative effort on local public works than do other deputies. It is noteworthy that five of the six Local Organizers said development projects are an important activity they do for their constituents, yet Local Organizers did not initiate any local public works bills.

Poor people may only be satisfied by delivery of the promised project. They can easily monitor if the project is delivered (e.g., construction starts and is completed), but it is difficult for them to verify a claim that a bill was proposed. If we use local public works bills that become law as a proxy for fulfilling a promise, again legislative records do not differ significantly across the roles. But for local public works laws as a proportion of all bills deputies initiate that become law, the roles differ (p = 0.075), with local public works laws constituting a significantly smaller percentage of the successful legislative agenda of Congress Advocates than of Party Deputies. Since Congress Advocates should be at least as adept as their colleagues at getting their bills passed into law (probably more adept), this presumably indicates that they exert more effort pursuing their "policy" bills than their "local project" bills.

In sum, if delivering local development projects represents poor people, Constituency Servers and Congress Advocates are more likely to be representatives of the poor than are Party Deputies. I am certainly not arguing that poor people do not have national policy interests. Peasant farmers' protests against the Central American Free Trade Agreement (CAFTA) with the United States are examples that poor people can care about national policies. It is simply easier for poor people to monitor whether elected officials delivered on promises of local infrastructure projects, and the benefit of those projects is clear.[18] A deputy should be able to take credit for his or her local public works legislation (Mayhew 1974, 52–61) by taking part in the ceremony to inaugurate the project, and many deputies mentioned the pleasure such events give them. One deputy (PLH, Cortes) told about a two-hour delay in

18. The value of a national policy, in contrast, often depends on enforcement (Desposato 2001). Poor people have reason to be skeptical about whether they will benefit from a new law, even if it approximates their policy preference, due to a long history in Latin American countries of making laws but not enforcing them (Hirschman 1973). The Honduran government has often negotiated with poor sectors of society and made concessions rather than rely solely on repression (e.g., peaceful settlement of the 1954 dockworkers strike, land reform in the 1970s, grants of communal lands to indigenous people in the 1990s), but poor people still criticize the government for lack of follow-through in implementing pledges.

the ceremony to dedicate an electricity generator because the whole town was watching an Italian soccer match on TV, something they were now able to do because of their new electricity service. By contrast, a deputy who promises protections for *maquilla* workers cannot deliver such legislation without the cooperation of many other deputies and the executive branch, judiciary, and private companies to implement the law. It is difficult for a deputy to take credit for a policy law, and even once a law is passed, it must be enforced or policy outputs will not satisfy poor people.

Table 7.5 summarizes the types of local projects deputies propose, with Constituency Servers standing out for their activity. Schools are the most common, including bills to construct new schools and to expand school curricula. Utility and road projects are also common. Some bills make services more convenient (e.g., setting up a local court so people do not need to go to another town). Others provide funds for the community (e.g., giving the local government a building, creating a municipality, granting a tax exemption to import a truck). Extending industrial duty-free zone rights to a community expands its chances to attract factories and increase employment opportunities.

Deputies can also introduce bills to make policies to benefit poor sectors of society, so we can examine deputies' legislative records to see if the incidence of such bills varies across roles. I evaluated bill titles to determine if the target was a poor sector of society. This coding is crude, but a more refined measure was not feasible since the full text of bills was not available.[19] Given the necessity of crude coding, I used a broad definition of "beneficial to the poor" to include any bill that targeted sectors of the economy or the society in which the poor are dominant, such as small agricultural producers, the elderly, disabled people, and children. I included bills that would make it easier for people of limited resources to defend their rights (e.g., property rights, freedom from unfair treatment in the penal system), and bills that allow organizations that help poor people to import supplies tax-free (e.g., orphanages, medical groups).

Congress Advocates on average initiated more bills that target the poor than did deputies who adopted other roles (F value for Anova significant at $p = 0.017$). Congress Advocates also were the most successful at getting those bills passed ($p = 0.029$) (see table 7.4). Differences across roles in bills or

19. Obtaining the full text of bills would make unreasonable demands on the staff of the Congress Archive (the Secretaria Adjunta), and would necessitate many weeks in the Archive to read and take notes on bill content, as the Congress has no facility for photocopying by a researcher. When the link is functioning and updated, the Congress Web page now offers the full text of bills initiated in the current term, but only some older laws are available, primarily for major legislation.

Table 7.5 Local projects by role type, 1990–93, 1994–97, and 1998–2001 Congresses

	Role type				
	Congress Advocates (n = 12)	Party Deputies (n = 21)	Constituency Servers (n = 30)	No role[a] (n = 8)	All *propietarios*[b] (n = 128)
School	9 / 3	4 / 3	16 / 4	6 / 5	29 / 18
Utilities (electricity, water)	7 / 4	2 / 1	5 / 3	2 / 2	8 / 4
Road, bridge, allow municipality to buy road equipment tax-free	6 / 5	3 / 3	4 / 2	3 / 2	13 / 10
Park	3 / 2	0 / 0	1 / 1	1 / 0	3 / 1
Local court	2 / 1	0 / 0	3 / 0	2 / 2	11 / 10
Donate land or building to local government	1 / 1	4 / 3	2 / 1	0 / 0	8 / 4
Statue or monument	0 / 0	1 / 1	2 / 2	1 / 1	6 / 5
Industrial free zone	1 / 0	0 / 0	2 / 1	1 / 0	7 / 4
Give town title of city, create municipality	1 / 1	1 / 1	2 / 2	3 / 2	15 / 12
Allow municipality to import vehicle tax-free	0 / 0	1 / 1	2 / 1	0 / 0	3 / 3
Other[c]	0 / 0	2 / 0	4 / 1	3 / 1	17 / 8
TOTAL	30 / 17	18 / 13	43 / 18	22 / 15	120 / 79

NOTE: Table entries present the number of bills initiated followed by number of bills passed into law.

[a] Deputies who participated in the study but did not fit any of the three roles.

[b] Data about the legislative records of all *propietarios* are from the 1994–97 Congress.

[c] For Party Deputies includes: funds for a local holiday celebration, and requiring the Tela Railroad Co. to give funds to every municipality in which it has operations. For Constituency Servers includes: writing off municipal debts, an emergency shelter, a home for the elderly, and a rehabilitation center for youth. For the "no role" category includes: declaring the southern region an environmental emergency zone and a priority zone for reconstruction, as well as the provision of a local library and a cultural center. Additional projects in the "other" category for "all *propietarios*" include: declaring an area an ecological reserve, transferring funds from the Anthropology Institute to the municipal government where a tourist attraction is located, creating a land customs office, transferring funds from customs offices to municipal governments in municipalities where there are customs offices, construction of a day care center, and funds for church construction.

laws that target the poor as a proportion of deputies' total legislative agenda are not statistically detectable (p = 0.142 for bills, p = 0.358 for laws).[20]

Table 7.6 shows the types of bills deputies initiated and the number that became law. Many Constituency Servers' bills target small farmers or cooperatives, specific organizations that work with the poor (e.g., a group running a home for senior citizens), or other local initiatives, such as scholarships to schools in a particular department. Once again, their legislation is consistent

20. Local Organizers stand out from other deputies in the proportion of their legislative agenda that targets policy for poor people, but Local Organizers initiated just three such bills, all from the same deputy, and none became law.

Table 7.6 Legislation beneficial to the poor by role type, 1990–93, 1994–97, and 1998–2001 Congresses

	Role type				
	Congress Advocates (n = 12)	Party Deputies (n = 21)	Constituency Servers (n = 30)	No role[a] (n = 8)	All *propietarios*[b] (n = 128)
Price controls for basic goods	2 / 1	1 / 0	1 / 0	1 / 1	4 / 1
Defense of property	3 / 0	0 / 0	2 / 1	0 / 0	4 / 0
Help for small farmers, fisherman, cooperatives, land reform	2 / 2	5 / 1	8 / 1	2 / 1	15 / 4
Human rights and protection from imprisonment	1 / 1	2 / 0	0 / 0	0 / 0	5 / 2
Women's rights	3 / 1	0 / 0	0 / 0	0 / 0	3 / 1
Rights of elderly and disabled	1 / 0	1 / 0	3 / 0	4 / 2	6 / 3
Care for children	2 / 0	0 / 0	1 / 0	1 / 0	6 / 4
Tax-free status for organization working for the poor	3 / 1	0 / 0	3 / 3	1 / 1	1 / 1
Other[c]	7 / 3	1 / 1	3 / 0	5 / 1	13 / 4
TOTAL	24 / 9	10 / 2	21 / 5	14 / 6	57 / 20

NOTE: Table entries present the number of bills initiated followed by number of bills passed into law.

[a] Deputies who participated in the study but did not fit any of the three roles.

[b] Data about the legislative records of all *propietarios* are from the 1994–97 Congress.

[c] For Congress Advocates includes: amnesty for military deserters, suspending military recruitment, protection against immigrant smugglers, worker's rights, a night school program, and allowing teachers elected to municipal government in communities where the government salary is lower than the teacher's salary to keep their teacher's salary. For Party Deputies includes: providing chlorinated water for public health. For Constituency Servers includes: a scholarship program for schools, new doctor positions for government health network, a program requiring high school and college students to teach illiterate people to read. For the "no role" category includes: donating government buildings to the Lenca Indian organization, and declaring the southern zone an environmental emergency zone and priority area for reconstruction. Additional projects in the "other" category for "all *propietarios*" include: a law to regulate tipping, unemployment benefits, condemning interest on a housing project, making condoms more readily available and affordable, and tax-free import of cars and equipment by people returning from living illegally in the United States.

with these deputies' geographically defined concept of constituents. Congress Advocates initiated more bills intended to address a problem affecting a class of people all over the country (e.g., women, poor families, workers), which is consistent with their interest in policymaking. Party Deputies initiated very few bills that met even a crude criterion of benefiting the poor.

Congress Advocates initiate more bills that target poor sectors of society than do Party Deputies or Constituency Servers, but in general Honduran deputies initiate few bills to make policy for the poor. This may simply be rational behavior when parties prefer benefits they can target at party supporters. It also may indicate recognition of the difficulty individual deputies have had in passing national policy legislation, especially if it lacks party backing. Deputies who want to represent poor people, but who realize they will only benefit poor people if they can *deliver,* may view local development projects and particularistic benefits as a more efficient use of their time.

Deputies can support any bills the executive branch might initiate to attend to the policy interests of the poor by speaking in support of the bill or voting for the bill, but such bills are rare in the legislative agenda of the executive branch. The executive initiated only twelve bills targeting policy for the poor during the 1994–97 government, and only eight of these bills became law. The executive's bills included amending the Constitution to make military service voluntary, creating the Institute for Human Rights, an emergency law to deal with the problem of people spending long periods of time in prison without being charged, two bills concerning titles to coffee farms, and a bill exempting imports of donated fertilizers and agricultural equipment from tax. The executive can also initiate bills for local development projects. In the 1994–97 term, the executive initiated eighty-eight local development project bills, eighty-two of which became law (sixty-five of these bills were to build roads).

Roles and Representation of the Poor: Conclusions

Deputies who adopt different roles behave differently in ways that reinforce the identities and preferences about the deputy's job that define those roles. Deputies' roles are shaped by the institutions making up the Honduran political environment at the time of the study, and there is evidence that deputies who adopt some types of roles want to represent poor people.

Constituency Servers in the study are more likely than their colleagues to work to address poor people's need for local development. The defining characteristic of the Constituency Server role is a desire to develop communities. That is why these deputies want to be in the Congress, their knowledge of their communities is what they think qualifies them to be deputies, and working on projects is how they enjoy spending their time. Unlike their colleagues who adopt other roles, Constituency Servers express intense frustration when partisan or factional politics keeps them from having access to state resources for their communities or from helping a community or organization because it is associated with the opposition party.

Fearon (1999) used the term "good type" to refer to an agent who wants to do the same things the principal wants, so that the principal does not need to monitor the agent. It would seem that if poor people wanted their representatives in the Congress to deliver local public works, they should try to elect Constituency Servers because they are "good types." With closed-list PR elections, however, poor people did not, until 2005, have the capacity to make such choices because they had to vote for a party's entire slate; further, the party-based form of clientelism gave the poor person an incentive to vote for his or her party's slate to maintain access to party-based clientelistic resources, even if the party did not place Constituency Servers in electable slots on the list.

In the pre-2005 reality of Honduras, if poor people wanted their representatives to address national policy issues that affected the poor (e.g., workplace benefits, trade policies to protect small agricultural producers), none of the roles in my study would be certain, or even likely, to represent them. Congress Advocates want to legislate, but they are most likely to get to continue their political career if they apply their efforts to improving the quality of legislation that their party backs, and neither traditional party is likely to reward a Congress Advocate who aggressively promotes policies that could benefit poor people but would harm elites. A poor person would need to know a Congress Advocate's legislative interests in order to select a "good type," and that kind of information was unlikely to be available to poor people; moreover, the closed-list ballot did not allow a voter to select a particular deputy candidate whose policies they liked. In addition, Congress Advocates in the study know how the legislative process works, and that passing legislation over the opposition of the executive or party leaders is unrealistic in Honduras. A Congress Advocate might personally be interested in national policy that would benefit poor people but not want to promote policy initiatives that are doomed to failure. The defining characteristics of Congress Advocates are their desire to produce better laws and strengthen the Congress. Their best strategy for achieving those goals may be to focus their legislative efforts on bills that have a good chance of passage and of aggressive implementation: high-profile legislation such as revising the penal or tax codes, or transferring the police to civilian control.

Party Deputies in the study see their job as representing their party, specifically their faction leader. State resources are very limited in Honduras, so it has been more efficient for the governing party to reward party militants with particularistic benefits than with community development projects (unless the community is known for supporting the party) or with national policies that would also benefit supporters of other parties. This means that some party supporters would get a job, scholarship, or permit, and many receive food at a campaign rally, a T-shirt, or help from a doctor or lawyer working for the party. Since clientele networks in Honduras have long been party-based, Party Deputies should want to help people (poor or not) who are affiliated with their party faction leader (the deputy's political patron). This means that a poor person who is not a known supporter of the Party Deputy's party or faction is unlikely to receive even clientelistic representation from that Party Deputy.

What do these micro-level implications of the theory indicate about whether the poor count? The answer depends on what type of representation poor people want. If poor people assign a low expected value to abstract national policies because they are uncertain what the policy would really do for them and whether it will be enforced, they may prefer that deputies deliver local development projects and personalistic benefits. The Constituency Servers of my study are the only type of deputy whose identity and work in the Congress represent poor people—*if* local development projects are the type of representation poor people desire. Yet Constituency Servers do not always get their bills sponsoring local development projects passed into law. Whether this is due to insufficient legislative experience, their party or faction being out of power, or parties wanting to target benefits to party loyalists rather than the general public, it means that even the Constituency Servers who want to help communities are not always successful.

We can combine the macro- and micro-level analyses of incentives to represent poor people from chapters 5–7 to draw conclusions about whether, when, and how poor people count in Honduras. Poor people have virtually no ability to monitor national policy work, but they can easily monitor whether politicians deliver local development projects and personalistic benefits. Party-based clientele networks mean poor people pay a high personal cost for switching their vote to sanction their party (i.e., severing their ties to their patron party); further, they also give parties an incentive to reward loyal clients with benefits that can be targeted at individuals, which makes it less desirable for government to build public works for a community (unless the community is known to be loyal to the party or the use of the service can be targeted to party militants). Yet within this institutional environment, deputies can choose how they will do their job. Congress Advocates wanted to develop better laws and their legislative work could represent poor people, though sponsoring controversial policy may harm a Congress Advocate's future political career prospects. Poor people lack the monitoring resources to be aware of a Congress Advocate's efforts, and had no capacity or reason to reward the deputy for unsuccessful policy efforts. Constituency Servers wanted to develop their communities. They were a well-known type within the Congress, and most who wanted to continue in politics have been able to do so (see table 6.3). Yet it is noteworthy that some Constituency Servers did not *want* to be reelected. Their frustrations with partisan politics led them to conclude that they could do as much for their communities from outside of government. Party Deputies saw themselves as agents of their party or faction leader, so their work for poor people was likely to be limited to providing particularistic benefits to party militants.

We can conclude that in the institutional milieu of Honduran politics, poor people have counted in a narrow fashion. Their votes have been important to traditional parties, but since state resources are very limited, parties have wanted deputies to focus on benefits that are targetable to party supporters. Constituency Servers and Congress Advocates could work on projects that produce collective benefits for poor people (for a community, a sector of society, or the entire nation), but their party might not back their efforts. Honduras's form of clientelism has prompted poor people to be risk averse and to support their traditional party to maintain their connection to their party-based clientele network because even small personalistic benefits are too valuable to lose. The high cost and probably low benefit a poor person would receive from supporting a new (nontraditional) party has prompted poor people to support the traditional parties. Defecting in this setting is costly as long as poor people expect that they will receive some benefits from maintaining their clientelistic link to their party, and that they may obtain additional representation from Constituency Server deputies if the governing party happens to nominate such a "good type" from their town.

The behavior of voters in 2005, when open-list ballots were used for the first time, indicates that poor people understand the value of voting for a traditional party. Voters used the open-list ballots to sanction many party caudillos or "dinosaurs," who lost their reelection bid, but they did not elect more deputies from nontraditional parties.[21] Presumably, poor voters used the new election

---

21. In Honduras's open-list elections (both primaries and general elections), voters can cast a separate vote for as many candidates as their department's DM.

rules that gave them the capacity to support particular deputies within their party to elect candidates who they thought would be more active representatives of their needs. Election Day interviews quoted poor people saying that they hoped the elections would produce officials who remembered their communities and worked for poor people (Corona 2005; Molina 2005).

EIGHT

---≫≫≫≫≪≪≪≪---

DO THE POOR COUNT IN
LATIN AMERICAN DEMOCRACIES?

This book explores whether, when, and how representation and accountability exist in a context of poverty. It asks, do the poor count in Latin American politics? . . . or was O'Donnell (1992) correct to worry that poor people would once again be ignored? These are important questions for democratic consolidation because in most Latin American countries poor people make up a large part of the population. It is hard to imagine that democratic regimes can deepen if a large sector of society does not receive representation because it lacks the capacity to hold elected officials accountable. Yet poor people in some countries appear to support the democratic regime and continue to vote for established parties. In other countries poor people have turned away from established parties, backing populist, antiparty, even antidemocracy politicians. In this book I have offered an institutional explanation for this difference. Institutions can enhance or limit the capacity of poor people to sanction elected officials. Institutions can also give elected officials incentives to build their career on support from poor voters, and they can prompt politicians to adopt an identity or preferences about holding office that make them want to attend to the needs of poor people. In such institutional settings, while democracy may not deepen, poor people are given a reason to work within the democratic system to address their needs.

The questions driving this book were prompted by reading chapters by Ferejohn and Fearon in *Democracy, Accountability, and Representation*, edited by Przeworski, Stokes, and Manin (1999). These renowned formal theorists present models of democratic accountability between citizens and elected officials. While not explicitly writing about the challenges of creating accountability in countries with advanced industrialized economies, their models seem to assume a reasonably uniform capacity across citizens to monitor and sanction officials. They acknowledge that most people, even highly educated, financially well-off citizens, do not expend much effort monitoring elected representatives—but the potential is there, and that potential for being monitored, and for being sanctioned if citizens find their performance lacking, is what creates an incentive for elected officials to represent the interests of the people who elect them. Lack of vigilant monitoring creates the opportunity for elected officials to not faithfully represent constituents' preferences; but if shirking becomes too blatant, the potential exists that constituents will take notice and punish the official. Reading those elegant formal theories about the mechanisms that promote accountability in democracy prompted the question, does accountability break down when some people have much less capacity than others to monitor and sanction elected officials? A stark difference in the capacity to monitor and in the tools available for sanctioning unacceptable performance is a challenge for democracy in a context of poverty. It is one of the differences between rich and poor people that disadvantages the poor, even in democratic regimes based on the principle of one person, one vote. This question led me to consider how institutions affect the ability of poor and rich people to sanction, and how combinations of institutions shape legislators' preferences for wanting a government post and constrain their strategies for building a political career, thereby creating incentives to represent different types of constituents.

There is a vast literature about democratization in Latin America, some of which alludes to how lack of representation of poor people will impede the consolidation of democracy (e.g., Karl 1990; O'Donnell 1992; Huber, Rueschemeyer, and Stephens 1999; Lievesley 1999; Hagopian 2005; Seligson 2007). Also, there is an expanding literature about how the design of democratic institutions affects how democratic regimes function in Latin America, but this literature focuses on the elite level of executive-legislative relations and party control over officials. Literature about electoral rules explores whether institutions give politicians an incentive to seek a personal or a party vote, but does not differentiate among groups in the mass public or address whether the differing capacity of groups to monitor and sanction elected officials means politicians will have a greater incentive to seek the approval of some people rather than others. This book links these literatures and combines rational choice and historical institutionalism to theorize and examine how institutions shape whether, when, and how the poor count in democratic politics.

This chapter briefly explores implications for government policy outputs of this theory of incentives to represent poor people. Then I draw conclusions about whether, when, and how institutions create incentives to represent poor people, and end with a discussion of the implications for consolidating democracy.

Institutions and Incentives to Represent the Poor: Implications for Policy Outputs

What are the implications of this theory of incentives to represent poor people for the policy outputs of governments? This topic merits discussion because the theory presented in this book predicts that under many institutional settings, elected officials do not have an incentive to provide policy representation to poor people; and when legislators do have such an incentive, it will take the form of clientelistic representation. Yet there are cases where governments have proposed and implemented high-profile programs for poor people, such as Bolsa Familia in Brazil. How was this possible? Literature on social sector policy reform in Latin America expects that such efforts come mainly from the executive branch (Grindle 2004, 20; Kaufman and Nelson 2004a, 14), so here I briefly explore the theoretical implications for how legislators have an incentive to react to pro-poor programs from the executive, followed by analyses of pro-poor social policies in Honduras and Brazil.

This book has advanced a theory about how the differing capacity of poor versus rich people to monitor elected officials, along with the capacity institutions give to poor and rich people to sanction, affects elected officials' incentives to represent poor people. Some officials (presidents or legislators) want to make policy that benefits poor people, and the theory has implications for what form such policy is likely to take given what is necessary to get a policy adopted and implemented before the next election so that poor people will want to reward officials. The theory thus helps predict when an official who has a preference for making policy benefiting poor people will be able to pursue this goal. Lacking a personal preference for pro-poor policy, the theory also helps predict when legislators have an incentive to work for poor constituents and what form that work is likely to take (national-level policy proposals, local projects, or particularistic benefits). The theory also helps explain when the preferences and threats of sanction from better-off citizens are likely to influence elected officials, in which case programs for the poor are unlikely to move beyond political rhetoric.

One point this theory highlights is that poor people are unlikely to reward elected officials who make promises (about policy or goods) but do not deliver tangible benefits. Poor people have heard many promises without results, so promises are unlikely to maintain the loyalty of poor voters (see Grindle 2004, 11–12). It is difficult, if not infeasible, for a poor person to monitor whether a politician is actually working within the halls of government to deliver on a policy promise. Thus, if a poor person does not receive or observe concrete benefits from the policy before the next election, that person should not be expected to reward the politician who says "I'm working on it."[1] Politicians or parties can provide policy, local development projects, or personalistic benefits to poor people *if* they can get these measures adopted and implemented before the next election and can avoid being successfully sanctioned by opponents.[2] A sanction or threat of sanction (e.g., business taking investments out of the country because a policy will raise the cost of labor, or strikes by unions that fear a policy's redistributive consequences) could sufficiently raise the political cost of a policy so that legislators will oppose a bill that would deliver services to poor people, causing the bill to die in congress or be watered down (Angell and Graham 1995, 210; Kaufman and Nelson 2004b, 474; Weyland 2006).[3] The political need to provide concrete deliverables before the next election may also prompt modifications to make the policy more likely to produce clientelistic resources, thereby turning a *policy* proposal into *clientelistic representation*. As Kaufman and Nelson (2004b, 482) explain, "Politicians and political parties regard building schools and clinics as vote-getters, but fear that more contentious or slow-acting reforms may lose more votes than they gain."

Simply put, *wanting* to make policy for poor people, or viewing it as *electorally rational* to do so, is not enough. To receive electoral support from poor people, a politician needs to deliver benefits. That means that the politician

1. Honduran deputies who adopted a Constituency Server role explained that one of their jobs was to explain to constituents why a promised project had not yet materialized—for example, explaining that a road project had to go through an engineering feasibility stage, a project approval stage (often involving getting a road bill passed into law), and a project funding stage, after which construction could finally begin.

2. Poor people are often not organized and active in politics, so they are unlikely to pressure for policy reform (Angell and Graham 1995, 199; Nelson 2004; Arretche 2004, 166). According to Nelson (2004, 40), "Where popular pressures for better service do emerge (often channeled through local NGOs or parties), they are likely to focus on improved service from local facilities, not on major revisions of national policy" (see also Hochstetler 2000, 180). This indicates that politicians are unlikely to be rewarded by poor people unless they deliver concrete benefits, so local development projects and personalistic benefits are more likely to be politically valuable than national policy reforms.

3. For example, when health sector reform was being formulated in Colombia in 1993, teachers' and petroleum workers' unions resisted reforms "that would alter their traditional generous health and pension provisions," and were ultimately exempted from the legislation (Nelson 2004, 35n7; Ramirez 2004, 132).

must: get the policy passed into law (method A); find a way to implement a program that does not require new legislation (method B); or have resources to deliver local development projects or particularistic benefits to poor people (method C). Below I elaborate on each method, and then provide examples from Honduras and Brazil illustrating how legislators have responded to conditional cash transfer programs developed by the executive.

Method A: Getting a Policy Passed into Law

Getting a policy passed into law requires a majority in the legislature. This often involves building a coalition to vote for the policy, and may require policy concessions, logrolling, and issue bundling (Kaufman and Nelson 2004b, 510).[4] Concessions are particularly likely if actors with extensive monitoring resources and sharp sanctioning tools are threatened by the policy, making legislators concerned that without concessions they will be sanctioned by opponents.[5] Meanwhile, the president or legislators who support the policy will not be rewarded by poor people for their efforts unless the policy is passed and implemented so that it actually delivers concrete benefits to poor people. The social policy reform literature refers to creating new stakeholders who benefit from the new policy, but those stakeholders will not defend the politicians who made the policy happen until they are receiving the new benefits. Until they actually receive benefits, the policy is just another promise that lacks credibility.

Method A is more feasible during a time of economic expansion, when benefits can be extended to new groups without taking resources away from groups who are already beneficiaries of state policy. For example, between the 1950s and the 1970s many Latin American governments expanded access to education, increasing the percentage of children enrolled in school and reducing illiteracy. Such programs were popular, producing benefits for poor

4. If a president enjoys strong partisan powers (Shugart and Mainwaring 1997), he or she may be able to use this control to get the congress to approve a policy reform even in the face of opposition from affected actors. This was how President Fujimori in Peru passed the Entidades Prestadoras de Salud scheme in 1997 (Weyland 2006, 191–93). Where presidents have decree powers, they may be able to avoid submitting a reform bill to the legislature (Grindle 2004, 49). Alternatively, a president may be able to cement a governing coalition through patronage appointments (Kellam 2007).

5. Grindle (2004) elaborates conditions that limit political clout of unions: fragmentation, loss of prestige, or lack of affiliation with the party in power (see also Garland 2000, 6–7; Kaufman and Nelson 2004b, 501–2).

people and creating jobs for teachers and school administrators, construction workers building schools, and textbook companies. They "provided citizens with increased benefits and politicians with tangible resources to distribute to their constituencies" (Grindle 2004, 5). Method A may also be feasible when policy entrepreneurs view social sector policy reform as a way to reinforce the democratic political system. This could explain Colombia's health sector reform that began with the 1991 Constituent Assembly. Key senators demanded major reform, and the 1991 Constitution established a time line for the legislation (Ramirez 2004, 127). The initial reform proposal of President César Gaviria's health team was rejected by the Senate's Social Affairs Commission, which "urged a more comprehensive approach" (Ramirez 2004, 131). Law 100 of December 1993 was a radical reform of the health sector that was mainly the product of initiatives by reformers in the Ministry of Health and in the Senate (Nelson 2004, 31, 39, 44–45). But even under these auspicious circumstances, reformers had to compromise. To obtain the support of public sector health workers, provisions were made to raise their salaries. The Ministry of Health established Health Solidarity Enterprises in the electoral bailiwicks of some senators to give them a clientelistic stake in the reform. The reforms that were ultimately adopted also provided clientelism opportunities, since local governments determined who would receive the state subsidy to cover individuals who were too poor to pay for the obligatory insurance (Ramirez 2004, 137, 140, 150).

Leftist parties that lack a majority in the legislature may be able to block policy changes such as privatization (Grindle 2004, 11), but they cannot pass pro-poor policies without building broader support, which typically requires making policy concessions. Kaufman and Nelson (2004b, 501) conclude that leftist or reformist parties "generally did not have a consistent influence on social service reforms."[6] They can contribute to the scope of policy ideas discussed (e.g., proposing equity-enhancing programs or implementing pilot programs at the local level), but on their own they cannot get their initiatives adopted as policy reform laws. When such ideas are adopted, they are often taken over

6. There have been exceptions, such as the leftist victory to include universal health care in Brazil's 1988 Constitution. In 2000, a constitutional amendment obliging states and municipalities to spend at least 7 percent of revenues on health care (increasing to 12 percent), and increasing federal funding for health care, was the initiative of a PT deputy. The legislator "gained support of the health policy community and from a broad alliance in the legislature," but it was also important that he had the support of Health Minister Jose Serra, who expected "that constitutional guarantees for levels of health spending could serve as a defense against fiscal cutbacks advocated by the finance minister" (Arretche 2004, 179–80).

by patronage politicians—what Weyland (2006, 170) calls the "politically driven erosion of targeting." For years, Brazil's PT has confronted these problems. PT members of Congress were unable to get redistributive policies from the party's platform adopted, and poor people did not reward the PT for its rhetoric and instead voted for traditional parties and politicians who could deliver concrete (clientelistic) benefits (Meneguello 1995; Hunter and Power 2005, 136; 2007, 9; Zucco 2007).

Method B: Implementing a Program Without New Legislation

Implementing a program requires funds and cooperation from the bureaucracy. Where this method is feasible, legislators have little ability to prevent implementation of an executive program they do not support. Weyland (2006, 172) explains that many Latin American countries already had a legal policy of universal health care, so equity-enhancing programs "did not require legal changes, which could have aroused redistributive conflicts over how to finance this equity-enhancing change. Instead, it could be pursued through low-profile administrative rules." Kaufman and Nelson (2004a, 5) list "relatively small steps that slide under the radar screen of national politics: ministerial decrees, shifts in administrative practices, or local initiatives that may escape the attention of actors outside the sector" as a way that social sector reform occurs in Latin America. Policy "add-ons" are particularly feasible if they appear to be distributive programs that extend benefits to new groups "without taxing the better-off" (Weyland 2006, 9; see also Nelson 1992).[7]

Yet the executive's capacity to pursue add-on policy reforms may still be limited by legislators. Reforms that will provide new services to benefit the poor may threaten middle-class stakeholders in the existing policy. For example, organized actors such as doctors and other medical service personnel often object to reforms that move resources from sophisticated hospital care used by the middle class to simple preventive medicine services that will primarily benefit the poor. Unions that oppose a reform may enlist the help of legislators from parties supported by the union (Weyland 2006, 178; Nelson 2000, 58).[8] Grindle (2004, 7) points out that "when reformers failed in efforts to introduce

7. For example, Chile's Concertación government invested funds to improve the quality of elementary schools in poor areas, but most of the funds came from a World Bank loan (Angell and Graham 1995, 210).

8. Health sector workers in El Salvador used this tactic, appealing to FMLN legislators to block a health reform project (Weyland 2006, 196–97).

significant quality-enhancing reforms [in education], politicians were pleased to fill the gap by reverting to more popular activities like building schools and improving infrastructure." Pro-poor policies that appear to be policy add-ons can eventually require some action by the legislature (e.g., to approve a loan, continue a tax, or amend a law). "External donors can offer support available solely for pro-poor programs, thus transforming them from redistributive into distributive measures" (Nelson 1992, 233; see also Kaufman and Nelson 2004b, 479–80; Weyland 2006), making it possible for the executive to start a pro-poor program and avoid a budget fight with the congress, though the congress still gets to play a role if loans require the legislature's approval. This is illustrated below in Honduras and Brazil. The congress may have to wait for an opportunity to influence program approval, but when it does, policy opponents may be able to use the legislature to change or derail a policy that is not overtly redistributive.

This book's theory of incentives to represent the poor underscores why poor people are unlikely to become beneficiaries of extensive social sector policy reform even when they represent a large percentage of the potential electorate. Poor people lack effective means for monitoring what politicians are doing as they try to develop social sector policy reforms, and they have little reason to reward efforts that have not yet produced concrete benefits. Meanwhile, organized middle-class interests (e.g., health care workers or teachers) often have knowledge of policy changes that are in the development stage, and their well-organized unions can mobilize quickly to protest (Kaufman and Nelson 2004a, 12). In addition, politicians who are benefiting from clientelistic resources in the existing health care or education system have little incentive to support policy reform, particularly if structural adjustment policies have caused them to lose many of the state resources they formerly used for clientelism (Nelson 1992, 238–39; Weyland 2006, 163, 167–68).[9] Legislators may also spoil a pro-poor policy by "buying into it." If legislators become aware of a small targeted program implemented by the bureaucracy, for example to extend health care benefits to a small category of the most needy poor people, they

---

9. Reform that decreases patronage opportunities can occur, particularly if the party that will be hurt is not in the reforming government's coalition. The Fernando Cardoso government in Brazil pursued reform in the education sector, which had long been controlled by "conservative, pork-barrel politicians." Mayors were willing to accept the loss of control over education money to the schools themselves because the amount of funds was small and divided across many schools, which made the administrative and accounting costs relatively high. By contrast, school meal funds were retained under the control of mayors, as they were considered to be an important patronage resource (Draibe 2004, 394–95).

may pass a law expanding the program to increase its benefit as a clientelism instrument, undermining the ability to implement the policy to benefit all the people who met the narrowly defined programs' qualifications. In sum, distributive programs, typically on a small scale and often funded by external donors, may be the type of policy for the poor that is politically feasible, but even that is uncertain.

Method C: Delivering Local Development Projects or
Particularistic Benefits to Poor People

Delivering local or particularistic benefits requires either getting legislation passed authorizing the local project or benefit, or obtaining access to the executive so that a legislator can procure funds from the bureaucracy to deliver on such promises. According to Kaufman and Nelson (2004b, 479), "Building schools, clinics and hospitals is especially appealing to politicians, because a one-time outlay creates a visible and durable benefit; in contrast, expanding staff and ensuring supplies require ongoing expenditures."

Method C typically requires the legislator to be in the governing party in a single-party majority government (possibly even in the party's dominant faction), to be part of the coalition that backs the president, or to vote for the president's legislative agenda in exchange for resources. The latter is common in Brazil as minority presidents must form coalitions, exchanging resources for votes in order to pass major items in their legislative agendas (see Power 1998; Desposato 2001; Grindle 2004, 104, 150). Honduran deputies who adopted a Constituency Server role often complained that if they were not in the president's faction of the ruling party, they could not get access to resources to build development projects in their district.

CCTs in Honduras and Brazil:
Legislator Response to Pro-poor Programs

This section illustrates some of the theoretical implications of the theory of incentives to represent poor people by examining conditional cash transfer programs (CCTs) in Honduras and Brazil. CCTs "provide money to poor families conditional upon investments in human capital, usually sending children to school and/or bringing them to health centers on a regular basis. The cash transfer is aimed at providing short-term assistance to families often in extreme poverty without the means to provide for adequate food consumption, while the conditionalities aim to promote longer term human capital investments, especially among the young" (Rawlings 2004, 1). The largest CCT in Latin America is Brazil's Bolsa Familia from President Lula da Silva's administration (2003–), built on the Bolsa Escola CCT from the Cardoso administration (1995–2002). The Honduran executive began the Programa de Asignación Familiar CCT (PRAF) in 1990 during the administration of Rafael Callejas (1990–94), which targets getting poor children into school and providing medical care for pregnant women and young children. Here I examine how presidents have been able to pursue these pro-poor programs given the incentives legislators have to represent poor people in each country's institutional milieu. Why an executive wants to pursue a pro-poor policy is exogenous to the present analysis, but reasons range from electoral strategy, to personal concerns of the president (as has been said about Lula's Fome Zero program), to pressure from international organizations to fight poverty. The focus here is on how legislators respond to executive initiatives, exploring implications based on the incentives that institutions create for legislators.

These CCT programs are associated with the executive. For example, Honduras's President Zelaya (PLH, 2006–9) took an active role in PRAF. When PRAF funds are disbursed there is often a community fair, and it is common for the president to attend and give a speech to the community. Local leaders may also speak and food staples are sold at low prices, and sometimes bags of beans are distributed (Moore 2008, 29). Brazilian municipalities originally developed CCTs in 1995, but in 2001 President Cardoso introduced the federal Bolsa Escola to replace the PGRM (Programa de Garantia de Renda Mínima, established in 1997 to provide federal financing to local-level CCTs) (De Janvry et al. 2005, 6; Lindert et al. 2007, 11–12). Lula brought Bolsa Escola into his broader Bolsa Familia program, which was originally directly linked to the office of the president but in January 2004 was moved to the new Ministry of Social Development (Hall 2006, 697). Yet even though these CCT programs are associated with the executive, in both countries the congress has had opportunities to become involved, and legislators have acted in ways that fit expectations of the theory of incentives to represent the poor. The Honduran Congress has consistently supported PRAF, making it possible for the program to continue and expand through several loan approvals and changes to supporting laws. The Brazilian Congress did not create obstacles to the Bolsas until 2007, when conservative senators used a supermajority requirement to suspend a primary source of funding for Lula's signature pro-poor program.

These CCT programs were developed and expanded with funds that were either already controlled by the executive branch or with new funds from international banks, so they did not appear to be redistributive. Also of import, neither program was paired with a hostility-causing restructuring of the education or health sectors, so they did not attract opposition from teachers or health provider unions. Honduras's PRAF is largely funded by loans from the Inter-American Development Bank and World Bank, though it also receives domestic funding that is particularly important for maintaining PRAF-I (Moore 2008, 1, 4). Brazil's Bolsas are funded by World Bank loans, a tax on bank transactions (Contribuição Provisória sobre Movimentação Financeira, CPMF) that already existed when Cardoso set up the federal Bolsa Escola,[10] and gains from efficiencies obtained when Lula combined several independent CCTs into the Bolsa Familia.

In Honduras, the Congress has approved several loans to fund PRAF. The Congress also had an opportunity to weigh in on an aspect of PRAF program design because PRAF-II required that supply-side funds, primarily to develop and train parent associations for schools, go from PRAF to NGOs to the parent associations.[11] PRAF-II encountered implementation problems because parent associations (Asociaciones de Padres de Familias, or APFs) had not been legally approved, so they could not receive the funds to develop and train parent associations for schools. According to Moore (2008, 15), "To solve this problem, PRAF-II personnel had to approach Congress to request either that the requirements on the NGOs, or that the restrictions on the APFs, be lifted. It proved easier for Congress to reduce the restrictions on the APFs than on the NGOs, so it passed a [law] making it legal for APFs to form and maintain a governing body, as well as to receive and use the money granted to them from the project." The Congress could have derailed the supply-side part of PRAF-II by not acting on the needed legislation. Instead, Congress passed a law reforming the rules so that funds could be dispersed to parent associations without going through NGOs. The Congress also played a role in formalizing PRAF, passing Law 135-92 in 1992 making the program of "indefinite duration" (ibid., 3).

Brazil's Congress had several opportunities to promote or hinder the Bolsas. The CPMF tax already existed before President Cardoso nationalized the Bolsa Escola CCT in 2001, as he had engineered its approval as part of his

10. The CPMF was earmarked exclusively for the Health Ministry (Power 1998, 70).
11. The reason for using NGOs was so that "the gains realized in the supply side could be preserved in spite of any changes in government administrations" (Moore 2008, 11).

policy agenda of neoliberal reforms (see Power 1998). The Congress reauthorized the tax in 2002, and its revenues were already known to be an important source of funds for government social programs. On January 9, 2004, Congress passed Law 10,836 approving Lula's Bolsa Familia, which had been set up by executive decree in late 2003. Initially there was clearly congressional support for the CCTs. In 2007, the CPMF tax again had to be reauthorized, but this time the Senate defeated the bill, creating a twenty-billion-dollar budget shortfall, since in 2007 the CPMF had paid for more than 80 percent of the Bolsa Familia program (Jungblut 2007; Clendenning 2007). Thus in 2007 conservative legislators checked the president's ability to pursue his policy preferences. Renewal of the tax required a two-thirds vote of approval in the Senate, so just a small coalition of senators could end a major source of funding for Lula's program. On December 12, 2007, the tax measure was defeated by a vote of forty-five to thirty-four, four votes shy of the forty-nine needed for renewal.

Why Has the Honduran Congress Supported PRAF?

Examination of PRAF implementation details indicates that the program works in a way that is valuable to the traditional parties.[12] PRAF has evolved through phases, beginning in 1990 with PRAF-I. It began as a "social safety net," and though PRAF-I included co-responsibilities, they were not enforced. From 1992 to 1997, PRAF-I reached an average of 233,000 people annually; a program expansion in 1998 allowed it to reach 318,000; and with further expansion, by 2005 PRAF-I reached 628,475 (about 10 percent of the population). PRAF-I includes a school voucher program and a maternal and child voucher. Later additions include funds for school supplies (1992), vouchers for senior citizens (1993), and a nutritional voucher for children (1998) (Moore 2008, 3–7). Communities that would receive PRAF-I funds were determined by identifying schools and health centers in areas with the highest malnutrition levels. The number of potential beneficiaries was capped, so the number of people who met program requirements could exceed the supply of vouchers.

---

12. PRAF is not the only social safety net program in Honduras. Food programs have existed since the 1950s. The other large safety net program—the FHIS—was created in 1990 with World Bank funds, and focuses on infrastructure development based on a workfare program. The program was intended to focus on the poorest parts of the country, but FHIS funds have been used in more populous areas, with activity typically channeled through private contractors and NGOs. The overall impact of FHIS "is still inconclusive, although its political power is well established" (Moore 2008, 3); thus traditional politicians and parties probably view the program favorably for its clientelistic value.

Teachers and employees at local health centers were supposed to decide which children came from the poorest households, but "anecdotal evidence suggests that the beneficiaries were often chosen based on political motivations rather than on the children's genuine needs" (Moore 2008, 5).[13]

In 1998, the Inter-American Development Bank funded PRAF-II to pilot a program that would serve as a guide for restructuring PRAF-I. PRAF-II was implemented in seventy rural municipalities and reached 60,000 households (109,649 beneficiaries) annually (approximately 1.7 percent of the population). PRAF-II is the real CCT in Honduras, because it tried to enforce the *conditional* part of the cash transfer. Yet beneficiary selection again is not transparent and enforcement of conditionality compliance has been lax. Therefore the program, while delivering benefits to poor people, has been targetable by the governing party to benefit party supporters. PRAF-II has components intended to increase the "demand" (number of children in school and use of health services) through distribution of stipends, and to improve "supply" with transfers of funds to health centers and primary schools. PRAF-II also included a Learning Development Initiative to strengthen parent organizations by helping them obtain legal status and financial transfers through local NGOs, which was the part of the program that required Congress to change a law to overcome the bottleneck in transferring funds to the parent associations (IFPRI 2000a, 3, 5; IFPRI 2000b, 6; IFPRI 2001, 5, 46, 50; Moore 2008, 7–9).

A new loan to finance PRAF-III was negotiated between the Zelaya government and the Inter-American Development Bank. PRAF-III operates within the framework of the Red Solidaria umbrella social protection program set up by President Zelaya, under the direction of the First Lady (Moore 2008, 16–17, 25).[14] PRAF-III has larger vouchers so that the transfers will represent "approximately 18–20 per cent of the expenditures of extremely poor rural families" instead of the much smaller size of the transfers under PRAF-II, making PRAF more like CCTs in Mexico and Brazil (ibid., 17). The PRAF-III loan will provide support for twenty thousand households, and the Honduran government will provide 10 percent of the funds for the program (ibid., 17–19).

13. "A survey conducted by CARE in 1996 found that 30 per cent of the beneficiaries of the School Voucher and 40 per cent of the beneficiaries of the Maternal and Child Voucher belonged to the richest two income quintiles of the population" (Moore 2008, 6).

14. Red Solidaria includes new benefits to poor people: a youth voucher (for fourteen-to-twenty-four-year-olds in the two major cities), DI-MUJER (Proyecto de Desarrollo Integral de la Mujer, for women aged eighteen to sixty, providing skills training and credit for micro-businesses), and a voucher program for the elderly (Moore 2008, 26–27).

PRAF-I began to adopt new practices, based on PRAF-II and PRAF-III, when the Zelaya government took office. While targeting regulations have been reformed in PRAF-I, there are still concerns about subjective components in the decision making about which villages are targeted, and program practitioners have mentioned political issues as well as supply-side considerations in the decision-making process. PRAF-I is now beginning to require that recipients comply with conditionalities, but at least in the first year of its implementation there was evidence that poor people were not aware that they now needed to meet such requirements to receive funds (ibid., 25, 28, 31–32).

External evaluations of PRAF indicate that it benefits very poor people, but the way the program has been implemented also allows the governing party to target benefits to its own poor supporters. The Congress has supported PRAF in all its phases because the program can be used for clientelism.[15] Formal and informal operating rules of the Congress allow the governing party to control what bills and amendments come up for votes as well as the vote outcome (see chapter 5). This makes it difficult for opposition deputies to oppose the executive branch using state resources for clientelistic activities. During the twenty years in which PRAF has existed, both traditional parties have benefited from its clientelistic aspects; for that reason, the traditional party that is out of power has an incentive to complain about political manipulation of funds, but lacks an incentive to change the way the program is implemented when it becomes the governing party. Deputies know that to oppose programs that give their party access to resources that can be used to reward party supporters would be disastrous for their political future, so this is not an issue that even deputies who adopt the Congress Advocate role would take on. In sum, while PRAF allows the president to reap the public credit for delivering services to poor people, PRAF also benefits the governing party and its deputies by providing resources with which to reward many poor clients. National administrative staff posts at PRAF are also used for patronage (Moore 2008).

The theory of incentives to represent the poor would predict that PRAF will continue to be supported by the governing party in Congress as long as

---

15. Both traditional parties have been incumbents and lost elections since PRAF began, indicating that PRAF is not able to buy election victories for the incumbent party. Yet both traditional parties have maintained the program because they value the clientelistic resources it provides. Structural adjustment reforms have decreased the state resources available to Honduras's traditional parties, so PRAF is a valuable resource for either party when in power. A review of Honduras's Poverty Reduction Strategy, which is part of its inclusion in the Heavily Indebted Poor Countries program, concludes that clientelism is "an obstacle to pro-poor growth" (Cuesta 2007, 334, also 353–54).

beneficiary selection methods continue to enable the governing party to target resources to party supporters. If international banks were able to force the Honduran government to change PRAF implementation so that it ceased to be a useful resource for distributing clientelistic benefits, deputy support for the program would likely diminish.

Why Did the Brazilian Congress Initially Support the Bolsas but Later Cut Funding to Lula's CCT?

When President Cardoso made the Bolsa Escola a national antipoverty program in 2001, it was funded with resources that were already available, so it fits what Weyland (2006) calls a policy add-on. Bolsa Escola did not spark strong opposition because it did not take funds away from existing programs that benefited groups with greater capacity than poor people to monitor or sanction elected officials (Hall 2006). The CPMF tax that provides significant funding for social programs was redistributive, since it taxed people in the middle and upper classes who have bank accounts, and most of the funds paid for health care benefits for poor people (Clendenning 2007). World Bank assessments argue that pro-poor programs such as the Bolsas were acceptable in Brazil (and by extension that it was acceptable to use CPMF funds for the program) because the nation has developed a sense that "people are poor due to the 'fault of an unjust society'" (Lindert et al. 2007, 9).[16]

Bolsa Escola was attractive to clientelistic politicians because the way it was implemented created opportunities for political patrons to help people become program beneficiaries. There were not enough stipends (*bolsas*) to cover all the children who qualified based on the means test, nor were there national standards for how people were to be signed up for the program, so some communities utilized enrollment methods (e.g., signing up for the program at the mayor's office) that would be easier for clients of specific politicians. Conditionalities were not enforced, so once enrolled a client was likely to continue to receive benefits (De Janvry et al. 2005, 11–13, 18, 23; Hall 2006). In Brazil, Congress members are responsible for their own election, many

---

16. In the World Values Survey (1995–97), "76% of Brazilians believe that the poor are poor because 'society is unjust' and that the poor 'have very little chance to escape from poverty' on their own" (Lindert et al. 2007, 9). The 1988 Constitution included social rights for the needy. In the 1990s, Senator Eduardo Suplicy (PT, São Paulo) got the Senate to approve a guarantee of a minimum income to all Brazilian adults, but it did not become law until 2004 (at the same time that the law creating Bolsa Familia was passed) (Lindert et al. 2007, 10, 14; Hall 2006, 703–4).

legislators want posts in state or local government, and the form of clientelism does not require a poor person to be part of a party-based clientele network, so many poor people can cheaply shop for a new patron if they are not satisfied with the services they receive. Thus, in Brazil's institutional setting, there was no reason for legislators from conservative parties to oppose Cardoso's program. Instead, they could benefit from it, since it provided a new resource for clientelistic benefits to poor people.

In October 2003, Lula merged Bolsa Escola with other transfer programs into his flagship Bolsa Familia antipoverty program. Some funding was already in place (the checking account tax, and savings from consolidating administration of several transfer programs), which was augmented by World Bank and Inter-American Development Bank loans, the economic growth Brazil began experiencing in 2004, and an initiative to get corporations to make contributions to the program. Thus, while Lula's Bolsa Familia was a massive expansion of pro-poor programs with the intent of reaching all 11.2 million families (approximately 46 million people) who met the program's income requirements, it still was largely an add-on program that could be run from within the executive branch. Bolsa Familia did not take funds away from larger social welfare programs, such as pensions, that primarily benefited the middle class (Flynn 2005; Hunter and Power 2005, 136; Lindert 2005, 67–69; Hall 2006, 692–95, 698; Lindert et al. 2007, 19, 112).[17]

At first Bolsa Familia was useful to traditional politicians because it still created opportunities for political patrons to help clients. The program utilized the beneficiary identification regimes from the old programs, and there were gaps in the implementation of conditionality compliance (Lindert 2005, 70; Hall 2006, 696–703, 706; Hunter and Power 2007, 18; Hunter 2007). While these conditions existed, members of the Congress could use Bolsa Familia to benefit their political careers. Bolsa Familia and its huge number of beneficiaries are also credited with salvaging Lula's reelection despite the corruption scandals swirling around his first administration.[18] Hunter and Power (2007,

---

17. Bolsa Familia has reduced the number of people living in extreme poverty, but a large percentage of the population is still poor and income inequality is still one of the most extreme in Latin America. Critics argue that CCTs tie poor people to dependence on the state and do not generate the jobs and permanent infrastructure changes that will end the structural causes of poverty (Skidmore 2004; Hall 2006).

18. Votes from poor people were also important to Lula because his government had pursued policies (particularly social security reform) that had angered the PT's traditional constituency among the middle class and government employees (Hunter and Power 2005, 131; 2007, 16; Flynn 2005; Hall 2006; Zucco 2007).

9, 12–13) show that poor voters were less likely than better-off groups to be aware of the scandals, and they were not likely to sanction a politician for corruption who had delivered material benefits, which Lula had done. In fact, the regions with large percentages of Bolsa Familia recipients went overwhelmingly for Lula. Zucco (2007, 10) explains that "in highly impoverished regions the economy depends so much on governmental actions that the cumulative effect of [a] large percentage of the population receiving direct cash handouts not only affects the overall perceptions of the economy, but creates a sense that the government cares."

Yet the aspects of Bolsa Familia that initially made it useful to a broad spectrum of politicians would end if Lula's program met its goals. Improved targeting and conditionality enforcement were "fundamental to strengthening the 'investment' role of the program for long-term poverty reduction" (Lindert 2005, 68).[19] World Bank loans rewarded the Bolsa Familia for its targeting and enforcement successes, because successive parts of the loan disbursements were contingent on reaching early project goals (Lindert 2005, 69). Success in tightening up targeting and strengthening enforcement of conditionalities could be argued to have ended the Bolsa's usefulness for conservative politicians.

Based on the theory of incentives to represent the poor, Brazilian legislators who did not have a policy preference for pro-poor legislation would turn against Lula's signature program when it ceased to be politically useful to them. With bureaucratic procedures and refinements in beneficiary targeting machinery for Bolsa Familia, traditional politicians may no longer have viewed the program as a source of clientelistic resources.[20] When middle-class Brazilians became vocal about their frustration with their tax burden, it became useful for conservative members of Congress to be able to claim that they are representing the interests of Brazilians when they work to cut taxes and force the government to use its budget resources more efficiently. As mentioned above, the checking account tax was set to expire in December 2007, which gave a blocking coalition in the Senate an opportunity to check the president by cutting off a major source of funds for his signature antipoverty program. CPMF opponents

19. See Lindert et al. (2007, 34–45, 62–70) for in-depth information about how Bolsa Familia targeting and compliance monitoring is carried out.

20. Local governments still identify potential participants, but the national bureaucracy handles approval for the program, with multiple checks of validity and accuracy of data for determining which families meet the program's qualifications (Lindert et al. 2007, 34–45). Some scholars argue that clientelism is abating in Brazil (see Lyne 2007), and the relatively small coalition of senators who joined forces to defeat renewal of the CPMF after Bolsa Familia had become needs based instead of a source of clientelism may lend support to that contention.

presented their votes as an effort to respond to middle-class interests in lower taxes, not as a strike against a program for the poor (Clendenning 2007; Jungblut 2007; Brazil house passes financial tax 2008; Renato Souza 2008). Lula responded by issuing a decree extending the Bolsa Familia to families with children up to seventeen years old, though it was not clear how he would pay for this expansion.[21]

Bolsa Familia shows that representation of the poor on a massive scale is possible in a Latin American democracy, but the way Lula's administration built from a policy add-on—rather than by passing laws for programmatic structural change that would have been more in keeping with the PT's platform—shows that representation of the poor is most politically feasible when it takes the form of clientelistic representation. Poor voters have consistently rewarded incumbents, regardless of their party, but this has been interpreted as due to incumbents' ability to "deliver the goods" rather than their policy initiatives (unless those policies have already borne fruit that is valued by poor voters) (Zucco 2007, 11). Structural reforms would have been unlikely to produce the electoral returns of the CCT. In the 2006 election, Lula's competitors pledged that they would continue Bolsa Familia, indicating that conservative politicians realized the program's vote potential and the political cost of undoing it (Hunter and Power 2007, 18, 24). Yet the Senate's actions in December 2007 indicate that the program is still vulnerable when it ceases to be of value as a clientelistic tool to politicians below the president, and when other social groups with greater monitoring ability, such as the middle class, demand policy change that makes funding uncertain.

These case studies illustrate that an executive can face challenges from legislators in implementing pro-poor programs even when the program is a policy add-on. They also show that an executive can obtain the legislature's support for a pro-poor program when it operates in ways that respond to the needs of legislators and parties for clientelistic resources.

Institutions and Incentives to Represent Poor People

To address the question of whether the poor count, I have examined the capacity of poor and rich people to monitor, the ability institutions give poor and

21. In June 2008, the Chamber of Deputies passed a bill essentially recreating the CPMF, but Senate passage was uncertain, and CPMF opponents said they would take the law to the Supreme Court (Renato Souza 2008).

rich people to sanction their elected officials, and how institutions constrain the preferences and strategies of politicians. Politicians are influenced by institutions in various ways: they shape the person to whom a legislator must appeal to build a political career, and they shape the identity, self-image, and preferences of legislators regarding their reasons for wanting a post in government and their goals in their job.

All else being equal, a rational career-seeking politician will represent people who can monitor the politician's actions and sanction when those actions are not close enough to their policy/service preferences. This strategy often indicates that legislators should represent rich people. The monitoring resources of the rich often make it possible for them to know if a politician is acting contrary to their interests within the halls of government, even in behind-closed-doors negotiations, while poor people generally lack access to information about what is going on within policy negotiations or debates.[22] Being aware of a representation gap is, however, only the first half of the problem for people, rich or poor, who want to hold their elected representatives accountable. To change the situation, they must have a cost-effective means to sanction. Institutions in a polity determine the capacity of poor *and* rich people to sanction elected officials. Some institutions make it difficult for either rich or poor people to punish politicians without overcoming an enormous collective action problem, but other institutions give all citizens, even poor ones, some capacity to sanction officials without paying a high personal cost. Table 8.1 summarizes when institutions give poor and rich people greater or lesser capacity to sanction, focusing on the cost (c) a person pays for attempting to sanction (even if the sanction is not successful) and on the number of participants who must sanction for a politician to be punished (n^*).

One macro-level observable implication of the theory is the relationship between how electoral rules, nomination procedures, and forms of clientelism empower poor people and how they evaluate their national legislature. Categorization of institutions in nine countries by whether they empower poor people, paired with World Values Survey and Latinobarómetro data assessing how poor people evaluate their congress, indicates that there is a relationship

---

22. In this project I focused on contrasting the monitoring and sanctioning capacity of poor versus rich people and how this affects the career strategy of politicians. The middle class could also be included in the theory as another actor. As explained in chapter 2, the middle class typically have greater monitoring capacity than poor people, they could have a distinct set of policy/service preferences, and they could form a coalition with rich or with poor people to pressure for the policies and services they desire.

Table 8.1 Sanctioning capability different institutions give poor and rich people

Institution	Sanctioning ability of:	
	Poor people	Rich people
Types of electoral rules		
SMD-P	*weak:* people can vote for or against incumbent, but many voters must sanction in the same election for incumbent to lose (n^* is large, c is small)	*weak:* people can vote for or against incumbent, but many voters must sanction in the same election for incumbent to lose (n^* is large, c is small) *moderate:* if person can make important campaign contributions ($n^* \rightarrow 1$)
Open-list PR	*weak:* people can vote for or against incumbent, but many voters must sanction in the same election for incumbent to lose (n^* is large, c is small)	*weak:* people can vote for or against incumbent, but many voters must sanction in the same election for incumbent to lose (n^* is large, c is small) moderate: if person can make important campaign contributions ($n^* \rightarrow 1$)
Closed-list PR	*very weak:* people must vote for entire party slate, sanction only affects politicians if party does so badly that even "safe" list slots do not win (n^* is very large, c is small)	*very weak:* people must vote for entire party slate, sanction only affects politicians if party does so badly that even "safe" list slots do not win (n^* is very large, c is small)
Types of nomination procedures		
Competitive primary	*weak:* people can vote for or against incumbent, but many voters must sanction in the same primary for incumbent to lose (n^* is large, c is small)	*weak:* people can vote for or against incumbent, but many voters must sanction in the same primary for incumbent to lose (n^* is large, c is small) *moderate:* if person can make important campaign contributions ($n^* \rightarrow 1$)
Party convention	*moderate:* if person can participate in the convention they can vote for or against incumbent and lobby others to do the same (n^* is relatively small, c is potentially large)	*moderate:* if person can participate in the convention they can vote for or against incumbent and lobby others to do the same (n^* is relatively small, c is potentially large)

| | Sanctioning ability of: | |
Institution	Poor people	Rich people
National party leaders select candidates	*very weak*: must influence party leaders to reward or sanction incumbent (n^* is very large)	*strong*: if person has resources to influence party leaders (campaign contributions; business, family, friendship connections) ($n^* \longrightarrow 1$)
Forms of clientelism		
Market of patrons	*strong*: people can search market for new patron if incumbent reneges on promised benefits (n^* is large, $c \longrightarrow 0$)	*strong*: if person can make valuable campaign contributions to incumbent or other potential patrons ($n^* \longrightarrow 1$)
Party-based clientele networks	*weak*: must switch parties to find new patron, and may need time to prove loyalty to new party before receiving patronage benefits *very weak*: if few parties have clientelism linkages to voters (n^* is large, c is large)	*strong*: if person can make valuable campaign contributions to party (or new party) for providing clientelistic benefits to voters ($n^* \longrightarrow 1$)
Any patron can obtain access to state resources	*strong*: person can switch patrons and diverse legislators will have access to state resources for patronage (n^* is large, $c \longrightarrow 0$)	*weak*: lowers threat of taking away campaign contributions because patron can make deals w/executive for state resources (n^* is large)
Only governing party has access to state resources	*weak*: if person switches patrons they must consider if the new patron's party will be in government (n^* is large, c is large)	*strong*: if patron's party is in opposition, campaign contributions are very valuable to politician ($n^* \longrightarrow 1$)

NOTE: (1) n^* is the number of participants required for the sanctioning effort to harm a politician. (2) c is the cost to the person of attempting to sanction.

between institutional context and how poor people view the representative branch of their government. In general, more people express confidence in their legislature in countries where institutions give poor people a greater capacity to sanction officials without having to pay a high personal price.

An in-depth study of Honduras explored how institutions interact to affect incentives for legislators to attend to poor people. Party-based clientelism is an established force in Honduras, creating incentives for elected officials to act as patrons to obtain access for their clients to scarce state resources. Long ago resource scarcity made clientelistic connections essential for individuals or communities to receive needed services, and this influenced both poor people's expectations as well as politicians' reasons for aspiring to a seat in Congress. Poor clients of traditional parties in Honduras remain loyal because doing so is the surest way to obtain clientelistic benefits the next time the party is in power. Closed-list elections and nominations controlled by national party leaders made it very difficult for poor people to sanction deputies who did not attend to their needs.[23] The Honduran president has not needed to form coalitions to pass legislation, so only deputies from the governing party have had access to state resources for clientelism, which limits clientele network options for poor people, thereby raising the cost to them of trying to sanction. Yet party alternation in power has given poor people an incentive to stick with their traditional party, in order to maximize their chances of receiving clientelistic benefits the next time their party wins.[24]

In Honduras, where representation has almost always taken the limited form of clientelistic benefits, traditional parties have been able to retain popular support by continuing to provide these limited benefits to their supporters when in control of the government. Poor people in Honduras would like greater attention from their politicians, but for a poor person it is not worth attempting to sanction one's party (to which one is connected via party-based clientele networks) because, based on historical experience, a poor person has no reason to think switching parties would secure more policy representation or even more clientelistic benefits. History has taught poor Hondurans to have low expectations, and traditional parties understand the electoral benefit of using scarce state resources to meet the expectations of their militants. Honduran deputies also are influenced by this history, and many adopt a Constituency Server role. As long as the community they want to help is known to back the deputy's party, or the deputy pursues local development in ways that are targetable to party supporters, the clientelistic representation provided by

23. When open-list primaries and general elections were adopted in 2005, voters used their new capacity to sanction and did not reelect some deputies with long careers in the Congress.

24. Clientelism in Honduras has much in common with the brokerage politics that Valenzuela (1977, 167) described in Chile before Augusto Pinochet. Valenzuela attributed the predominance of clientelistic-like networks in Chile's local political arena to structural features of the system: "the scarcity of resources, the centralization of the polity, and the presence of parties as networks to the center." Congress members in Chile responded to this situation by adopting a Constituency Server role, where much of their time was spent seeking out resources for towns, organizations, and individuals in their district (132–33).

these Constituency Server deputies is compatible with strong, vertically organized traditional parties controlled by national leaders that protect elite interests. This clientelistic representation also gives party supporters a reason to continue to back their party.

Brazil offered an interesting comparison with Honduras because open-list elections and a multiparty system enhance the sanctioning capacity of poor people (or lower the immediate cost to a poor person of sanctioning) and create incentives for legislators. As in Honduras, clientelism is an old institution in Brazilian politics, though the form of clientelism in Brazil is different, with more patron options for clients. Clientelism and poverty have shaped both poor people's expectations of representation and legislators' identities, making a patron image common in Brazilian politics. Particularly in the poor regions of the country, receipt of a small particularistic benefit has been valuable to enough poor voters for them to elect clientelistic politicians (Desposato 2001). The form of clientelism (i.e., a competitive market of patrons instead of two party-based clientele networks) and open-list elections reinforce incentives for legislators to provide clientelistic representation, at least at the minimal level necessary to retain the electoral support of poor voters, otherwise legislators risk losing in intensely competitive elections.[25] Clientelism helped Lula to implement his Bolsa Familia antipoverty initiative, creating a reason for legislators to support the program initially, and it gave Lula the popular support to win his reelection bid. By fulfilling (or exceeding) poor people's expectations for clientelistic representation, Lula won massive electoral support from poor people, and the strategy of a CCT program meant he avoided the risk of not delivering in time for the election (which would have been a danger of pursuing a programmatic legislative route for his reforms). As targeting for Bolsa Familia has become more efficient and bureaucratic, however, the program is no longer a good source for clientelism resources for politicians, and in December 2007 enough conservative senators were able to vote as a block to suspend a major source of program funding.

In sum, some combinations of institutions give politicians incentives to represent poor people. But the limited capacity of poor people to monitor *policy* activity by their elected officials, especially when paired with negative past experiences with politicians making policy promises and not delivering,

---

25. Competition is intense in open-list elections because you must run against candidates from other parties *and* co-partisans, and it is not feasible to compete against co-partisans on the basis of party ideology or platform (Carey and Shugart 1995).

is likely to prompt poor people to place greater value on personalistic benefits and local development projects that they can easily monitor. This means that when institutions give politicians an incentive to represent poor people, it is more likely to take the form of clientelistic representation than programmatic policy. As a Honduran deputy who adopted the Congress Advocate role explained, a poor person cannot eat a bill.[26] Unless a politician has another way to safeguard their political future (e.g., campaign contributions to their party so they will receive a safe position on the party's list, or nomination by a party such as Brazil's PT that values programmatic policy), an ambitious politician must deliver concrete benefits to poor voters if they have the capacity to deny the legislator a political future. If it is personally very costly for a poor person to attempt to sanction a legislator who does not attend to their needs, even a clientelism institution with a lengthy historical base will not prompt all legislators to adopt a patron or local development agent role. If too few politicians have incentives to represent poor people even with clientelistic representation, a crisis of representation can result.

Implications for Democratic Consolidation

What are the implications for democratic consolidation of the observation that elected representatives in some institutional settings have an incentive to provide clientelistic but not policy representation for poor people, and that some institutional settings do not even provide a strong incentive for clientelistic representation? If policy representation is a necessary condition for poor people to become vested in democracy, the prognosis is not good. The electoral rules, nomination procedures, and forms of clientelism that are common in Latin American countries do not give legislators an incentive to represent *policy* interests of poor people as a strategy to build a political career.[27] If the policies poor people want threaten the rich or the macroeconomic

---

26. Interestingly, Valenzuela (1977, 133) encountered the same response from some of the Chilean congress members he interviewed in the late 1960s.

27. Professionalization alone should not change this incentive structure to provide clientelistic representation to poor people, because professional legislators will want to be reelected, and therefore they must make strategic choices to get themselves renominated to a safe spot on their party's list or to get enough personal votes to be reelected. Unless party leaders or sufficient numbers of voters start rewarding policy work over short-term, concrete clientelistic representation, more professional legislators will still face an incentive to provide clientelistic representation because it is less risky for their career (see Desposato 2005).

situation of the state, rich people can be expected to work to keep such reform off the policy agenda. If elected representatives do not have incentives to represent the poor, however, poor people can become frustrated with legislators, the legislature, dominant parties, or even democracy itself. If people perceive that they are not receiving sufficient representation, they start to think that the legislature and legislators' salaries are a waste of money. Their frustration could lead them to reject established parties, as occurred in Venezuela. Popular unrest, even if it does not lead to democratic breakdown, creates uncertainty and deters economic investment, thereby exacerbating the challenges of addressing the policy and service preferences of all types of citizens.

Yet some combinations of institutions do create incentives for clientelistic representation. Although clientelism can make changing national policy more difficult (Geddes 1994; Weyland 1996; Mainwaring 1999), clientelistic representation may prompt the poor people who received clientelistic benefits to give a positive answer to the question "What has government done for me lately?" It can also give poor people who expect to receive clientelistic benefits the next time their party is in power a reason to continue to support established parties. The cost of sanctioning established, dominant parties is high for a person who values clientelistic benefits if that person is likely to forfeit clientelistic benefits by attempting to sanction. An individual who might be willing to forfeit clientelistic benefits to try to change the system should consider whether enough other people are likely to attempt a sanction so that it will be successful, since punishing an elected official or a party requires collective action. If many poor people receive clientelistic benefits, or expect to if their party wins the next election, it is unlikely that they will sanction. This means that consistent clientelistic representation, which is the most feasible type of representation for poor people to monitor, reduces the likelihood of sanctions by poor people. The democratic regime may not deepen, but it will not destabilize. Clientelistic representation may be one explanation for the persistence of what scholars have called "frozen" democracies in Latin America—democracies that do not fall, but that also do not make progress toward consolidation.

The incentives that some institutional environments create for clientelistic representation could make clientelism an accommodating informal institution. Such institutions "may enhance the stability of formal institutions by dampening demands for change" (Helmke and Levitsky 2004, 729). This is particularly worth considering if the alternative to clientelistic representation is no representation at all for poor people—as happened in Venezuela when oil revenues shrank and AD and COPEI used scarce state resources to try to shore up their support from other sectors of society (Karl 1986, 219; Myers 2000, 283; Roberts 2003, 51; Canache 2004).

Scholars often decry clientelism as a source of many of Latin America's problems (e.g., Hagopian 1992, 248; O'Donnell 1996; Weyland 1996; Diamond 1997; Mainwaring 1999; Dominguez 2003, 378). Yet this study suggests that a *lack* of clientelistic benefits for poor people may be dangerous as well. Clientelism can be a barrier to making policy to provide universalistic benefits and social services, because politicians benefit more from being able to dole out benefits to individuals in exchange for votes than they would from working for reform—though the brief analysis of why the Honduran and Brazilian Congresses supported CCT programs indicates that clientelism can facilitate some sorts of pro-poor policies. But removing clientelism does not guarantee that government will provide universalistic benefits (Kitschelt 2000). Career-seeking politicians may still represent the policy interests of rich people because they are more likely than poor people to sanction. Further, government may lack the *resources* to provide universalistic benefits—witness the cuts in welfare benefits during neoliberal economic restructuring, even in the world's most developed economies.

If democratic government does not provide universalistic policy to benefit poor people (whether due to lack of resources or lack of political will), and poor people do not receive personalistic benefits or local development projects, what reason do poor people have to support democracy? Many hoped that democracy in Latin America would bring justice for victims of human rights violations, increased civil liberties, and widespread economic prosperity (Hagopian 2005). Poor people were even willing to accept harsh restructuring policies to turn around the economic crises left by authoritarian regimes (Stokes 1999). But high hopes and willingness to sacrifice are unlikely to last unless democracy delivers on at least some of poor people's expectations. "Justice" was certainly harsh during authoritarian regimes, but justice is not applied equally to people of all socioeconomic strata in democratic regimes either. Without benefits (universalistic policy or clientelistic perks), safety, or justice, poor people cannot be expected to give a positive answer to the question "What has government done for me lately?"

Clientelistic representation does not meet democratic ideals about representative democracy and accountability. If poor people receive clientelistic representation, they are likely to remain cynical about democracy because it does not make structural changes to improve opportunities for the poor. Even Lula's Bolsa Familia, which has reduced the number of people living in extreme poverty, is criticized for not addressing the causes of poverty. According to Mainwaring (1999, 208), "Patronage can win votes, and trading favors can win political support, but clientelism does not create legitimacy." Brazil is a case where several institutions give politicians an incentive to provide clientelistic representation, but more than half of poor people said they had little confidence in Congress, which indicates that clientelistic representation is not good enough to produce a truly positive assessment of the representative branch of government. But clientelistic representation can be stabilizing if *many* poor people receive clientelistic benefits or expect to receive them the next time their party is in power. If the number of beneficiaries is small or shrinking, if benefits are decreasing, or if poor people who are not currently receiving clientelistic benefits do not expect that their fortunes will change with the next election, they will lose nothing if they attempt to sanction. This could be viewed as a variation on Lyne's (2007) "voter's dilemma." Poor people no longer vote based on a clientelistic benefit they perceive as valuable, not because they do not *value* clientelistic benefits, but because they are *not receiving* any (and do not expect to in the future). Poor people may still pay a cost for participating in a strike or protest (e.g., arrest or police brutality), but they will not lose personal benefits if they attempt to sanction their elected officials.

Do the poor count in Latin American democracies? It appears the answer is a qualified "no." If institutions give elected officials any incentive to represent poor people, it is most likely to take the form of clientelistic representation, not policy representation. Personalistic benefits and local development projects do not fulfill most concepts of "representation." But the electoral rules, nomination procedures, and forms of clientelism typically found in Latin American democracies make it a risky strategy for a career-seeking legislator to try to represent the national policy preferences of poor people—just trying will not be sufficient, and in fact may be punished. Scholars point to the poverty in Latin America as a reason to question "the real existence of citizenship rights" (Vilas 1997, 21). This study indicates that it is not poverty itself that negates citizenship rights (though poverty makes monitoring policy difficult). Rather, it is poverty in combination with institutions that make it more difficult for poor people than elites to sanction elected officials, and that constrain the viable strategies of politicians in ways that punish them for trying to represent poor people that create a representation deficit for the poor.

Appendix

CODING INFORMAL ROLES

Methodology for Uncovering Informal Roles or Identities

To determine deputy preference roles, I used Searing's (1994, appendix B) methodology. Information gained from elite interviews needed to be turned into empirically comparable indicators of deputy preferences, from which systematic evidence of different deputy roles could be lifted. As Searing (1994, 411–12) explains, these roles "are not Weberian ideal types that deliberately distort experience for theoretical purposes. Yet they are not photographic representations either. The [three] principal backbench roles are instead 'extracted types' constructed from the transcribed language and concepts of the role players themselves." To determine the roles that exist in the Honduran Congress, I had to uncover the motivational cores of those roles as expressed by the deputies themselves in the interviews and surveys.

Each deputy was asked three questions, taken from Searing (1994):

(1) Thinking broadly about your role as a deputy, what are the most important duties and responsibilities involved?
(2) Thinking for a moment very broadly about Honduran society, how important is your work as a deputy to the functioning of society as a whole?
(3) Thinking about your political activity, what do you personally find most satisfying about it? What would you miss most if you left politics?

I looked for major patterns to the responses, and identified three backbench roles: Congress Advocate, Party Deputy, and Constituency Server. I did not enter this project with the intent of finding three roles; rather, it was while conducting the interviews that I noticed a few "types" of deputies. The Constituency

Server role was most obvious, as many of these deputies referred to themselves as "Rangers" and contrasted their view of a deputy's job, which focuses
on constituency service, with the Constitution's, which says that the job of
deputies is to legislate. The Congress Advocate role also stood out, as some
deputies wanted to strengthen the Congress's ability to legislate, and viewed
constituency service as a drain on their time. These two role types were
clearly aware of each other, and indicated a cleavage in the Congress. A third
type of deputy stood out because of their interest in working for their party
and party leaders, rather than for their district or voters in general.

Once all the interviews were complete and after repeated readings of the
interviews and surveys, I identified a short list of motivational themes for
each type.

Congress Advocate Themes

Improve the quality of legislation (better researched and organized)
Decrease the partisan aspect of government (make deputies more independent of party leaders, and the legislature more independent of the executive)
Strengthen democracy (improve checks and balances and electoral rules,
reduce corruption)
Deputies need to be well trained (educated, expert in legislating, not just
interested in immunity)
Desire to build expertise in specific policy areas
Emphasis on legislating to help the people of the country, rather than
focusing on providing development projects for a department or services
for individuals

Party Deputy Themes

Build the party (or faction) and work in campaigns
Political oversight (checking the executive for *political* reasons)
Belief that the job of the deputy is to legislate (be responsible in attending
congressional sessions, follow directions from party leaders)
Represent your party, or your faction
Being a deputy is desirable because it gives you influence in government
Service to the people, but with no mention of concrete works of service
Acceptance that you will not be able to do much if your party is in the
opposition

Constituency Server Themes

Stay in contact with your department, do not move to the capital and
lose touch

Deliver development project to your community

Help individuals with problems

Resolve collective problems in your district

Influence government policy to help the people

Complaints that if your party (or faction) is out of power you cannot do
much to help your district

Based on the instances of each type of motivational theme in their answer, each deputy was given a score for each role question for the three deputy types, producing nine scores for each deputy, ranging from zero to three. A question was scored zero for a role type if the deputy made no mention of any of the motivational themes of that role type. A score of one meant that a motivational theme was mentioned but it was not central to the answer. If a motivational theme was central to the deputy's answer, it was scored two. If the motivational theme was central to the answer, and the deputy provided an example to illustrate their discussion, the question was scored three on that role type.[1] The three scores across the three role questions for a particular type were summed to produce a composite score for each role type, ranging from zero to nine. Deputies were assigned to the role for which they received the highest composite score, which produced the empirical typology of deputy roles in the Honduran Congress.[2]

I agree with Searing (1994, 415) that differences in behavior across roles serve as evidence of the validity of the different roles, and chapter 7 shows many

1. Searing distinguishes between cases where a motivational theme was central to an answer and where the MP also provided an example, because "backbenchers who seemed to care most about a theme not only made it central to their discussions but also reinforced it with striking examples" (1994, 485n10). I adopted the same scoring scheme because this distinction also applied for deputies in Honduras.

2. For eight deputies (11.3 percent of study participants), no role assignment was possible. Five deputies received the same composite score for two or more roles, and the factor analysis yielded very low or negative scores for the deputy on all three roles. Two deputies' composite scores on all three roles were low and very similar, and the factor analysis yielded negative scores on all three roles. For one deputy no role assignment was possible because of missing information. These cases are presented in tables throughout the book in a column labeled "no role." Searing (1994) was unable to make role assignments for 11.5 percent of the British MPs who took part in his study. Cornbach's alpha reliability coefficients for the three composite scores are as follows: Congress Advocate $\alpha = 0.81$, Constituency Server $\alpha = 0.79$, Party Deputy $\alpha = 0.71$.

behavior differences. That the deputies themselves are aware of these roles, and speak of themselves as Rangers or as representatives who buck the historical pattern because they are concerned with legislating, is further evidence of different roles or identities. In addition to these informal kinds of evidence of the validity of the roles, factor analysis of the deputies' scores on the three motivational themes for the three role questions also indicates the existence of three distinct factors.

The factor analysis indicates that the three roles created by the additive indices structure the original data (see table A.1). First, I performed a maximum-likelihood factoring analysis to test hypotheses about the number of factors that were optimal for this data. The maximum-likelihood factoring test indicated that a three-factor model significantly improves on a no-factor model (x^2 [27] = 297.91, p = 0.0000), but that a three-factor model is *not* significantly worse than a perfect-fit model (x^2 [12] = 8.75, p = 0.7239). Thus I retained three factors from principal factoring analysis with a varimax rotation.[3]

The factor analysis shows that the factors correspond to the three general roles constructed with the additive indices. The sets of three questions/scores used to produce the composite scores for the deputies cluster together to define the three different factors/roles. With few exceptions, they also load negatively on the other factors. Factor 1 represents the Party Deputy dimension. The three Party Deputy themes dominate this factor, and it produces no other notable positive loadings. It produces some notable negative loadings for the Constituency Server themes, however, and chapter 6 shows that lack of interest in constituents is a trait of the Party Deputy. Factor 2 is dominated by the Congress Advocate themes, and produces no other positive loadings, though it indicates a fairly strong negative association with Party Deputy themes. This is consistent with the motivational theme of this role of decreasing the partisan nature of government. The Constituency Server themes dominate Factor 3,

---

3. The analysis was conducted with Stata 7.0. The eigenvalue for factor 1 was 2.97, factor 2 had an eigenvalue of 2.44, and factor 3's eigenvalue was 0.54. (See below for explanation of which factors correspond to which roles.) While it is common in factor analysis to retain factors with eigenvalues greater than one, doing so only detected the Congress Advocate and Party Deputy factors/roles. Since the maximum-likelihood factoring analysis indicated that three factors created a better fit for the data than just two, and since "constituency service" motivational themes clustered on the third factor, I retained the first three factors. Other types of factor analysis (e.g., oblique rotation, principal components) produced factors for the Congress Advocate and Party Deputy roles. The Constituency Server role was, however, a weaker and less consistent factor. This is due to the heterogeneity of the deputies who adopt that role, as is discussed below and in chapter 6, and resembles the challenges Searing encountered with the Parliament Man role, as that category was heterogeneous and the subtypes of Parliament Men quite distinct (1994, 487n22).

Table A.1 Factor analysis of indicators used to produce composite scores for deputy roles

Indicators	Factor 1	Factor 2	Factor 3
Congress Advocate			
Question 1	0.046	0.858	0.028
Question 2	0.197	0.799	−0.116
Question 3	0.044	0.649	−0.351
Constituency Server			
Question 1	−0.492	−0.431	0.308
Question 2	−0.825	−0.281	0.369
Question 3	−0.261	−0.098	0.948
Party Deputy			
Question 1	0.495	−0.504	−0.258
Question 2	0.584	−0.323	−0.186
Question 3	0.311	−0.420	−0.519
Percent variance explained	46	38	8

	Interfactor Correlations		
Factor	Factor 1	Factor 2	Factor 3
1	1.000	—	—
2	0.029	1.000	—
3	−0.056	−0.007	1.000

NOTE: Principal factoring analysis using a varimax rotation, based on data from all seventy-one deputies who participated in this study.

and it produces no other notable loadings. Interfactor correlations are low, consistent with the hypothesis that the roles are distinct.

Note About the Number of Deputies Who Participated in This Study

Searing's (1994) landmark study of MP roles in the British Parliament set a high standard for research about political elites. Searing and his research team interviewed 338 backbench MPs, and asked them to answer a survey. This study of deputy roles in the Honduran Congress includes a smaller percentage of the chamber's members, and there are several reasons for this lower rate of participation. One is the difficulty of making contact with Honduran deputies, since they do not have offices in the Congress or in their district. A second difficulty is some deputies' lack of trust of foreigners snooping around in the Congress. While I followed the standard academic research protocol of explaining the nature of my study when seeking to set up an interview, it was difficult for some deputies to accept my story. When they asked how it was possible for me to be doing this research, I explained that I had a grant from my university to fund the project. This did not seem plausible to many deputies, because Honduran academics do not have access to such research funds, and most hold multiple jobs simply to pay their living expenses.

That the participation rate in this study is lower than that of Searing's study does not invalidate the findings. It is possible that the deputies who avoided interviews would exhibit a fourth role type, as might deputies who rarely attend the Congress. I expect, however, that many of those deputies would fit the Party Deputy role. They are the deputies who are least interested in constituency outreach and who tended to have gotten their seat because of their close relationship with a party leader, rather than by building a record of party activism in their department. Thus they are the type of deputies who would tend to view talking to a visiting researcher as "not part of their job" (attending to the needs of constituents is not a major part of their job either). The participation rate of deputies in this study is similar to or higher than participation rates other scholars have obtained, as displayed in the following list of projects.

Casework in the Israeli Knesset (Uslaner 1985)—interviews with 21 of 120 MKs

Constituent orientation in Malaysian state legislatures (Kumbhat and Marican 1976)—questionnaires returned by 92 of 301 backbenchers

Personal vote seeking by members of the British Parliament (Cain, Ferejohn, and Fiorina 1984)—interviews with MPs or party agents in 101 of 133 constituencies included in their sample

Role orientations in English local councils (Newton 1974)—interviews with 66 of 156 members of the Birmingham County Borough Council

Study of representation by Venezuelan legislators (Kulisheck 1998)—interviews with 65 deputies (31.4 percent of Chamber)[4]

Study of representation by legislators in Argentina, Brazil, and Chile in 1997, 1998, and 1999–2001 (Hagopian 2001)—survey with 31 percent response in Argentina and Chile, surveys and interviews with 25 percent response in Brazil

4. Kulisheck (1998, 12n3) writes, "The N reported here is comparable to other research on legislative behavior: Bianco (1994) examines constituent-legislator trust in the United States using a sample of 37.3 percent of the House of Representatives. Lancaster and Patterson (1990) analyze representation in the West German Bundestag using responses from 37.1 percent of the MPs. As parts of the Parliamentary Elites of Latin America (PELA) project, Ramos (1997) relies on a sample of 31.9 percent of the Venezuelan Chamber of Deputies and while Kenney (1996) uses a sample of 72.5 percent of the Peruvian Congress, he interviewed a total of eighty-seven legislators."

References

Abstencionismo electoral, tercera fuerza en el país. 2005. *La Prensa*, December 11.

Acker, Alison. 1988. *Honduras: The making of a banana republic.* Boston: South End Press.

Agosto, Gabriela, and Francisco Cuelo Villamán. 2001. República Dominicana. In *Partidos políticos de América Latina: Centroamérica, México, y República Dominicana,* ed. Manuel Alcántara Sáez and Flavia Freidenberg, 615–98. Salamanca, Spain: Ediciones Universidad Salamanca.

Ajenjo Fresno, Natalia. 2001. Honduras. In *Partidos políticos de América Latina: Centro-américa, México, y República Dominicana,* ed. Manuel Alcántara Sáez and Flavia Freidenberg, 179–273. Salamanca, Spain: Ediciones Universidad Salamanca.

———. 2007. Honduras: Nuevo gobierno liberal con la misma agenda política. Special issue, *Revista de Ciencia Política* 27:165–81.

Altman, David, and Rossana Castiglioni. 2006. The 2004 Uruguayan elections: A political earthquake foretold. *Electoral Studies* 25 (1): 147–54.

Álvaro, Miriam. 2007. La parapolítica: La infiltración paramilitar en la clase política Colombiana. Paper presented at the Fifth European Congress of Latinamericanists, CEISAL, April 11–14, in Brussels, Belgium.

Amaya Banegas, Jorge Alberto. 1997. *Los árabes y palestinos en Honduras.* Tegucigalpa, Honduras: Editorial Guaymuras.

———. 2000. *Los judíos en Honduras.* Tegucigalpa, Honduras: Editorial Guaymuras.

Ames, Barry. 1994. The reverse coattails effect: Local party organization in the 1989 Brazilian presidential election. *American Political Science Review* 88 (1): 95–111.

———. 1995. Electoral strategy under open-list proportional representation. *American Journal of Political Science* 39 (2): 406–33.

———. 2001. *The deadlock of democracy in Brazil.* Ann Arbor: University of Michigan Press.

Amorim Neto, Octavio. 1998. Cabinet formation in presidential regimes: An analysis of ten Latin American countries. Paper presented at the Latin American Studies Association conference, September 24–26, in Chicago, Ill.

Angell, Alan, and Carol Graham. 1995. Can social sector reform make adjustment sustainable and equitable? Lessons from Chile and Venezuela. *Journal of Latin American Studies* 27 (1): 189–219.

Aoki, Aya, Barbara Bruns, Michael Drabble, Mmantsetsa Marope, Alain Mingat, Peter Moock, Patrick Murphy, Pierella Paci, Harry Patrinos, Jee-Peng Tan, Christopher Thomas, Carolyn Winter, and Hongyu Yang. 2002. Education. In *Sourcebook for poverty reduction strategies,* ed. Jeni Klugman, 231–75. Washington, D.C.: World Bank.

Arancibia Córdova, Juan. 1991. *Honduras: Un estado nacional?* 2nd ed. Tegucigalpa, Honduras: Editorial Guaymuras.

Archer, Ronald. 1990. The transition from traditional to broker clientelism in Colombia: Political stability and social unrest. Working Paper 140, Kellogg Institute for International Studies, University of Notre Dame.

Argueta, Mario. 1989. *Tiburcio Carías: Anatomía de una época, 1923–1948.* Tegucigalpa, Honduras: Editorial Guaymuras.

Arretche, Marta. 2004. Toward a unified and more equitable system: Health reform in Brazil. In *Crucial needs, weak incentives: Social sector reform, democratization, and globalization in Latin America,* ed. Robert R. Kaufman and Joan M. Nelson, 155–88. Baltimore: Johns Hopkins University Press.

Auyero, Javier. 2006. *Poor people's politics: Peronist survival networks and the legacy of Evita.* Durham: Duke University Press.

Avelino, George, David S. Brown, and Wendy Hunter. 2005. The effects of capital mobility, trade openness, and democracy on social spending in Latin America, 1980–1999. *American Journal of Political Science* 49 (3): 625–41.

Bachrach, Peter, and Morton S. Baratz. 1970. *Power and poverty: Theory and practice.* New York: Oxford University Press.

Barro, Robert J. 1973. The control of politicians: An economic model. *Public Choice* 14 (1): 19–42.

Becker, David G. 1988. Democracy and civil society in Peru and Venezuela. Paper presented at the Latin American Studies Association, March 17–19, in New Orleans, La.

Bendel, Petra. 1993. Honduras. In *Encyclopedia electoral Latinoamericana y del Caribe,* ed. Dieter Nohlen, 393–411. San José, Costa Rica: Instituto Interamericano de Derechos Humanos.

Bendor, Jonathan, and Adam Meirowitz. 2004. Spatial models of delegation. *American Political Science Review* 98 (2): 293–310.

Bethell, Leslie. 1991. From the Second World War to the cold war, 1944–1954. In *Exporting democracy: The United States and Latin America,* ed. Abraham F. Lowenthal, 41–70. Baltimore: Johns Hopkins University Press.

Bianco, William T. 1994. *Trust: Representation and constituents.* Ann Arbor: University of Michigan Press.

Binns, Jack R. 2000. *The United States in Honduras, 1980–1981: An ambassador's memoir.* Jefferson, N.C.: McFarland and Company.

Boix, Charles. 1999. Setting the rules of the game: The choice of electoral systems in advanced democracies. *American Political Science Review* 93 (3): 609–25.

Bollen, K. A. 1990. Political democracy: Conceptual and measurement traps. *Studies in Comparative International Development* 25 (1): 7–24.

Booth, John A., and Amber Aubone. 2007. Las elecciones del 2005 y la participación electoral en Honduras en perspectiva regional comparada. Paper presented at the Reunión Internacional sobre los Procesos Electorales en América Latina, May 29–30, in Madrid, Spain.

Bowman, Kirk. 2002. *Militarization, democracy, and development: The perils of praetorianism in Latin America.* University Park: Pennsylvania State University Press.

Bowman, Kirk, Fabrice Lehoucq, and James Mahoney. 2005. Measuring political democracy: Case expertise, data adequacy, and Central America. *Comparative Political Studies* 38 (8): 939–70.

Bratton, Michael, Yun-Han Chu, and Marta Lagos. 2006. Who votes: Implications for new democracies. Working Paper 1, Global Barometer, Santiago, Chile.

Brazil house passes financial tax. 2008. Associated Press, June 12.

Brockett, Charles D. 1988. *Land, power, and poverty: Agrarian transformation and political conflict in Central America.* Boston: Unwin Hyman.

Brown, David J., Christopher Brown, and Scott W. Desposato. 2002. Left turn on green? The unintended consequences of international funding for sustainable development in Brazil. *Comparative Political Studies* 35 (7): 814–38.

Brown, David, and Wendy Hunter. 2004. Democracy and human capital formation. *Comparative Political Studies* 37 (7): 842–64.

Brusco, Valeria, Marcelo Nazareno, and Susan C. Stokes. 2004. Vote buying in Argentina. *Latin American Research Review* 39 (2): 66–88.

Burton, Michael, Richard Gunther, and John Higley. 1992. Introduction: Elite transformations and democratic regimes. In *Elites and democratic consolidation in Latin America and southern Europe,* ed. John Higley and Richard Gunther, 1–37. Cambridge: Cambridge University Press.

Cain, Bruce E., John Ferejohn, and Morris Fiorina. 1984. The constituency service basis of the personal vote for U.S. representatives and British members of Parliament. *American Political Science Review* 78 (1): 110–25.

———. 1987. *The personal vote: Constituency service and electoral independence.* Cambridge: Harvard University Press.

Calvo, Ernesto. 2007. The responsive legislature: Public opinion and law making in a highly disciplined legislature. *British Journal of Political Science* 37 (2): 263–80.

Calvo, Ernesto, and Maria Victoria Murillo. 2004. Who delivers? Partisan clients in the Argentine electoral market. *American Journal of Political Science* 48 (4): 742–57.

Canache, Damarys. 2004. Urban poor and political order. In *The unraveling of representative democracy in Venezuela,* ed. Jennifer L. McCoy and David J. Myers, 33–49. Baltimore: Johns Hopkins University Press.

Carey, John M. 1996. *Term limits and legislative representation.* Cambridge: Cambridge University Press.

———. 2000. Parchment, equilibria, and institutions. *Comparative Political Studies* 33 (6–7): 735–61.

Carey, John M., and Andrew Reynolds. 2007. Parties and accountable government in new democracies. *Party Politics* 13 (2): 255–74.

Carey, John M., and Matthew Soberg Shugart. 1995. Incentives to cultivate a personal vote: A rank ordering of electoral formulas. *Electoral Studies* 14 (4): 417–39.

Carlin, Ryan E. 2006. The socioeconomic roots of support for democracy and the quality of democracy in Latin America. *Revista de Ciencia Política* 26 (1): 48–66.

Casper, Gretchen, and Michelle M. Taylor. 1996. *Negotiating democracy: Transitions from authoritarian rule.* Pittsburgh: University of Pittsburgh Press.

CEPAL (Comisión Económica para América Latina y el Caribe). 1992. *El perfil de la pobreza a comienzos de los años 90.* Santiago, Chile: CEPAL.

Chandra, Kanchan. 2004. *Why ethnic parties succeed: Patronage and ethnic head counts in India.* New York: Cambridge University Press.

———. 2007. Counting heads: A theory of voter and elite behavior in patronage democracies. In *Patrons, clients, and policies: Patterns of democratic accountability and political competition,* ed. Herbert Kitschelt and Steven I. Wilkinson, 84–109. New York: Cambridge University Press.

Cleary, Matthew R., and Susan C. Stokes. 2006. *Democracy and the culture of skepticism: Political trust in Argentina and Mexico*. New York: Russell Sage Foundation.

Clendenning, Alan. 2007. Brazil financial tax rejected, handing Silva big political defeat. *International Herald Tribune*, December 13.

Cohen, Ernesto, Rolando Franco, and Pablo Villatoro. 2006. Honduras: El programa de asignación familiar. In *Transferencias con corresponsabilidades: Una mirada Latinoamericana,* ed. Ernesto Cohen and Rolando Franco, 283–320. Mexico City: SEDESOL/FLASCO.

Collier, David, and Steven Levitsky. 1997. Democracy with adjectives: Conceptual innovation in comparative research. *World Politics* 49 (3): 430–51.

Collier, Ruth Berins, and David Collier. 1991. *Shaping the political arena*. Princeton: Princeton University Press.

Collier, Ruth Berins, and Samuel P. Handlin. 2005. Shifting interest regimes of the working classes in Latin America. Working Paper 122-05, Institute of Industrial Relations, University of California, Berkeley.

Colomer, Josep M. 2004. *Handbook of electoral system choice*. London: Palgrave Macmillan.

Conaghan, Catherine M. 1996. A deficit of democratic authenticity: Political linkage and the public in Andean politics. *Studies in Comparative International Development* 31 (3): 32–55.

———. 2001. Making and unmaking authoritarian Peru: Re-election, resistance, and regime transition. Agenda Paper 47, North-South Center, University of Miami.

Coppedge, Michael. 1993. Parties and society in Mexico and Venezuela: Why competition matters. *Comparative Politics* 25 (3): 253–74.

———. 1994. *Strong parties and lame ducks: Presidential partyarchy and factionalism in Venezuela*. Stanford: Stanford University Press.

Corona, Tania. 2005. A seis grados centígrados votaron en Intibucá. *La Prensa,* November 28.

Cox, Gary W. 1997. *Making votes count: Strategic coordination in the world's electoral systems*. Cambridge: Cambridge University Press.

Cox, Gary W., and Scott Morgenstern. 2002. Epilogue: Latin America's reactive assemblies and proactive presidents. In *Legislative politics in Latin America,* ed. Scott Morgenstern and Benito Nacif, 446–68. Cambridge: Cambridge University Press.

Crisp, Brian F. 1997. Presidential behavior in a system with strong parties: Venezuela, 1958–1995. In *Presidentialism and democracy in Latin America,* ed. Scott Mainwaring and Matthew Soberg Shugart, 160–98. New York: Cambridge University Press.

———. 2000. *Democratic institutional design: The powers and incentives of Venezuelan politicians and interest groups*. Stanford: Stanford University Press.

———. 2006. The nature of representation in Andean legislatures and attempts at institutional reengineering. In *The crisis of democratic representation in the Andes,* ed. Scott Mainwaring, Ana María Bejarano, and Eduardo Pízarro Leongómez, 204–24. Stanford: Stanford University Press.

Crisp, Brian F., and Juan Carlos Rey. 2001. The sources of electoral reform in Venezuela. In *Mixed-member electoral systems: The best of both worlds?* ed. Matthew Soberg Shugart and Martin P. Wattenberg, 173–93. New York: Oxford University Press.

Croson, Rachel T. A., and Melanie Beth Marks. 2000. Step returns in threshold public goods: A meta- and experimental analysis. *Experimental Economics* 2 (3): 239–59.

Cruz, José Miguel, and Mitchell A. Seligson, with Siddhartha Baviskar. 2004. *The political culture of democracy in Honduras, 2004*. Nashville: Latin American Public Opinion Project.

Cuesta, Jose. 2007. Political space, pro-poor growth, and poverty reduction strategy in Honduras: A story of missed opportunities. *Journal of Latin American Studies* 39 (2): 329–54.

Dalton, Elizabeth H. 1994. The 1993 Honduran general elections: An experiment in increased voter choice. Paper presented at the Midwest Political Science Association, April 14–16, in Chicago, Ill.

Datos de opinion: Proyecto de Elites Latinoamericanos (PELA), Honduras. 1994–2005. Manuel Alcántara (dir.). University of Salamanca, Spain.

De Janvry, Alain, Frederico Finan, Elisabeth Sadoulet, Donald Nelson, Kathy Lindert, Bénédicte de la Brière, and Peter Lanjouw. 2005. Brazil's Bolsa Escola program: The role of local governance in decentralized implementation. SP Discussion Paper 542, Social Safety Net Primer Series, World Bank.

Del Cid, Rafael. 1991. Logros y perspectivas del proceso de democratización en Honduras. In *Honduras: Crisis económica y proceso de democratización política*, 1–24. Tegucigalpa: Centro de Documentación de Honduras.

De Luca, Miguel, Mark P. Jones, and María Inés Tula. 2002. Back rooms or ballot boxes? Candidate nomination in Argentina. *Comparative Political Studies* 35 (4): 413–36.

Desposato, Scott W. 2001. Institutional theories, societal realities, and party politics in Brazil. Ph.D. diss., University of California, Los Angeles.

———. 2005. Explaining patterns of oversight in Brazilian subnational governments. In *Trends in parliamentary oversight,* ed. Riccardo Pelizzo, Rick Stapenhurst, and David Olson, 33–39. Washington, D.C.: World Bank Institute.

———. 2006a. The impact of electoral rules in legislative parties: Lessons from the Brazilian Senate and Chamber of Deputies. *Journal of Politics* 68 (4): 1018–30.

———. 2006b. Parties for rent? Ambition, ideology, and party switching in Brazil's Chamber of Deputies. *American Journal of Political Science* 50 (1): 62–80.

———. 2007. How does vote buying shape the legislative agenda? In *Elections for sale: The causes and consequences of vote buying,* ed. Frederic Charles Schaffer, 101–22. Boulder, Colo.: Lynne Rienner.

Diamond, Larry. 1997. Consolidating democracy in the Americas. *Annals of the American Academy of Political and Social Science* 550 (March): 12–41.

Dion, Michelle. 2007. Poverty, inequality, policy, and politics in Latin America. *Latin American Research Review* 42 (1): 186–95.

Dixit, Avinash, and John Londregan. 1996. The determinants of success of special interests in redistributive politics. *Journal of Politics* 58 (4): 1132–55.

Dominguez, Jorge I. 2003. Constructing democratic governance in Latin America: Taking stock of the 1990s. In *Constructing democratic governance in Latin America,* ed. Jorge I. Dominguez and Michael Shifter, 351–81. 2nd ed. Baltimore: Johns Hopkins University Press.

Draibe, Sônia M. 2004. Federal leverage in a decentralized system: Education reform in Brazil. In *Crucial needs, weak incentives: Social sector reform, democratization, and globalization in Latin America,* ed. Robert R. Kaufman and Joan M. Nelson, 375–406. Baltimore: Johns Hopkins University Press.

Durand, Francisco, and Eduardo Silva, eds. 1998. *Organized business, economic change, and democracy in Latin America.* Miami: North-South Center Press.

Durston, John, Daniel Duhart, Francisca Miranda, and Evelyn Monzó. 2005. *Comunidades campesinas, agencias públicas, y clientelismos políticos en Chile.* Santiago, Chile: LOM Ediciones.

Easton, David. 1975. A re-assessment of the concept of political support. *British Journal of Political Science* 5 (4): 435–57.

Escobar-Lemmon, Maria. 2000. The causes and process of decentralization in Latin America. Ph.D. diss., University of Arizona.

Escobar-Lemmon, Maria, Claudia Nancy Avellaneda, and Felipe Botero. 2005. Latin America's proactive presidents and proactive assemblies. Paper presented at the Regional Latin Americanist Conference, April 29–30, in College Station, Tex.

Espíndola, Roberto. 2001. No change in Uruguay: The 1999 presidential and parliamentary elections. *Electoral Studies* 20 (4): 649–57.

Euraque, Darío A. 1990. Merchants and industrialists in northern Honduras: The making of a national bourgeoisie in peripheral capitalism. Ph.D. diss., University of Wisconsin, Madison.

———. 1994. Social, economic, and political aspects of the Carías dictatorship in Honduras: The historiography. *Latin American Research Review* 29 (1): 238–48.

———. 1996. *Reinterpreting the banana republic: Region and state in Honduras, 1870–1972.* Chapel Hill: University of North Carolina Press.

———. 2000. Los políticos Hondureños y la costa norte (1876–1950): Narrativa e interpretación. *Revista Política de Honduras* 2 (24): 113–56.

Faundez, Julio. 1997. In defense of presidentialism: The case of Chile, 1932–1970. In *Presidentialism and democracy in Latin America,* ed. Scott Mainwaring and Matthew Soberg Shugart, 300–320. New York: Cambridge University Press.

Fearon, James D. 1999. Electoral accountability and the control of politicians: Selecting good types versus sanctioning poor performance. In *Democracy, accountability, and representation,* ed. Adam Przeworski, Susan C. Stokes, and Bernard Manin, 55–99. Cambridge: Cambridge University Press.

Fenno, Richard. 1978. *Home style: House members in their districts.* Boston: Little, Brown.

Ferejohn, John. 1986. Incumbent performance and electoral control. *Public Choice* 50 (1–3): 5–25.

———. 1999. Accountability and authority: Toward a theory of political accountability. In *Democracy, accountability, and representation,* ed. Adam Przeworski, Susan C. Stokes, and Bernard Manin, 131–53. Cambridge: Cambridge University Press.

Fernández, Arturo. 1988. *Partidos políticos y elecciones en Honduras, 1980.* 2nd ed. Tegucigalpa, Honduras: Editorial Guaymuras.

Fleisher, Richard, and Jon R. Bond. 2004. The shrinking middle in the U.S. Congress. *British Journal of Political Science* 34 (3): 429–51.

Flynn, Peter. 2005. Brazil and Lula, 2005: Crisis, corruption, and change in political perspective. *Third World Quarterly* 26 (8): 1221–67.

Fox, Jonathan. 1994. The difficult transition from clientelism to citizenship: Lessons from Mexico. *World Politics* 46 (2): 151–84.

Funes, Matías. 1995. *Los deliberantes: El poder militar en Honduras.* Tegucigalpa, Honduras: Editorial Guaymuras.

García Montero, Mercedes, and Flavia Freidenberg. 2001. Perú. In *Partidos políticos de América Latina: Países andinos,* ed. Manuel Alcántara Sáez and Flavia Freidenberg, 410–84. Salamanca, Spain: Ediciones Universidad Salamanca.

Garland, Allison M. 2000. The politics and administration of social development in Latin America. In *Social development in Latin America: The politics of reform,* ed. Joseph S. Tulchin and Allison M. Garland, 1–14. Boulder, Colo.: Lynne Rienner.

Gay, Robert. 1990. Popular incorporation and prospects for democracy: Some implications of the Brazilian case. *Theory and Society* 19 (4): 447–63.

Geddes, Barbara. 1994. *Politician's dilemma: Building state capacity in Latin America.* Berkeley and Los Angeles: University of California Press.

Gerring, John. 2004. What is a case study and what is it good for? *American Political Science Review* 98 (2): 341–54.

Gibson, Edward L. 1997. The populist road to market reform: Policy and electoral coalitions in Mexico and Argentina. *World Politics* 49 (3): 339–70.

Gleijeses, Piero. 1991. *Shattered hope: The Guatemalan revolution and the United States, 1944–1954.* Princeton: Princeton University Press.

Goeree, Jacob K., and Charles A. Holt. 2005. An explanation of anomalous behavior in models of political participation. *American Political Science Review* 99 (2): 201–13.

Goldfrank, Benjamin, and Aaron Schneider. 2006. Competitive institution building: The PT and participatory budgeting in Rio Grande do Sul. *Latin American Politics and Society* 48 (3): 1–31.

Goldfrank, Benjamin, and Andreas Schrank. 2006. Who's left in the city? What's right in the hinterland? Urban political economy in contemporary Latin America. Paper presented at the American Political Science Association, August 30–September 3, in Philadelphia, Pa.

González, José Dolores. 2001a. Carías Andino y Zúñiga Huete en 1932. *Revista Política de Honduras* 3 (27): 105–7.

———. 2001b. Las candidaturas en los partidos históricos. *Revista Política de Honduras* 3 (29): 175–78

Grindle, Merilee S. 2004. *Despite the odds: The contentious politics of education reform.* Princeton: Princeton University Press.

Gutiérrez, Norma C. 2009. Honduras: Constitutional law issues. Report for U.S. Law Library of Congress, August. http://www.loc.gov/law/help/honduras/constitutional-law-issues.php, accessed March 9, 2010.

Hagopian, Frances. 1990. Democracy by undemocratic means? Elites, political pacts, and regime transition in Brazil. *Comparative Political Studies* 23 (2): 147–70.

———. 1992. The compromised consolidation: The political class in the Brazilian transition. In *Issues in democratic consolidation: The new South American democracies in comparative perspective,* ed. Scott Mainwaring, Guillermo O'Donnell, and J. Samuel Valenzuela, 243–93. Notre Dame: University of Notre Dame Press.

———. 2001. Economic liberalization, political competition, and political representation in Latin America. Paper prepared for the Comparative Politics Workshop, University of Chicago, December 6.

———. 2005. Conclusions: Government performance, political representation, and public perceptions of contemporary democracy in Latin America. In *The third wave of democratization in Latin America: Advances and setbacks,* ed. Frances Hagopian and Scott Mainwaring, 319–62. Cambridge: Cambridge University Press.

———. 2009. Parties and politicians in Latin America: Polarization, program, and patronage in the post-reform era. Paper presented at the Midwest Political Science Association, April 2–5, in Chicago, Ill.

Hall, Anthony. 2006. From Fome Zero to Bolsa Família: Social policies and poverty alleviation under Lula. *Journal of Latin American Studies* 38 (4): 689–709.

Hall, Peter A., and Rosemary C. R. Taylor. 1996. Political science and the three new institutionalisms. *Political Studies* 44 (4): 936–57.

Harmel, Robert, and Kenneth Janda. 1994. An integrated theory of party goals and party change. *Journal of Theoretical Politics* 6 (3): 259–87.

Hartlyn, Jonathan. 1994. Crisis-ridden elections (again) in the Dominican Republic: Neopatrimonialism, presidentialism, and weak electoral oversight. *Journal of Interamerican Studies and World Affairs* 36 (4): 91–144.

———. 1998. *The struggle for democratic politics in the Dominican Republic*. Chapel Hill: University of North Carolina Press.

Hellman, Judith Adler. 1994. Mexican popular movements, clientelism, and the process of democratization. *Latin American Perspectives* 21 (2): 124–42.

Helmke, Gretchen, and Steven Levitsky. 2004. Informal institutions and comparative politics: A research agenda. *Perspectives on Politics* 2 (4): 725–40.

Hirschman, Albert O. 1973. *Journeys toward progress: Studies of economic policy-making in Latin America*. New York: Norton.

Hite, Katherine. 1997. Preface. In *The new politics of inequality in Latin America: Rethinking participation and representation*, ed. Douglas A. Chalmers, Carlos M. Vilas, Katherine Hite, Scott B. Martin, Kerianne Piester, and Monique Segarra, v–vii. Oxford: Oxford University Press.

Hochstetler, Kathryn. 2000. Democratizing pressures from below? Social movements in the new Brazilian democracy. In *Democratic Brazil: Actors, institutions, and processes*, ed. Peter R. Kingstone and Timothy J. Power, 162–82. Pittsburgh: University of Pittsburgh Press.

Hochstetler, Kathryn, and Elisabeth Jay Friedman. 2008. Can civil society organizations solve the crisis of partisan representation in Latin America? *Latin American Politics and Society* 50 (2): 1–32.

Honduran National Census. 2001. *Censo nacional de población y vivienda, 2001*. Instituto Nacional de Estadística, Tegucigalpa, Honduras. http://www.ine-hn.org/, accessed April 10, 2010.

Huber, Evelyne, Thomas Murillo, and John D. Stephens. 2008. Politics and social spending in Latin America. *Journal of Politics* 70 (2): 420–36.

Huber, Evelyne, Dietrich Rueschemeyer, and John D. Stephens. 1999. The paradoxes of contemporary democracy: Formal, participatory, and social dimensions. In *Transitions to democracy*, ed. Lisa Anderson, 168–92. New York: Columbia University Press.

Human Rights Watch. 1994. *Honduras: The facts speak for themselves: The preliminary report of the National Commissioner for the Protection of Human Rights in Honduras*. New York: Human Rights Watch.

Hunter, Wendy. 1997. Continuity or change? Civil-military relations in democratic Argentina, Chile, and Peru. *Political Science Quarterly* 112 (3): 56–80.

———. 2007. The normalization of an anomaly: The Workers' Party in Brazil. *World Politics* 59 (3): 440–75.

Hunter, Wendy, and Timothy J. Power. 2005. Lula's Brazil at midterm. *Journal of Democracy* 16 (3): 127–39.

———. 2007. Rewarding Lula: Executive power, social policy, and the Brazilian elections of 2006. *Latin American Politics and Society* 49 (1): 1–30.

IFPRI (International Food Policy Research Institute). 1999. *PRAF II project: Evaluation and capacity building*. Washington, D.C.: IFPRI.

———. 2000a. *PRAF/IDB phase II: Monitoring and evaluation system*. Washington, D.C.: IFPRI.

————. 2000b. *PRAF/IDB phase II: Project coordinating unit.* Washington, D.C.: IFPRI.

————. 2001. *PRAF/IDB phase II: Analysis of the situation before the beginning of distribution of vouchers and project implementation.* Washington, D.C.: IFPRI.

Inglehart, Ronald, and Christian Welzel. 2003. Political culture and democracy analyzing cross-level linkages. *Comparative Politics* 36 (1): 61–79.

Iversen, Torben, and David Soskice. 2006. Electoral institutions and the politics of coalitions: Why some democracies redistribute more than others. *American Political Science Review* 100 (2): 165–81.

Jones, Mark P. 2008. The recruitment and selection of legislative candidates in Argentina. In *Pathways to power: Political recruitment and candidate selection in Latin America,* ed. Peter Siavelis and Scott Morgenstern, 41–75. University Park: Pennsylvania State University Press.

Jones, Mark P., Sebastian Saiegh, Pablo T. Spiller, and Mariano Tommasi. 2002. Amateur legislators-professional politicians: The consequences of party-centered electoral rules in a federal system. *American Journal of Political Science* 46 (3): 656–69.

Jungblut, Cristiane. 2007. Oposição derruba a prorrogação da CPMF no Senado: Governo consegue só 45 votos. *O Globo,* December 13.

Karl, Terry Lynn. 1986. Petroleum and political pacts: The transition to democracy in Venezuela. In *Transitions from authoritarian rule,* ed. Guillermo O'Donnell, Philippe Schmitter, and Laurence Whitehead, 196–219. Baltimore: Johns Hopkins University Press.

————. 1990. Dilemmas of democratization in Latin America. *Comparative Politics* 23 (1): 1–22.

————. 1995. The hybrid regimes of Central America. *Journal of Democracy* 6 (3): 72–86.

Katznelson, Ira, and Barry R. Weingast. 2005. Intersections between historical and rational choice institutionalism. In *Preferences and situations: Points of intersection between historical and rational choice institutionalism,* ed. Ira Katznelson and Barry R. Weingast, 1–24. New York: Russell Sage Foundation.

Kaufman, Robert R. 1974. The patron-client concept and macro-politics: Prospects and problems. *Comparative Studies in Society and History* 16 (3): 284–308.

Kaufman, Robert R., and Joan M. Nelson. 2004a. Introduction: The political challenges of social sector reform. In *Crucial needs, weak incentives: Social sector reform, democratization, and globalization in Latin America,* ed. Robert R. Kaufman and Joan M. Nelson, 1–19. Baltimore: Johns Hopkins University Press.

————. 2004b. Conclusions: The political dynamics of reform. In *Crucial needs, weak incentives: Social sector reform, democratization, and globalization in Latin America,* ed. Robert R. Kaufman and Joan M. Nelson, 473–519. Baltimore: Johns Hopkins University Press.

Kaufman, Robert R., and A. Segura-Ubiergo. 2001. Globalization, domestic politics, and social spending in Latin America. *World Politics* 53 (4): 553–87.

Kellam, Marisa. 2007. When politics is local: Coalition instability in Latin America. Ph.D. diss., University of California, Los Angeles.

Kenney, Charles D. 1996. Outsiders on the inside: Preliminary results from the parliamentary elites of Latin America survey in Peru. Paper presented at the Midwest Political Science Association, April 18–20, Chicago, Ill.

Kettering, Sharon. 1988. The historical development of political clientelism. *Journal of Interdisciplinary History* 18 (3): 419–47.

King, Gary, Robert O. Keohane, and Sidney Verba. 1994. *Designing social inquiry: Scientific inference in qualitative research.* Princeton: Princeton University Press.

Kitschelt, Herbert. 2000. Linkages between citizens and politicians in democratic politics. *Comparative Political Studies* 33 (6–7): 845–79.

Kitschelt, Herbert, and Steven I. Wilkinson. 2007. Citizen-politician linkages: An introduction. In *Patrons, clients, and policies: Patterns of democratic accountability and political competition,* ed. Herbert Kitschelt and Steven I. Wilkinson, 1–49. New York: Cambridge University Press.

Klugman, Jeni, ed. 2002. *Sourcebook for poverty reduction strategies.* Washington, D.C.: World Bank.

Kulisheck, Michael R. 1998. Who's in and who's out: An analysis of representation patterns in the Venezuelan Chamber of Deputies. Paper presented at the Latin American Studies Association, September 24–26, in Chicago, Ill.

Kumbhat, M. C., and Y. M. Marican. 1976. Constituent orientation among Malaysian state legislators. *Legislative Studies Quarterly* 1 (3): 389–404.

Lagos, Marta. 2003. Public opinion. In *Constructing democratic governance in Latin America,* ed. Jorge I. Dominguez and Michael Shifter, 137–61. 2nd ed. Baltimore: Johns Hopkins University Press.

Lamarchand, Rene, and Keith Legg. 1972. Political clientelism and development: A preliminary analysis. *Comparative Politics* 4 (2): 149–78.

Lambsdorff, Johann Graf. 2003. 2002 corruption perceptions index. In *Global corruption report, 2003,* ed. Robin Hodess, 262–65. London: Profile Books.

———. 2008. The big picture: Measuring corruption and benchmarking progress in the fight against corruption. In *Global corruption report, 2008,* 296–320. Berlin: Transparency International. http://www.transparency.org/publications/ger/ger _2008, last accessed April 19, 2009.

Lancaster, Thomas D. 1986. Electoral structures and pork barrel politics. *International Political Science Review* 7 (1): 67–81.

Lancaster, Thomas D., and W. David Patterson. 1990. Comparative pork barrel politics: Perceptions of the West German Bundestag. *Comparative Political Studies* 22 (4): 458–77.

Langston, Joy. 2006. The changing Party of the Institutional Revolution: Electoral competition and decentralized candidate selection. *Party Politics* 12 (3): 395–413.

———. 2008. Legislative recruitment in Mexico. In *Pathways to power: Political recruitment and candidate selection in Latin America,* ed. Peter Siavelis and Scott Morgenstern, 143–63. University Park: Pennsylvania State University Press.

Langston, Joy, and Francisco Aparicio. 2008. Political career structures in democratic Mexico, 1997–2006. Paper presented at the American Political Science Association, August 28–31, in Boston, Mass.

Latinobarómetro Report. 2005. *1995–2005: A decade of public opinion, 176,554 interviews in 18 countries.* Santiago, Chile: Corporación Latinobarómetro.

Latinobarómetro survey. 2006 and 2007. http://www.latinobarometro.org/, accessed April 10, 2010.

Lazo, César. 2001. Partidos autoritarios y elecciones. *Revista Política de Honduras* 3 (29): 53–55.

Levi, Margaret. 1997. A model, a method, and a map: Rational choice in comparative and historical analysis. In *Comparative politics: Rationality, culture, and structure,* ed. Mark Irving Lichbach and Alan S. Zuckerman, 19–41. Princeton: Princeton University Press.

Lievesley, Geraldine. 1999. *Democracy in Latin America: Mobilization, power, and the search for a new politics.* Manchester: Manchester University Press.

Lijphart, Arend. 1971. Comparative politics and the comparative method. *American Political Science Review* 65 (3): 682–93.

———. 1999. *Patterns of democracy: Government forms and performance in thirty-six countries.* New Haven: Yale University Press.

Lindert, Kathy. 2005. Brazil: Bolsa Familia program: Scaling-up cash transfers for the poor. In *Emerging good practice in managing for development results: Source book,* ed. OECD-DAC Joint Venture on Managing for Development Results, 67–74. Washington, D.C.: World Bank.

Lindert, Kathy, Anja Linder, Jason Hobbs, and Bénédicte de la Brière. 2007. The nuts and bolts of Brazil's Bolsa Familia program: Implementing conditional cash transfers in a decentralized context. Social Protection Discussion Paper 709, World Bank.

Linz, Juan J., and Alfred Stepan. 1996. *Problems of democratic transition and consolidation: Southern Europe, South America, and post-communist Europe.* Baltimore: Johns Hopkins University Press.

Lodge, Milton G., and Charles Taber. 2000. Three steps toward a theory of motivated political reasoning. In *Elements of political reason: Cognition, choice, and the bounds of rationality,* ed. Arthur Lupia, Mathew D. McCubbins, and Samuel L. Popkin, 183–213. New York: Cambridge University Press.

Lukes, Steven. 1974. *Power: A radical view.* London: Macmillan.

———. 2005. *Power: A radical view.* 2nd ed. Hampshire, UK: Palgrave Macmillan.

Lyne, Mona M. 2007. Rethinking economics and institutions: The voter's dilemma and democratic accountability. In *Patrons, clients, and policies: Patterns of democratic accountability and political competition,* ed. Herbert Kitschelt and Steven I. Wilkinson, 159–81. New York: Cambridge University Press.

Magaloni, Beatriz, Alberto Diaz-Cayeros, and Federico Estévez. 2007. Clientelism and portfolio diversification: A model of electoral investment with applications to Mexico. In *Patrons, clients, and policies: Patterns of democratic accountability and political competition,* ed. Herbert Kitschelt and Steven I. Wilkinson, 182–205. New York: Cambridge University Press.

Mahoney, James. 2001. *The legacies of liberalism: Path dependence and political regimes in Central America.* Baltimore: Johns Hopkins University Press.

Mainwaring, Scott. 1999. *Rethinking party systems in the third wave of democratization: The case of Brazil.* Stanford: Stanford University Press.

Mainwaring, Scott, Ana María Bejarano, and Eduardo Pizarro Leongómez. 2006. The crisis of democratic representation in the Andes: An overview. In *The crisis of democratic representation in the Andes,* ed. Scott Mainwaring, Ana María Bejarano, and Eduardo Pizarro Leongómez, 1–44. Stanford: Stanford University Press.

Mainwaring, Scott, Daniel Brinks, and Aníbal Pérez-Liñán. 2001. Classifying political regimes in Latin America, 1945–1999. *Studies in Comparative International Development* 36 (1): 37–65.

Mainwaring, Scott, and Christopher Welna, eds. 2003. *Democratic accountability in Latin America.* Oxford: Oxford University Press.

Mansbridge, Jane. 2003. Rethinking representation. *American Political Science Review* 97 (4): 515–28.

Marenghi, Patricia, and Mercedes García Montero. 2006. El rompecabezas de la representación: Qué intereses defienden y cómo se comportan los legisladores latinoamericanos. In *Políticos y política en América Latina,* ed. Manuel Alcántara Sáez, 29–82. Madrid: Siglo XXI.

Mayhew, David. 1974. *Congress: The electoral connection.* New Haven: Yale University Press.

McDonald, Ronald H., and J. Mark Ruhl. 1989. *Party politics and elections in Latin America.* Boulder, Colo.: Westview.

Mejía Acosta, Andrés. 2002. *Gobernabilidad democrática sistema electoral, partidos políticos, y pugna de poderes en Ecuador, 1978–1998.* Quito, Ecuador: Fundación Konrad Adenauer-Stiftung.

———. 2003. Through the eye of a needle: Veto players, informal institutions, and economic reform in Ecuador. Paper presented at the Informal Institutions and Politics in Latin America conference, April 24–25, in Notre Dame, Ind.

Meneguello, Rachel. 1995. Electoral behaviour in Brazil: The 1994 presidential elections. *International Social Sciences Journal* 146 (December): 627–41.

Mezey, Michael. 1979. *Comparative legislatures.* Durham: Duke University Press.

Micozzi, Juan Pablo. 2009. The electoral connection in multilevel systems with non-static career ambition. Ph.D. diss., Rice University.

Moe, Terry M. 2005. Power and political institutions. *Perspectives on Politics* 3 (2): 215–33.

Molina, Efraín. 2005. Bajas temperaturas no detuvieron a yoreños. *La Prensa,* November 28.

Molina, José E., and Carmen Pérez. 1998. Evolution of the party system in Venezuela, 1946–1993. *Journal of Interamerican Studies and World Affairs* 20 (2): 1–26.

Moncada Silva, Efrain. 1986. Democracia, sufragio, y sistemas electorales en Honduras. In *Legislación electoral comparada: Colombia, México, Panamá, Venezuela, y Centroamérica,* 179–244. San José, Costa Rica: Centro de Asesoria y Promoción Electoral.

Moore, Charity. 2008. Assessing Honduras' CCT programme PRAF, Programa de Asignación Familiar: Expected and unexpected realities. Country Study 15, International Poverty Center, UNDP.

Moraes, Juan Andrés. 2008. Why factions? Candidate selection and legislative politics in Uruguay. In *Pathways to power: Political recruitment and candidate selection in Latin America,* ed. Peter Siavelis and Scott Morgenstern, 164–85. University Park: Pennsylvania State University Press.

Moreno, Erika, and Maria Escobar-Lemmon. 2008. Mejor solo que mal acompañado: Political entrepreneurs in Colombia. In *Pathways to power: Political recruitment and candidate selection in Latin America,* ed. Peter Siavelis and Scott Morgenstern, 119–42. University Park: Pennsylvania State University Press.

Morgan, Jana. 2007. Partisanship during the collapse of Venezuela's party system. *Latin American Research Review* 42 (1): 78–98.

Morgenstern, Scott, and Javier Vazquez-D'Elia. 2007. Electoral laws, parties, and party systems in Latin America. *Annual Review of Political Science* 10 (June): 143–68.

Morris, James A. 1984. *Honduras: Caudillo politics and military rulers.* Boulder, Colo.: Westview.

Müller, Wolfgang C., and Thomas Saalfeld, eds. 1997. *Members of parliament in western Europe: Roles and behaviour.* London: Frank Cass.

Munro, Dana G. 1967. *The five republics of Central America: Their political and economic development and their relations with the United States.* 2nd ed. New York: Russell and Russell.

Myers, David J. 2000. Venezuela: Shaping the "new democracy." In *Latin American politics and development,* ed. Howard J. Wiarda and Harvey F. Kline, 259–94. 5th ed. Boulder, Colo.: Westview.

Navia, Patricio. 2008. Legislative candidate selection in Chile. In *Pathways to power: Political recruitment and candidate selection in Latin America,* ed. Peter Siavelis and Scott Morgenstern, 92–118. University Park: Pennsylvania State University Press.

Nelson, Joan M. 1992. Poverty, equity, and the politics of adjustment. In *The politics of economic adjustment: International constraints, distributive conflicts, and the state,* ed. Stephan Haggard and Robert R. Kaufman, 221–69. Princeton: Princeton University Press.

———. 2000. Reforming social sector governance: A political perspective. In *Social development in Latin America: The politics of reform,* ed. Joseph S. Tulchin and Allison M. Garland, 53–69. Boulder, Colo.: Lynne Rienner.

———. 2004. The politics of health sector reform: Cross-national comparisons. In *Crucial needs, weak incentives: Social sector reform, democratization, and globalization in Latin America,* ed. Robert R. Kaufman and Joan M. Nelson, 23–64. Baltimore: Johns Hopkins University Press.

Newton, Kenneth. 1974. Role orientations and their sources among elected representatives in English local politics. *Journal of Politics* 36 (3): 615–36.

Nichter, Simeon. 2008. Vote buying or turnout buying? Machine politics and the secret ballot. *American Political Science Review* 102 (1): 19–31.

Nickson, Andrew R. 1995. *Local government in Latin America.* Boulder, Colo.: Lynne Rienner.

Norsworthy, Kent, and Tom Barry. 1993. *Inside Honduras.* Albuquerque, N.Mex.: Interhemispheric Education Resource Center.

Nylen, William R. 2003. *Participatory democracy versus elitist democracy: Lessons from Brazil.* New York: Palgrave Macmillan.

O'Donnell, Guillermo. 1992. Transition, continuities, and paradoxes. In *Issues in democratic consolidation: The new South American democracies in comparative perspective,* ed. Scott Mainwaring, Guillermo O'Donnell, and J. Samuel Valenzuela, 17–56. Notre Dame: University of Notre Dame Press.

———. 1994. Delegative democracy. *Journal of Democracy* 5 (1): 55–69.

———. 1996. Another institutionalization: Latin America and elsewhere. Working Paper 222, Kellogg Institute for International Studies, University of Notre Dame.

———. 2003. Horizontal accountability: The legal institutionalization of mistrust. In *Democratic accountability in Latin America,* ed. Scott Mainwaring and Christopher Welna, 34–54. Oxford: Oxford University Press.

OEA recomienda a Honduras despolitizar el sistema electoral. 2001. *La Prensa,* December 5.

O'Neill, Kathleen. 2006. Decentralized politics and political outcomes in the Andes. In *The crisis of democratic representation in the Andes,* ed. Scott Mainwaring, Ana María Bejarano, and Eduardo Pizarro Leongómez, 171–203. Stanford: Stanford University Press.

Organization of American States. 2005. Misión de OEA destaca compromiso de los Hondureños de vivir en democracia. Press release, December 7. http://www.oas .org/OASpage/press_releases/press_release.asp?sCodigo=MOE-HON-8, accessed February 8, 2006.

Otero, Laura Wills, and Aníbal Pérez-Liñán. 2005. La evolución de los sistemas electorales en América: 1900–2004. *Colección* 16:47–82.

Otis, John. 2003. A fruitless labor: Ruled by fear, banana workers resist unions. *Houston Chronicle,* September 14.

Patzelt, Werner J. 1997. German MPs and their roles. In *Members of parliament in western Europe: Roles and behaviour,* ed. Wolfgang C. Müller and Thomas Saalfeld, 55–78. London: Frank Cass.

Paz Aguilar, Ernesto. 2008. La reforma política electoral en Honduras. In *Reforma política y electoral en América Latina, 1978–2007*, ed. Daniel G. Zovatto and José de Jesús Orozco Henríquez, 623–51. Mexico City: Universidad Nacional Autónoma de México.

PELA (Proyecto de Elites Latinoamericanas). 1998. Manuel Alcántara (dir.). University of Salamanca, Spain.

———. 2002. Manuel Alcántara (dir.). University of Salamanca, Spain.

Petrovsky, Nicolai, and Michelle M. Taylor-Robinson. 2005. Do the poor in Latin America vote? Paper presented at the Midwest Political Science Association, April 7–10, in Chicago, Ill.

Piattoni, Simona. 2001. Clientelism in historical and comparative perspective. In *Clientelism, interests, and democratic representation: The European experience in historical perspective*, ed. Simona Piattoni, 1–30. Cambridge: Cambridge University Press.

Pitkin, Hanna F. 1967. *The concept of representation*. Berkeley and Los Angeles: University of California Press.

Posas, Mario. 1981. *Luchas del movimiento obrero Hondureño*. San José, Costa Rica: EDUCA.

———. 1989. *Modalidades del proceso de democratización en Honduras*. Tegucigalpa, Honduras: Editorial Universitaria.

———. 1992. El proceso de democratización en Honduras. In *Puntos de vista: Temas políticos*, 1–37. Tegucigalpa: Centro de Documentación de Honduras.

Posas, Mario, and Rafael Del Cid. 1983. *La construcción del sector público y del estado nacional en Honduras, 1876–1979*. 2nd ed. San José, Costa Rica: EDUCA.

Posner, Paul W. 1999. Popular representation and political dissatisfaction in Chile's new democracy. *Journal of Interamerican Studies and World Affairs* 41 (1): 59–85.

Powell, G. Bingham, Jr. 1989. Constitutional design and citizen electoral control. *Journal of Theoretical Politics* 1 (2): 107–30.

Power, Timothy J. 1998. Brazilian politicians and neoliberalism: Mapping support for the Cardoso reforms, 1995–1997. *Journal of Interamerican Studies and World Affairs* 40 (4): 51–72.

Przeworski, Adam. 1991. *Democracy and the market*. Cambridge: Cambridge University Press.

Przeworski, Adam, Michael E. Alvarez, José A. Cheibub, and Fernando Limongi. 2000. *Democracy and development: Political institutions and well-being in the world, 1950–1990*. Cambridge: Cambridge University Press.

Przeworski, Adam, Susan C. Stokes, and Bernard Manin, eds. 1999. *Democracy, accountability, and representation*. Cambridge: Cambridge University Press.

Psacharopoulos, George. 1994. Returns to education: A global update. *World Development* 22 (9): 1325–43.

Ramirez, Patricia. 2004. A sweeping health reform: The quest for unification, coverage, and efficiency in Colombia. In *Crucial needs, weak incentives: Social sector reform, democratization, and globalization in Latin America*, ed. Robert R. Kaufman and Joan M. Nelson, 124–54. Baltimore: Johns Hopkins University Press.

Ramos, Marisa Luisa. 1997. Creencias y valores de los parlamentarios en Venezuela. *Nueva Sociedad* 148 (March–April): 44–51.

Randall, Vicky, and Lars Svåsand. 2002. Party institutionalization in new democracies. *Party Politics* 8 (1): 5–29.

Rawlings, Laura B. 2004. A new approach to social assistance: Latin America's experience with conditional cash transfer programs. Social Protection Discussion Paper 416, Social Protection Unit, Human Development Network, World Bank.

Remmer, Karen L. 1995. New theoretical perspectives on democratization. *Comparative Politics* 28 (1): 103–22.

———. 2007. The political economy of patronage: Expenditure patterns in the Argentine provinces, 1983–2003. *Journal of Politics* 69 (2): 363–77.

Renato Souza, Paulo. 2008. Governistas aprovam nova CPMF. Web page of Congress Deputy Renato Souza, June 11. http://www.paulorenatosouza.com.br/reportage mmanchete.asp?id=368, last accessed July 7, 2008.

Roberts, Bryan R., and Alejandro Portes. 2006. Coping with the free market city: Collective action in six Latin American cities. *Latin American Research Review* 41 (2): 57–83.

Roberts, Kenneth M. 2002. Social inequalities without class cleavages in Latin America's neoliberal era. *Studies in Comparative International Development* 36 (4): 3–33.

———. 2003. Social correlates of party system demise and populist resurgence in Venezuela. *Latin American Politics and Society* 45 (3): 35–57.

Roett, Riordan. 1984. *Brazil: Politics in a patrimonial society*. 3rd ed. New York: Praeger.

Roniger, Luis. 2004. Political clientelism, democracy, and market economy. *Comparative Politics* 36 (3): 353–75.

Roniger, Luis, and Ayse Günes-Ayala. 1994. *Democracy, clientelism, and civil society*. Boulder, Colo.: Lynne Rienner.

Ropp, Steven C. 1974. The Honduran army in the sociopolitical evolution of the Honduran state. *The Americas* 30 (3): 504–28.

Rosenberg, Mark B. 1987. Political obstacles to democracy in Central America. In *Authoritarians and democrats: Regime transition in Latin America*, ed. James M. Malloy and Mitchell A. Seligson, 193–215. Pittsburgh: University of Pittsburgh Press.

———. 1989. Can democracy survive the democrats? From transition to consolidation in Honduras. In *Elections and democracy in Central America*, ed. John A. Booth and Mitchell A. Seligson, 40–59. Chapel Hill: University of North Carolina Press.

Ross, Michael. 2006. Is democracy good for the poor? *American Journal of Political Science* 50 (4): 860–74.

Rothstein, Frances. 1979. The class basis of patron-client relations. *Latin American Perspectives* 6 (2): 25–35.

Rubenstein, Jennifer. 2007. Accountability in an unequal world. *Journal of Politics* 69 (3): 616–32.

Ruhl, J. Mark. 1984. Agrarian structure and political stability in Honduras. *Journal of Interamerican Studies and World Affairs* 26 (1): 33–68.

———. 1996. Redefining civil-military relations in Honduras. *Journal of Interamerican Studies and World Affairs* 38 (1): 33–66.

———. 1997. Doubting democracy in Honduras. *Current History* 96 (February): 81–86.

———. 2000. Honduras: The limits of democracy. In *Latin American politics and development*, ed. Howard J. Wiarda and Harvey F. Kline, 512–26. 5th ed. Boulder, Colo.: Westview.

Rustow, Dankwart. 1970. Transitions to democracy. *Comparative Politics* 2 (2): 337–63.

Saez strikes a deal with COPEI. 1998. *Latin American Weekly Report*, May 12.

Sagás, Ernesto. 1997. The 1996 presidential elections in the Dominican Republic. *Electoral Studies* 16 (1): 103–7.

———. 1999. The 1998 congressional and municipal elections in the Dominican Republic. *Electoral Studies* 18 (2): 282–90.

———. 2003. Elections in the Dominican Republic, May 2002. *Electoral Studies* 22 (4): 792–98.

Salomón, Leticia. 1982. *Militarismo y reformismo en Honduras.* Tegucigalpa, Honduras: Editorial Guaymuras.

———. 1992. *Política y militares en Honduras.* Tegucigalpa: Centro de Documentación de Honduras.

———. 1994. *Democratización y sociedad civil en Honduras.* Tegucigalpa: Centro de Documentación de Honduras.

Samuels, David. 2003. *Ambition, federalism, and legislative politics in Brazil.* New York: Cambridge University Press.

———. 2008. Political ambition, candidate recruitment, and legislative politics in Brazil. In *Pathways to power: Political recruitment and candidate selection in Latin America,* ed. Peter Siavelis and Scott Morgenstern, 76–91. University Park: Pennsylvania State University Press.

Sapiro, Virginia. 1981. Research frontier essay: When are interests interesting? The problem of political representation of women. *American Political Science Review* 75 (3): 701–16.

Schady, Norbert R. 2000. The political economy of expenditures by the Peruvian social fund (FONCODES), 1991–95. *American Political Science Review* 94 (2): 289–304.

Scharpf, Fritz W. 1989. Decision rules, decision styles, and policy choices. *Journal of Theoretical Politics* 1 (2): 149–76.

Schattschneider, E. E. 1960. *The semi-sovereign people: A realist's view of democracy in America.* New York: Holt, Rinehart and Winston.

Schedler, Andreas. 2001. Measuring democratic consolidation. *Studies in Comparative International Development* 36 (1): 66–92.

Scheiner, Ethan. 2007. Clientelism in Japan: The importance and limits of institutional explanations. In *Patrons, clients, and policies: Patterns of democratic accountability and political competition,* ed. Herbert Kitschelt and Steven I. Wilkinson, 276–97. New York: Cambridge University Press.

Schlesinger, Joseph A. 1966. *Ambition and politics: Political careers in the United States.* Chicago: Rand McNally.

Schlesinger, Stephen, and Stephen Kinzer. 1982. *Bitter fruit: The story of the American coup in Guatemala.* New York: Doubleday.

Schmidt, Gregory D. 2003. The 2001 presidential and congressional elections in Peru. *Electoral Studies* 22 (2): 344–51.

———. 2007. Back to the future? The 2006 Peruvian general election. *Electoral Studies* 26 (4): 813–19.

Schulz, Donald, and Deborah Sundloff Schulz. 1994. *The United States, Honduras, and the crisis in Central America.* Boulder, Colo.: Westview.

Schwindt-Bayer, Leslie A., and William Mishler. 2005. An integrated model of women's representation. *Journal of Politics* 67 (2): 407–28.

Scott, James C. 1969. Corruption, machine politics, and political change. *American Political Science Review* 63 (4): 1142–58.

Searing, Donald D. 1985. The role of the good constituency member and the practice of representation in Great Britain. *Journal of Politics* 47 (2): 348–81.

———. 1994. *Westminster's world: Understanding political roles.* Cambridge: Harvard University Press.

Seligson, Mitchell A. 2007. The rise of populism and the Left in Latin America. *Journal of Democracy* 18 (3): 81–95.

Shepherd, Philip L. 1986. Honduras confronts its future: Some closing, but hardly final thoughts. In *Honduras confronts its future: Contending perspectives on critical issues,* ed. Mark B. Rosenberg and Philip L. Shepherd, 229–55. Boulder, Colo.: Lynne Rienner.

Shugart, Matthew Soberg. 1998. The inverse relationship between party strength and executive strength: A theory of politician's constitutional choice. *British Journal of Political Science* 28 (1): 1–29.

Shugart, Matthew Soberg, and Scott Mainwaring. 1997. Conclusion: Presidentialism and the party system. In *Presidentialism and democracy in Latin America,* ed. Scott Mainwaring and Matthew Soberg Shugart, 394–439. New York: Cambridge University Press.

Siavelis, Peter M. 1997. Executive-legislative relations in post-Pinochet Chile: A preliminary assessment. In *Presidentialism and democracy in Latin America,* ed. Scott Mainwaring and Matthew Soberg Shugart, 321–62. New York: Cambridge University Press.

———. 2000. *The president and congress in postauthoritarian Chile: Institutional constraints to democratic consolidation.* University Park: Pennsylvania State University Press.

Siavelis, Peter, and Scott Morgenstern, eds. 2008a. *Pathways to power: Political recruitment and candidate selection in Latin America.* University Park: Pennsylvania State University Press.

———. 2008b. Political recruitment and candidate selection in Latin America: A framework for analysis. In *Pathways to power: Political recruitment and candidate selection in Latin America,* ed. Siavelis and Morgenstern, 3–37. University Park: Pennsylvania State University Press.

Sieder, Rachel. 1995. Honduras: The politics of exception and military reformism (1972–1978). *Journal of Latin American Studies* 27 (1): 99–127.

Sixty-three por ciento de los Hondureños voto en plancha. 2005. *La Prensa,* December 15.

Skidmore, Thomas E. 2004. Brazil's persistent income inequality: Lessons from history. *Latin American Politics and Society* 46 (2): 133–50.

Stokes, Susan C. 1995. *Cultures in conflict: Social movements and the state in Peru.* Berkeley and Los Angeles: University of California Press.

———. 1998. Constituency influence and representation. *Electoral Studies* 17 (3): 351–67.

———. 1999. What do policy switches tell us about democracy? In *Democracy, accountability, and representation,* ed. Adam Przeworski, Susan C. Stokes, and Bernard Manin, 98–130. Cambridge: Cambridge University Press.

———. 2005. Perverse accountability: A formal model of machine politics with evidence from Argentina. *American Political Science Review* 99 (3): 315–25.

Stokes, William S. 1950. *Honduras: An area study in government.* Madison: University of Wisconsin Press.

Strom, Kaare. 1997. Rules, reasons, and routines: Legislative roles in parliamentary democracies. In *Members of parliament in western Europe: Roles and behaviour,* ed. Wolfgang C. Müller and Thomas Saalfeld, 155–74. London: Frank Cass.

Studlar, Donley T., and Ian McAllister. 1996. Constituency activity and representational roles among Australian legislators. *Journal of Politics* 58 (1): 69–90.

Sullivan, Mark P. 1995. Government politics. In *Honduras: A country study,* ed. Tim L. Merrill, 145–208. 3rd ed. Washington, D.C.: Federal Research Division, Library of Congress.

Taylor, Michelle M. 1992. Formal versus informal incentive structures and legislator behavior: Evidence from Costa Rica. *Journal of Politics* 54 (4): 1053–71.

———. 1996. When electoral and party institutions interact to produce caudillo politics: The case of Honduras. *Electoral Studies* 15 (3): 327–37.

Taylor-Robinson, Michelle M. 2001. Old parties and new democracies: Do they bring out the best in one another? *Party Politics* 7 (5): 581–604.

———. 2003. The elections in Honduras, November 2001. *Electoral Studies* 22 (3): 553–59.

———. 2006a. The difficult road from caudillismo to democracy, or can clientelism complement democratic electoral institutions? In *Informal institutions and democracy: Lessons from Latin America,* ed. Gretchen Helmke and Steven Levitsky, 106–24. Baltimore: Johns Hopkins University Press.

———. 2006b. La política Hondureña y la elecciones de 2005. *Revista de Ciencia Política* 26 (1): 114–24.

———. 2009. Honduras: Una mezcla de cambios y continuidad. *Revista de Ciencia Política* 29 (2): 445–63.

Taylor-Robinson, Michelle M., and Christopher Diaz. 1999. Who gets legislation passed in a marginal legislature and is the label *marginal legislature* still appropriate? A study of the Honduran Congress. *Comparative Political Studies* 32 (5): 590–626.

Taylor-Robinson, Michelle M., and Steven B. Redd. 2002. Framing and the poliheuristic theory of decision: The United Fruit Company and the 1954 U.S.-led coup in Guatemala. In *War and cognition: Applying the poliheuristic theory of decision to war and peace situations,* ed. Alex Mintz, 77–100. New York: Palgrave.

Tendler, Judith. 2000. Why are social funds so popular? In *Local dynamics in an era of globalization,* ed. Shahid Yusuf, Weiping Wu, and Simon Evenett, 114–29. New York: Oxford University Press.

Thelen, Kathleen. 1999. Historical institutionalism in comparative politics. *Annual Review of Political Science* 2 (June): 369–404.

Transparency International Corruption Perceptions Index. 2006. http://www.infoplease .com/ipa/A0781359.html, accessed September 20, 2007.

Trudeau, Robert H. 2000. Guatemala: Democratic rebirth? In *Latin American politics and development,* ed. Howard J. Wiarda and Harvey F. Kline, 493–511. 5th ed. Boulder, Colo.: Westview.

Tsebelis, George. 1995. Decision making in political systems: Veto players in presidentialism, parliamentarism, multicameralism, and multipartyism. *British Journal of Political Science* 25 (3): 289–325.

Ulloa, Fernando C., and Eduardo P. Carbó. 2003. The congressional and presidential elections in Colombia, 2002. *Electoral Studies* 22 (4): 785–92.

UNDP (United Nations Development Programme). 2003. *Human development report, 2003: Millennium development goals: A compact among nations to end human poverty.* New York: Oxford University Press.

———. 2006. *Informe sobre desarrollo humano Honduras, 2006: Hacia la expansión de la ciudadanía.* San José, Costa Rica: Litografía e Imprenta LIL.

———. 2007. *Human development report, 2007/2008: Fighting climate change: Human solidarity in a divided world.* New York: Palgrave Macmillan.

———. 2009. *Human development report, 2009: Overcoming barriers: Human mobility and development.* New York: Palgrave Macmillan.

Uslaner, Eric M. 1985. Casework and institutional design: Redeeming promises in the promised land. *Legislative Studies Quarterly* 10 (1): 35–52.

Valenzuela, Arturo. 1977. *Political brokers in Chile: Local government in a centralized polity*. Durham: Duke University Press.

Valenzuela, J. Samuel. 1992. Democratic consolidation in post-transitional settings: Notion, process, and facilitating conditions. In *Issues in democratic consolidation: The new South American democracies in comparative perspective*, ed. Scott Mainwaring, Guillermo O'Donnell, and J. Samuel Valenzuela, 57–104. Notre Dame: University of Notre Dame Press.

Vallejo Hernández, Hilario Rene. 1990. *Crisis histórica del poder político en Honduras*. Comayaguela, Honduras: ULTRA-Graph.

Valverde, Vanesa. 2009. El rol representativo de los legisladores latinoamericanos: Qué intereses defienden y cómo actúan? *Elites Parlamentarias Latinoamericanas, Boletín datos de opinión* 3 (April): 1–5.

Vilas, Carlos M. 1997. Introduction: Participation, inequality, and the whereabouts of democracy. In *The new politics of inequality in Latin America: Rethinking participation and representation*, ed. Douglas A. Chalmers, Carlos M. Vilas, Katherine Hite, Scott B. Martin, Kerianne Piester, and Monique Segarra, 3–42. Oxford: Oxford University Press.

Wampler, Brian. 2006. Does participatory democracy actually deepen democracy? Lessons from Brazil. Paper presented at the American Political Science Association, August 30–September 2, in Philadelphia, Pa.

Weyland, Kurt. 1996. *Democracy without equity: Failures of reform in Brazil*. Pittsburgh: University of Pittsburgh Press.

———. 1997. "Growth with equity" in Chile's new democracy? *Latin American Research Review* 32 (1): 37–67.

———. 1999. Neoliberal populism in Latin America and eastern Europe. *Comparative Politics* 31 (4): 379–401.

———. 2006. *Bounded rationality and policy diffusion: Social sector reform in Latin America*. Princeton: Princeton University Press.

Wilson, Thomas M. 1990. From patronage to brokerage in the local politics of eastern Ireland. *Ethnohistory* 37 (2): 158–87.

World Bank. 2006. *Honduras poverty assessment: Attaining poverty reduction*. Vol. 1, *Main report*. Washington, D.C.: Central America Department, Latin America and the Caribbean Region, World Bank.

Yiannakis, Diana Evans. 1982. House members' communication styles: Newsletters and press releases. *Journal of Politics* 44 (4): 1049–71.

Zucco, Cesar. 2007. The president's "new" constituency: Lula and the pragmatic vote in Brazil's 2006 presidential election. Unpublished manuscript.

Index

Made in the USA
Lexington, KY
24 August 2016